Enjoying Literature

LITERACY: MADE FOR ALL SERIES

Series Author: Arlene F. Marks

Literacy: Made for All is a classroom-ready, teacher-friendly resource for English and Writing teachers of Grades 9 through 12. Organized buffet style, it is designed to complement an existing English curriculum by providing a tested repertoire of strategies for teaching both writing skills and literary analysis techniques.

Benefits and Features:

- tested and proven effective at all learning levels, from Remedial to Pre-AP
- provides complete lesson plans including reproducible materials
- can be implemented as is or modified to suit individual teaching styles and/or students' needs
- each skill, assignment or project begins by "teaching the teacher," giving an inexperienced teacher the knowledge to provide effective instruction first time out and the confidence to modify and experiment thereafter
- comprised of reading, writing, literary criticism, and language-study components
- moves students from writing effectively to reading analytically (approaching text from the authoring point of view), a proven, highly successful methodology
- can turn any English course into a Literacy course
- extremely versatile and cost-effective
- can deepen an existing English course or complete the framework for a new one

Titles in the Series:

Story Crafting: Classroom-Ready Materials for Teaching Fiction Writing Skills in the High School Grades (2014)

Enjoying Literature: Classroom-Ready Materials for Teaching Fiction and Poetry Analysis Skills in the High School Grades (2014)

Wordsmithing: Classroom-Ready Materials for Teaching Nonfiction Writing and Analysis Skills in the High School Grades (2014)

Enjoying Literature

Classroom-Ready Materials for Teaching Fiction and Poetry Analysis Skills in the High School Grades

Arlene F. Marks

ROWMAN & LITTLEFIELD
Lanham • Boulder • New York • Toronto • Plymouth, UK

Published by Rowman & Littlefield
4501 Forbes Boulevard, Suite 200, Lanham, Maryland 20706
www.rowman.com

10 Thornbury Road, Plymouth PL6 7PP, United Kingdom

British Library Cataloguing in Publication Information Available

Library of Congress Cataloging-in-Publication Data

Marks, Arlene F., 1947–
  Enjoying literature : classroom ready materials for teaching fiction and poetry : analysis skills in the high school grades / Arlene F. Marks.
     pages cm. — (Literacy: made for all series)
  ISBN 978-1-4758-0739-4 (pbk. : alk. paper) — ISBN 978-1-4758-0740-0 (electronic) 1. English language—Composition and exercises—Study and teaching (Secondary) 2. Literature—Study and teaching (Secondary) 3. Literary form—Study and teaching. 4. Poetry—Study and teaching. I. Title.
  LB1631.M3855 2014
  808'.0420712—dc23
                                                                              2013049402

Printed in the United States of America

Contents

An introduction to the critical analysis of literature. Beneficial for all grade levels, but especially
recommended for grade 12.

PART III: WRITING THE LITERARY ESSAY

Skill 1: Developing a Topic
Unpacking a topic and brainstorming to arrive at a thesis question.

Skill 2: Organizing the Information
From chart to first-draft thesis statement.

Skill 3: Testing a Thesis
Arriving at a final draft thesis statement.

Skill 4: Generating Arguments
Pulling arguments out of a thesis statement by asking, "Why do I say that?"

Skill 5: Building Argumentation
Constructing compelling arguments using elaboration, examples, and supporting quotations. Writing a first draft of the body of an essay.

Skill 6: Writing the Introduction and Conclusion
Building a powerful opening and conclusion for a literary essay.
Reproducibles/Media: WLR 1–INTEGRATING QUOTATIONS INTO YOUR LITERARY ESSAY

Skill 7: Revision, Editing, and Proofreading
Completing the writing process and preparing the submission package.
Reproducibles/Media: WLR 2–PROOFREAD WITH A PARTNER: LITERARY
  ESSAY CHECKLIST
WLR 3–LITERARY ESSAY ASSESSMENT RUBRIC

PART IV: STUDYING POETRY

Aims and Objectives

BUILD YOUR TOOLKIT

Students familiarize themselves with literary terminology as they describe and discuss poetry at three levels of analytical complexity.

ANALYZING NARRATIVE POETRY   205
  Students practice using correct terminology as they consider and respond to questions on all three levels of analysis.

Assignment 1: The Story in the Poem   205
  Identifying and appreciating the narrative structure of the poem.

Assignment 2: Identify a Focus   207
  Formulating a focus question to be answered by the analysis of the poem.

Assignment 3: Perform a Close Reading   207
  Reading carefully to identify examples of poetical devices on all three levels of analysis.

Assignment 4: Analyze the Poem   208
  Answering the focus question by selecting and analyzing the strongest examples from the poem.

Introduction to *ENJOYING LITERATURE*

Welcome to book 2 of *Literacy: Made for All*, a buffet-style reading and writing program for the high school grades. *Enjoying Literature* will help your students discover and hone their critical and analytical skills as they delve into prose fiction and poetry, learning to appreciate—and use—the power of language to express and describe.

This student-centered approach to the study of literature, language, and writing is based on certain classroom-tested precepts:

1. **Reading and writing are equally essential to the development of a student's understanding of and appreciation for literature.**
   Students who practice using a variety of rhetorical and literary techniques in their own work not only become much better equipped to identify examples of a particular writing strategy, but they are also able to discuss more knowledgeably how and how well the strategy has been used.
2. **Literate readers are critical readers.**
   Because literate people understand and appreciate what words can do, they are not easily confused or manipulated by words. To be considered literate, therefore, students need to be able to assess the quality, the effect, and—most important—the *intent* of the language that is used to address them.
3. **Literature being studied must be read with purpose.**
   When we read strictly for entertainment, certain parts of the brain "gear down," sidelining the learning process. Students of literature, however, need to *think* about what they are reading. To ensure that this happens, they must read "with pen in hand," making notes or recording specific information as they go along.
4. **Discovery and learning come about when students feel confident enough to take risks and try new experiences.**
   Investigating something new always brings with it the risk of making mistakes. Children are taught from an early age to avoid mistakes if possible. However, students need to understand that while remaining in one's comfort zone may guarantee success, it also prevents growth; and while success may bring praise and make us feel good about ourselves, mistakes are how we learn.

At the same time, I have developed this program keeping in mind certain other rules of thumb, learned the hard way over years of teaching experience:

1. **Always begin with review.**
   No matter how basic the skill or how many grades ago the material should have been learned, there are bound to be students in your class who have never heard of it. That is why I have made laying the foundation a routine first step in each segment of *Literacy: Made for All*.
2. **The one who is doing the work is the one who is learning.**
   Since you already have earned the credit for the course you're teaching, students should be the ones practicing the skills, doing the investigating, bouncing ideas off one another, and drawing the conclusions. *Literacy: Made for All* gives students plenty of opportunity to do all of these.

3. **Repetition works.**

   By this, I don't mean rote learning but rather going back over already-charted territory. This kind of repetition hones skills and deepens understanding. It creates a level of comfort and encourages experimentation. And as long as you're asking students to repeat something they've enjoyed or found interesting in the past, they'll cheerfully revisit favorite lessons, activities, and assignments, over and over. In fact, I've had students *request* them.

4. **Practice may not make perfect, but it does make permanent.**

   Like a tattoo on the skin, something learned is very difficult to erase from the mind. That is why students need to learn things correctly the first time. And that is why modeling and guided practice are essential preliminary steps in each segment of *Literacy: Made for All.*

IMPLEMENTING THIS PROGRAM

This part of *Literacy: Made for All* contains four *modules*, each divided into a menu of teachable segments called *assignments*, which provide the teacher with complete, classroom-ready lesson plans as well as master copies of any media or reproducibles included in the lessons. Challenges and extensions have also been added to deepen or differentiate the material for senior-level or enriched classes.

Literacy: Made for All is designed to complement an English curriculum by providing a repertoire of strategies for teaching writing skills and literary analysis techniques, suitable for the study or production of any type of text. From this resource an educator can select the most effective and appropriate segment(s) to introduce, reinforce, or illuminate classroom discussions of literary works.

There is no prescribed order or number of assignments within a module. One or all of them may be selected, depending on the expectations to be fulfilled, the skill and interest levels of the students, the time allotted to the unit, and the instructional strategies favored by the teacher. There is also no prescribed duration for an assignment. Assignments can be compressed or extended to occupy whatever length of time the students require or the reading material demands.

When planning the English course at any high school grade level, a teacher may begin with any segment within the applicable module. However, for a final-year class destined for college or university, I highly recommend beginning with the ten-day module entitled "Literary Criticism 101," as critical thinking skills are essential to the understanding of literary and media works both within and outside of the classroom.

Each reading or writing assignment consists of four phases:

Introduction

- The literary/media element or writing skill under study is introduced and explained.
- In the process, students are introduced to the appropriate literary terminology.

Modeling/Guided Practice

- The learning strategy is modeled by the teacher.
- Students practice with partners or in groups, with the teacher's guidance.

Practice

- Students attempt the modeled skill individually.

Product

- Students form groups for the purpose of sharing and discussing the results of their practice.
- Each student then creates a tangible expression of his or her understanding, sharing it with the discussion group if time permits.

Student products may be written, visual, or auditory. At the teacher's discretion, the finished product of any assignment may be collected for formative assessment or may serve as the summative evaluation for the unit, provided it is complete and in final-draft form.

Each assignment is a basic framework—a recipe, if you like—tested and proven successful in my classroom. If you're having an off day or not feeling especially creative—and we all have times like that—you can follow the recipe as is and be assured of a positive result. As with any recipe, however, you may wish to adapt the ingredients or the process to suit individual tastes or needs. Please feel free to modify, combine, or embellish these activities as much as you like in order to tailor them to your own classes.

Above all, have fun with your students as they enjoy honing their literacy skills using *Literacy: Made for All.*

AIMS AND OBJECTIVES OF THE PROGRAM

Aims:

Students shall have opportunities to:

1. become aware of themselves as authors and come to realize the worth and uniqueness of their writing;
2. become proficient in the mechanics of written language and in the effective use of spoken and written language to think, learn, and communicate;
3. understand the role that language, literature, and the media play in the exploration of intellectual issues and in the establishment of personal and societal values;
4. develop critical skills and use them to respond to ideas communicated through various media; and
5. prepare for productive community membership by taking personal responsibility for their progress toward self-directed learning.

Objectives:

Through this program, students will be encouraged to:

1. become better communicators of their own opinions and observations;
2. develop a greater understanding and acceptance of other points of view through discussions and shared writing assignments;
3. develop a better understanding of themselves;
4. hone and channel their creative abilities by practicing the creative process;
5. establish a personal writing style;
6. become effective editors of their own writing and that of others; and
7. plan writing projects by determining the purpose and format and then organizing their time to allow for effective editing techniques.

STUDYING FICTION

	ASSIGNMENT	DESCRIPTION	NCCS ANCHORS ADDRESSED
1	Examine the Themes of the Story	Students look at the superficial and underlying themes in the story and how they are purposefully delivered by the characters, plot, setting and writing style of the author.	R.1, R.2, R.4, R.5, R.6, R.9, R.10, L.5, L.6
2	Appreciate the Realism in the Story	Students examine the interplay of plot logic, character consistency and setting description that combine to draw the reader into a story.	R.1, R.3, R.4, R.5, R.9, R.10
3	Chart the Dramatic Conflict in the Story	Students review the elements of dramatic conflict and discover its importance in creating an emotionally satisfying short story.	R.1, R.2, R.3, R.8, R.9, R.10, L.6
4	Explore the Structure of the Story	Students analyze the scene structure and plot structure of a short story, and learn how an author uses these to speed up or slow down the pace of a story.	R.1, R.2, R.3, R.5, R.9, R.10, L.6
5	Experience the Sensory Detail (Imagery) of the Story	Students identify the various types of sensory detail and learn what makes imagery an effective storytelling tool.	R.1, R.2, R.3, R.4, R.5, R.6, R.10, L.5, L.6
6	Evaluate the Simile and Metaphor in the Story	Students focus on these two types of figurative language and the contribution they make to the impact of a story.	R.1, R.2, R.4, R.5, R.10, L.5, L.6
7	Note the Use of Language in the Story	Students learn about the importance of word choices in story writing, to emphasize mood and define characters. Students also practice using a dictionary and thesaurus to expand their vocabulary.	R.1, R.2, R.4, R.6, R.9, R.10, L.3, L.4, L.5, L.6
8	Analyze the Main Characters in the Story	Students examine the role and nature of the protagonist and antagonist of a story and learn about the Dimensions needed in order to bring these characters to life for the reader.	R.1, R.2, R.3, R.6, R.10, L.6
9	Appreciate the Humor in the Story	Students analyze the techniques that create humor in a story and the role of humor in effective storytelling.	R.1, R.4, R.7, R.9, R.10, L.6
10	Explore the Setting of the Story	Students look at the techniques used by authors to create interesting settings, and the importance of setting details to the mood of a story.	R.1, R.3, R.4, R.5, R.6, R.9, R.10
11	Rate the Opening of the Story	Students identify the characteristics of a well-written story opening and practice evaluating the effectiveness of the first scene of a variety of story types.	R.1, R.5, R.9, R.10, L.6
12	Evaluate the Story	Students determine the characteristics of a well-written story and practice using these criteria to evaluate short stories.	R.1, R.10, L.6
13	Write a Literary Response	Students practice writing three different kinds of responses to fiction: dialectical, personal and analytical.	R.1, R.10, W.1, W.2, W.4, W.5, W.6, W.9, W.10, L.1, L.2, L.3, L.5, L.6

MODULE	DESCRIPTION	NCCS ANCHORS ADDRESSED
Literary Criticism 101	An introduction to literary analysis for students at all grade levels.	R.1, R.2, R.3, R.4, R.5, R.6, R.7, R.8, R.10 W.1, W.4, W.5, W.6, W.9, W.10 L.1, L.2, L.3, L.5, L.6
Writing the Literary Essay	A process for essay-writing that takes students from topic to final submission draft.	R.1, R.3, R.4, R.5, R.6, R.8, R.10 W.1, W.4, W.5, W.6, W.9, W.10 L.1, L.2, L.3, L.5, L.6

STUDYING POETRY

	SEGMENT	DESCRIPTION	NCCS ANCHORS ADDRESSED
1	Build Your Toolkit	In a series of activities, students learn and practice using literary terminology to describe and analyze poetry on three levels: technical, associative and thematic. They also practice answering effectiveness questions using correct literary terminology and may write a sight test.	R.1, R.2, R.4, R.5, R.9, R.10 W.2, W.4, W.5, W.9, W.10 L.1, L.2, L.3, L.5, L.6
2	Narrative Poetry (includes Teaching "David" by Earle Birney)	In a close examination of a narrative poem, students practice using correct terminology as they discuss and write answers to questions on all three levels of analysis. Written and creative challenges are provided and may serve as summative assignments.	R.1, R.2, R.3, R.4, R.5, R.6, R.9, R.10 W.2, W.3, W.4, W.5, W.9, W.10 L.1, L.2, L.3, L.5, L.6
3	Lyric Poetry: The Sonnet	In a close examination of the sonnet form, students practice using correct terminology as they discuss and write answers to questions on all three levels of analysis. Written and creative challenges are provided and may serve as summative assignments.	R.1, R.2, R.4, R.5, R.6, R.9, R.10 W.2, W.4, W.5, W.9, W.10 L.1, L.2, L.3, L.5, L.6
4	Dramatic Poetry (includes Teaching "Ulysses" by Alfred Lord Tennyson)	In a close examination of the dramatic monologue, students practice using correct terminology as they discuss and write answers to questions on all three levels of analysis. Written and creative challenges are provided and may serve as summative assignments.	R.1, R.2, R.4, R.6, R.9, R.10 W.2, W.4, W.5, W.9, W.10 L.1, L.2, L.3, L.5, L.6
5	Write a Literary Response to a Poem	Students practice writing three different kinds of responses to poetry: personal, dialectical and analytical. All work is put through the full writing process and may serve as a summative assignment.	R.1, R.2, R.4, R.5, R.6, R.10 W.2, W.4, W.5, W.6, W.9, W.10 L.1, L.2, L.3, L.5, L.6
6	Timed Writing Practice	Students learn and practice techniques that will help them do their best when writing essay-length responses to questions on English exams.	R.1, R.2, R.4, R.5, R.6, R.10 W.2, W.4, W.9, W.10 L.1, L.2, L.3, L.5, L.6

Studying Fiction

IMPLEMENTING THIS MODULE

STUDYING FICTION focuses on the close reading and analysis of short stories and longer prose fiction, up to and including novels, and is designed to be implemented either alone or in tandem with the corresponding Skill segments from *STORY CRAFTING*. Each of the reading assignments can be taught at any grade level, from Grade 9 through Grade 12. Extensions are provided to deepen the understanding of students in senior-level or enriched classes.

Here are some further recommendations to help ensure that both you and your students derive the greatest possible benefit from STUDYING FICTION:

1. There are writing activities included in every segment of this module. Should you decide to use one of these for formative or summative evaluation, give students the opportunity to practice peer- and self-evaluation of their work. Let them pair up or form groups to help edit or constructively critique one another's first or second drafts. It may be beneficial as well to teach a preliminary lesson on ways to deliver constructive criticism.

   I have three effective rules for the English classroom, which you may find useful in yours:
      a) *Every person in this class is entitled to form her/his own opinions, and every expressed opinion has value. (But in order to earn marks, an opinion must be convincingly supported by examples or quotations.)*
      b) *Every expressed criticism of another student's work must be constructive. (A chart may be posted on the wall to suggest constructive openings for critical comments, and to serve as a reminder that the purpose of criticism is to help the other author to improve.)*
      c) *Always try your best. (Areas where a student needs to improve will thus be easier to identify. Also, trying one's best to be constructive at all times will speed everyone's progress toward fluent, effective writing.)*

2. Do not hesitate to repeat any of the activities in this program if, in your opinion, the students need to deepen their understanding or improve their analytical skills. Rather than feeling bored because of lesson repetition, students will become more familiar with the structure of the activity and therefore more confident about undertaking it. Increased confidence makes students more willing to take risks, and risk-taking helps students to learn and grow. So, don't worry about repeating the segments in consecutive grades, or even about repeating a particular activity in two or more consecutive English periods. As your students 'get into' this program, you may even find them asking to repeat an activity that they have particularly enjoyed.

STUDYING FICTION and *STORY CRAFTING*, like your students' right and left legs, are designed to work together to move them along as naturally and efficiently as possible (in this case, toward literacy). *Literacy: Made for All* is non-grade-specific. It presents a methodology which can be used for the critical study of virtually any kind of literature, and which will help your students to develop their expressive faculties as they become confident, literate readers and viewers.

AIMS AND OBJECTIVES OF STUDYING FICTION

Aims:

Students shall have opportunities to:

1. compare themselves as authors with the writers whose work they are studying in class;
2. deepen their understanding of the ways in which authors use various writing techniques to make text effective;
3. understand the role that language, literature, and the media play in the exploration of intellectual issues and in the establishment of personal and societal values;
4. use their critical skills to respond to ideas communicated through the various media;
5. become thoughtful, literate readers of a range of texts.

Objectives:

Through this module, students will be encouraged to:

1. become better communicators of their own opinions and observations;
2. develop a greater understanding and acceptance of other points of view through group discussions;
3. develop a better understanding of themselves and others;
4. hone and channel their analytical abilities through close and thoughtful reading of a range of texts;
5. become effective editors of their own writing and that of others.

Studying Fiction Assignment 1

Examine the Themes of the Story

✍ YOU WILL NEED

- SFR 1–THEME IS EVERYWHERE chart (class set)
- Chart headings written across the board or on an overhead transparency

PLUS

- Class set of a short-short story (200–1200 words long) and 5 or 6 short stories selected for study (4 or 5 copies of each)

OR

- Class set of an anthology of short stories (with one selected for modeling) and a list from the anthology of 5 or 6 additional short stories

OR

- Class set of a short-short story selected for modeling and 5 or 6 selected 2–4 page excerpts from a novel under study

---

PURPOSE

Students identify the superficial and underlying themes in the story and examine how they are purposefully delivered by the characters, plot, setting, and writing style of the author.

INTRODUCTION

1. The teacher explains to the class the difference between the terms *superficial theme* and *underlying theme*:

   The superficial theme is the topic of the story, while the underlying theme is the message that the author wishes the reader to get from reading the story. For example, "war" would be a superficial theme; "the futility of war" would be an underlying theme. (The word *theme* is made up of the first five letters of "*the me*ssage.")

2. The teacher then reads aloud the short-short story selected for modeling as students follow along on their copies.

MODELING

1. In a whole-class discussion, the students identify the superficial and underlying themes of the story just read, and these are written above the chart headings on the board or the overhead transparency.

2. The teacher then explains that in a well-written story, the underlying theme can be found reflected in every part of the story. For example, how do the characters in the story just read *embody* the theme written on the board? How do their personalities, speeches, and behavior bring the theme to life? Is there one character who seems to be the author's "mouthpiece"? After some discussion, teacher and students fill in the chart on the board or overhead transparency under the "Characters" heading. *(An exemplar chart, filled in, has been provided for your own reference.)*

The teacher should take this opportunity to model the format s/he wishes students to use for referring to or quoting from the text. For example:

> *The sergeant tells the chaplain, "I'm not sure anymore what it is I'm supposed to be fighting for, padre, other than to keep us all alive."* (p. 13, para. 2)

GUIDED PRACTICE

1. The students form three groups and proceed to fill in the rest of the chart. Group 1 examines how the plot *enacts* the theme, Group 2 how the setting *reflects* it, and Group 3 how the language used by the author *reinforces* it throughout the story or excerpt.

SUGGESTION

1. Numbered heads. Students number off from one to three around the classroom. Each student works independently to find two or three examples that fit under his or her designated chart heading.

2. Numbered groups. Students then get into their three numbered groups to discuss and compare the examples they found.

3. After each group has identified five or six good examples, a representative goes to the board or overhead transparency and completes the group's section of the chart, with embedded references as previously modeled.

PRACTICE

1. After the group work has been shared in whole class, each student receives a blank copy of the THEME IS EVERYWHERE chart and is given or assigned a short story or novel excerpt to read and chart.

2. Each student then independently reads and charts the assigned short story or novel excerpt.

PRODUCT

1. Students assemble in groups of four or five who have read the same story or excerpt. Once assembled, they share the information they have charted and discuss one of the following questions:

   • In which element of your short story or excerpt does the theme come through most strongly? Why do you suppose the author made this choice?
   • How many underlying themes are you able to identify in this story? List them.
   • On a scale of one to five, how effectively does your author express the themes of this story? Give reasons for your opinion.

SUGGESTION

As a way of quantifying the discussion and making the students in each group accountable, you may wish to try the following:

Four-Corners Placemat. After reading through the story once, students get into groups of four.
1. Each group is given a sheet of chart paper with a circle drawn in the middle and straight lines extending from the circle to the edges or corners of the page, creating four equal-sized areas for jot notes.
2. Each member of the group then works individually, perhaps on a different part of the story, for some period of time, making notes on his or her quarter of the placemat.
3. The entire group can then pool and discuss their findings, using the center of the placemat to record their general conclusions before sharing them in whole-class discussion.

2. Following the time allotted for discussion, each student can do one of the following:

- write a first-draft opinion paragraph based on a discussion question
- create a poster for the story or novel, illustrating its main theme(s)
- script and deliver a radio ad to interest classmates in reading the story or novel

3. If time permits, students can reassemble in their discussion groups and share their products with the rest of their group.

EXTENSIONS FOR SENIOR CLASSES

1. Students can read and chart more than one of the selected six short stories or excerpts. Each student can then find a partner whose stories/excerpts are either the same as or different from his or her own. Pairs of students can compare their stories and charts to determine which story or excerpt delivers its theme most effectively through character, plot, setting, and language. This evaluation can serve as the basis for a whole-class discussion and subsequent product. Students can do one of the following:

- write a first-draft opinion piece
- script and present an imagined interview with one of the authors studied, focusing on the theme(s) of the story or novel
- rank the roles played by character, plot, setting, and language in delivering the theme(s) of a particular story or excerpt, then explain the rankings in a paragraph

If time permits, students can then form groups of four or five and share their products with the rest of the group.

2. (Alternative INTRODUCTION) Senior or enriched students studying a novel can engage in a whole-class discussion to identify the superficial and underlying themes of the entire book. Depending on their abilities, students may then work independently, in pairs, or in groups to select scenes or excerpts that they feel deliver the theme especially strongly and therefore merit closer study. *(From here, go to step 2 of "MODELING," above.)*

THEME IS EVERYWHERE

Title and Author of Story: _____

Superficial Theme: _____   Underlying Theme: _____

EMBODIED BY CHARACTERS (speech, actions, choices, thoughts)	ENACTED BY PLOT (plot events, twists, ironies)	REFLECTED BY SETTING (details, imagery, mood, era)	REINFORCED BY LANGUAGE (figures of speech, choice of words, imagery, syntax)

THEME IS EVERYWHERE

Title and Author: "Sophie, 1990" by Marian Engel

Superficial Theme: technology in society   Underlying Theme: Technology can be hazardous to the health of society.

EMBODIED BY CHARACTERS (speech, actions, choices, thoughts)	ENACTED BY PLOT (plot events, twists, ironies)	REFLECTED BY SETTING (details, imagery, mood, era)	REINFORCED BY LANGUAGE (figures of speech, choice of words, imagery, syntax)
– Bo and Roo symbolize what's happened to society—they look normal but are sickly and won't live long.	– The energy crisis led to an Accident (probably nuclear, since it was followed by a Freeze). Technology wasn't the answer to the energy crisis; it just made things much worse (irony).	– The sound curtain makes it possible to erect a wall anywhere—this is a society in which technology is keeping people isolated.	– "His poor little light going out before it was properly turned on." (p. 270, para. 1) A human life is compared to a light bulb—we've all become parts of society's great machine.
– Roo's mother represents the way most people feel: "We'll get through this day, Roo." (p. 270, para. 8) People aren't machines and can't be forced to live like machines.	– To stay warm during the Freeze, people burned their antique furniture (destroying ties to their past) and their books (taking away entertainment choices).	– "She handed him a little, white-stemmed violet" (p. 270, para. 2). Plants are supposed to be green—technology forces us to accept what isn't natural.	– "You put your tears behind the sound curtain, really." (p. 270, para. 5)—even human emotions are controlled by technology.
– Roo's mother is "sure someone is watching" (p. 270, para 8)—she's fearful and paranoid due to lack of human contact, thanks to technology.	– They relied on technology to entertain them—but machines are not creative.	– The government is very controlling, uses technology to keep people isolated—women can't have careers.	– "The boys were just figuring out how we should all live." (p. 269, para. 1)—technology makes it possible for one person's vision to be forced onto everyone.
– Sophie constantly looks for the positive side of what technology has done to society, but still says, "You can't have everything." (p. 270, para. 3)		– Technology's answer to the destruction of food sources during the Freeze is the Mixture (bland) seasoned with whatever people can grow hydroponically (parsley and onions—p. 269, para. 5).	

Studying Fiction Assignment 2
Appreciate the Realism in the Story

✍ **YOU WILL NEED**

- SFR 2–ELEMENTS OF REALISM I chart (class set)
- SFR 3–ELEMENTS OF REALISM II chart (class set)
- A copy of each chart on a transparency
- An overhead projector
- A short-short story of 2–3 pages, selected for modeling (class set)
                                 PLUS
- A class set of an anthology of short stories and a list from the anthology of 5–7 short stories containing strong elements of realism
                                 OR
- 5–6 selected 2–4 page excerpts from a novel under study, containing strong elements of realism

PURPOSE

Students examine the interplay of plot logic, character consistency, and setting description that combine to draw the reader into the world of a story.

INTRODUCTION

1. The teacher asks the class: How important is it for a story to be realistic? Why? In what ways can an author make a story realistic? The ensuing discussion should touch on at least the following points, which are written on the board and copied into students' notebooks:

   1. *Plot, characters, and setting all influence one another.*

   2. *Characters remain consistently "in character."*

   3. *The plot is logical, with a cause and effect progression.*

   4. *There is enough vivid descriptive detail to make us believe we are inside the story, watching it happen.*

MODELING

1. The teacher explains to the class that they will begin by focusing on the first item from the above list and elicits some examples from students of real-world people, places/times, and events influencing one another *(for example, the excitement surrounding the Super Bowl, Stanley Cup, or Olympics; international icons such as Nelson Mandela or Mother Teresa; a war zone or site of a natural disaster, and so on).*

2. The teacher projects the ELEMENTS OF REALISM I chart onto the screen and reminds the class that in order for a story to be realistic for the reader, it must contain characters, settings, and plot events that influence one another in the same way as the people, places/times, and events do in real life.

3. The class is then organized into three groups, each specializing in the influence or impact of one element of a story on the other two: (1) characters influencing plot and setting, (2) plot influencing characters and setting, and (3) setting influencing plot and characters.

4. To prepare students for the next step of this activity, the teacher provides a brief summary of the story to be read, outlining who the characters are, where and when the action of the story takes place, and what sort of action it is *(for instance, a school field trip, a daring car theft, a dreaded visit to the dentist, and so on).* This information may be written on the board for student reference.

5. As the teacher proceeds to read aloud the short-short story, the students in each specialist group listen carefully and make notes relating to their area of specialty.

6. In whole-class discussion, the students identify and compare the ways in which the plot, characters, and setting of this story influence one another. The teacher or a student secretary records the answers on the overhead transparency, modeling how the chart should be filled in.

GUIDED PRACTICE

1. The teacher places the ELEMENTS OF REALISM II chart on the overhead projector and explains that they will now be focusing on the second, third, and fourth items from the list on the board. Character realism is about *consistency*, plot realism is about *logic*, and setting realism is about *sensory detail*. These words should be printed on the chart directly under their respective headings.

2. To clarify, the teacher asks students to think of a time when they were asleep and suddenly realized they were in the middle of a dream. How did they know it was a dream? *(For instance, the students might describe events that defied logic, people who behaved contrary to their established personalities, or sensory detail that was at odds with the surroundings.)*

3. The teacher then points out that since an author's goal is to create the illusion of reality for the reader, what the teacher and students will be recording on this second chart will be examples from the story read earlier that show characters staying "in character" by their spoken words, thoughts, and actions; plot events that follow a chain of logical cause and effect; and vivid sensory details that help the reader to imagine that s/he is actually in the setting of the story.

   Depending on how much time has elapsed since the modeling phase, the teacher may wish to reread the short-short story to refresh everyone's memory.

4. Together, teacher and class proceed to discuss the short-short story and complete each section of the second chart on the transparency. The teacher should take this opportunity to model the format s/he wishes the students to use when referring to or quoting from text. For example:

   Allen is angry when his friend refuses to do him a favor. (p. 4, para. 5-6)

SUGGESTION

If time is limited, students can number off and form expert groups, each group concentrating on a single section of the chart. Then:

1. THINK. Each student takes a couple of minutes to record on paper the ways in which the author has created realism in the story using plot, character, or setting. Then:

2. PAIR. Students partner up within each numbered group to discuss and expand on each other's ideas. Then:

3. SHARE. Students volunteer ideas from their notes in a whole-class discussion on the elements of realism in the story, while the teacher or a student secretary fills in the chart on the overhead transparency.

PRACTICE

Each student receives a blank copy of both ELEMENTS OF REALISM I and ELEMENTS OF REALISM II and is assigned either a preselected short story from the anthology or an excerpt from the novel being studied to read and chart, working independently.

PRODUCT

1. Students assemble in groups of four or five to share the information they have charted and discuss one of the following questions:

   • What are the most realistic and least realistic parts of your assigned short story or excerpt? Give reasons for your answers.
   • How does the realism of your short story or excerpt make it more effective and/or more enjoyable for the reader?
   • Is realism still important if a story has strong fantasy elements? Why or why not?

2. Following the time allotted for discussion, each student can do one of the following:

   • write a first-draft opinion paragraph based on one of the questions
   • draft a letter to the author based on a discussion question
   • draw a picture illustrating a particularly realistic scene from his or her assigned story or excerpt (including all details from the story)

3. If there is time, students can reassemble in their discussion groups and share their products with the rest of their group.

SUGGESTION

3-2-1. The teacher selects important points that each student needs to have learned from the small-group discussion and asks students to write them down—and possibly hand them in—as per the following example:

• Three natural and realistic things the main character says or does
• Two vivid and realistic details from the setting of the story
• One thing about realism that you would like to say to the author of this story

EXTENSION FOR SENIOR CLASSES

Students can read and chart more than one of the selected short stories or novel excerpts. Each student can then find a partner whose stories or excerpts are either the same as or different from his or her own. Pairs of students can compare the elements of realism in their stories or excerpts and/or charts, to determine which story or excerpt is the most realistic and why. This evaluation can serve as the basis for a whole-class discussion and subsequent product. Students can do one of the following:

- write a first-draft multi-paragraph comparison of two short stories or novel excerpts
- script and deliver a monologue based on one of the stories or excerpts, beginning with either "It seemed so real," or "I couldn't believe it was happening"
- rank the roles played by character consistency, plot logic, and setting description in creating the illusion of reality in a particular story or excerpt, then write a paragraph explaining the rankings

If time permits, students can form groups of four or five and share their completed products with the rest of the group.

ELEMENTS OF REALISM I

Title and Author of Story: _____

HOW DOES	PLOT INFLUENCE	CHARACTER INFLUENCE	SETTING INFLUENCE
PLOT (sequence of events, cause and effect, plot twists, ironies, comic events, tragic events, building suspense, crises, climax, anticlimax)			
CHARACTER (basic needs, fears, and desires, goals, conflicts, physical presence, emotional reactions, vices and virtues, conscious and subconscious thoughts, personality traits)			
SETTING (time and place, weather conditions, social customs, morals, political climate, economic conditions, level of technology, public tastes, medical knowledge, ecological awareness)			

ELEMENTS OF REALISM II

Title and Author of Story: _____

HOW IS REALISM CREATED IN THIS STORY USING:

CHARACTERS	PLOT	DESCRIPTIVE DETAIL

Studying Fiction Assignment 3
Chart the Dramatic Conflict in the Story

PURPOSE

Students review the elements of Dramatic Conflict and discover its importance to creating an emotionally satisfying story.

INTRODUCTION

1. The teacher discusses and reviews with the class the parts of a Dramatic Conflict:
   Protagonist (Who?)
   Goal (wants to do What?)
   Motivation (Why?)
   Antagonists (What stands in the way?)

2. The teacher either draws on the board or puts up on a screen a copy of the THREE TYPES OF CONFLICT chart, with these parts as column headings.

3. The teacher then reviews with the class the three main categories of antagonist in a Dramatic Conflict: *person vs. person, person vs. environment,* and *person vs. self.*

   It should be explained to the students that the first two are categories only, not specific types of conflict. Person vs. environment, for example, includes such antagonists as society, nature, and technology. Person vs. person can include as an antagonist a wild animal, a family pet, or an angry ghost. (Strictly speaking, person vs. supernatural is not in itself a conflict. The supernatural elements of a story exist to create conflict that falls into one of the three aforementioned categories.)

MODELING

1. The teacher selects a children's story or fairy tale that the class is likely to be familiar with, such as *Cinderella* or *Little Red Riding Hood*. In whole-class discussion, the Dramatic Conflict of the story is analyzed, and the teacher records the information under the appropriate headings of the chart on the board or the overhead transparency.

SUGGESTIONS

1. Reading the story aloud to the class is a good way to ensure that all students have heard it at least once before you attempt the whole-class discussion and modeling.

2. In a class of students from diverse ethnic backgrounds, consider using a non-European folktale as your example. You could even ask the students to bring their favorite former bedtime story with them to class for this lesson. (Be sure to allow time for translation, if necessary.)

3. If repeating this lesson, you can inject variety into it by basing the modeling activity on a visually presented story: a comic book, video cartoon, or live-action half-hour television program.

The teacher should take this opportunity to discuss with students how best to identify the protagonist of a story, recording at least the following points on the board for students to copy into their notes:

A protagonist is:

> *the character with the most important goal (the main plot of the story)*
> *the character the reader is supposed to care about and cheer for*
> *the character who learns and changes in the course of the story*
> *usually the point-of-view character*
> *often the first character introduced or discussed in the story*

GUIDED PRACTICE

1. Each student receives a copy of the THREE TYPES OF CONFLICT chart and selects from the list of titles provided by the teacher the three short stories the student will read in the anthology.

2. Working independently, each student reads the first story selected, recording information about its Dramatic Conflict on the first line of the chart. The teacher circulates, providing assistance where needed.

PRACTICE

Each student continues to read and chart the second and third selected short stories, recording each one's Dramatic Conflict on its own line of the chart.

PRODUCT

1. Students assemble in groups of four or five to share the information they have charted and discuss one of the following questions:

   • Which of your three stories has the most gripping conflict? What makes it the most exciting?
   • How important is it that the protagonist achieve his or her goal? Is a "happy ending" essential to an enjoyable story?

- Choose a story with a human antagonist and retell the story from his or her point of view. Are all the parts of a Dramatic Conflict still present? Does it strengthen a story when the antagonist is embroiled in his or her own conflict, or does it weaken it? Give reasons for your answer.

SUGGESTION

    1. Numbered heads. Students number off from one to three around the classroom. Then:
    2. Numbered groups. Students get into their three numbered groups. Then:
    3. Breakout groups. Each numbered group divides itself into two or three smaller groups to discuss and compare the corresponding numbered line (1, 2, or 3) of their charts.

2. Following the time allotted for discussion, each student can do one of the following:

- write a first-draft opinion paragraph based on one of the discussion questions
- choose the most effective short story from his or her chart and create a visual representation of the various conflicts that are present
- write and deliver a short speech in which the antagonist explains and justifies his or her words and actions in the story

3. If there is time, students can reassemble in their discussion groups and share their products with the rest of their group.

EXTENSION FOR SENIOR CLASSES

1. The teacher writes the headings for a conflict chart across the board: *Protagonist, Goal, Motivation, Antagonist(s).* The teacher then tells the class about a protagonist who used to be an avid mountain climber. One year ago, this person had a fall while climbing a peak. He wasn't badly injured, but since then he has been "too busy" to go climbing with his friends, and they are beginning to think he's lost his nerve. At the beginning of the story, he is on his way with two buddies to tackle a very dangerous mountain. Teacher and students together fill in the chart on the board:

> *Protagonist:* mountain climber
> *Goal:* to climb the mountain
> *Motivation:* to prove that he hasn't lost his nerve
> *Antagonists:* the mountain, weather conditions, and the like

2. The teacher now explains that the protagonist in any Dramatic Conflict actually has two goals, not one. For example, this mountain climber's stated goal is to climb the mountain, but what does he really want? *(He wants to prove that he hasn't lost his nerve.)* Can he achieve his real goal without reaching his stated goal? *(Yes, by taking a risk to help one of his buddies who gets in trouble during the climb, or by performing some other feat of courage or strength while on the mountainside.)* As long as he reaches his real goal, will the protagonist be satisfied? *(Yes.)* Will the reader be satisfied? *(Let's find out. . .)*

If this example has already been used to teach a writing skill, the teacher may wish to substitute one of the following protagonists:

- *a school track-and-field athlete who wasn't able to finish her event at the regional finals due to an injury (Stated goal: to win a prize in the next competition. Real goal: to feel like a contender, to make up for letting everyone down last time).*
- *a person who keeps looking for a sibling who went missing (Stated goal: to find the sibling. Real goal: to achieve closure).*

3. Each student receives a copy of the REAL GOALS AND STATED GOALS worksheet to fill out. Students revisit the three stories already charted and record the requested information on the worksheet, one story per line.

4. The students can then form small groups to compare the endings of their three charted stories and discuss which one is the most emotionally satisfying for the reader and why.

5. Following the discussion, students can do one of the following:

   • write a first-draft opinion piece based on the discussion
   • collect examples of TV or print advertising in which the viewer's real goals are purposely replaced with the stated goal of buying a product
   • write and deliver a radio advertisement in which the listeners' real goals are replaced with the stated goal of buying a product or service

6. If time permits, students can then reassemble in their discussion groups and share their products or findings with the rest of their group.

THREE TYPES OF CONFLICT

	PROTAGONIST	GOAL	MOTIVATION	ANTAGONISTS (versus person, environment, or self)
1				(1) (2) (3)
2				(1) (2) (3)
3				(1) (2) (3)

REAL GOALS AND STATED GOALS

	PROTAGONIST	STATED GOAL	REAL GOAL	ANTAGONIST OVERCOME (and how overcome)	CONCLUSION (and what was learned)
1					
2					
3					

Studying Fiction Assignment 4

Explore the Structure of the Story

(This Is a Two-Part Assignment)

✍ **YOU WILL NEED**

- SFR 6–STORY OUTLINE chart, double-sided (class set)
- SFR 7–SCENE STRUCTURE chart, on the board or on an overhead transparency
- SFR 8–SCENE DEVELOPMENT chart (class set)
- A copy of each chart on the board or an overhead transparency
- Overhead projector
- A short-short story (200–1200 words long) with well-defined story structure (Part 2, MODELING)

  PLUS

- A class set of an anthology of short stories and a preselected list from the anthology of 5–7 stories with well-defined story structures

  OR

- 5 or 6 selected 2–4 page excerpts from a novel under study, each chosen from a different part of the story (*Introduction, Story Event, Rising Action, Crisis, Climax, Denouement*) and each containing more than one scene

  AS WELL AS

- A complete scene selected from one of the above (for Part 1, INTRODUCTION)

PURPOSE

Students analyze the scene structure and plot structure of a short story, and learn how an author uses these to speed up or slow down the pace of a narrative.

PART 1: SCENE STRUCTURE

INTRODUCTION

1. The teacher puts the SCENE STRUCTURE diagram on the board or screen and labels it while explaining to the class that a scene consists of five parts:

- Purpose (the immediate goal of the character entering the scene)
- Action (the steps taken by the character to achieve this goal)
- Peak (the Achievement, Confrontation, or Revelation that ends the Action)
- Reaction (the character considers or reacts emotionally to what has just happened)
- Decision (the character decides what to do next—this decision becomes the Purpose of the next scene involving the character)

2. The teacher reads aloud a complete scene chosen from one of the preselected short stories or novel excerpts. Teacher and students discuss and identify the parts of the scene and the type of peak that ends the character's attempts to achieve his or her goal:

- Achievement (the goal is achieved, so no further effort is required)
- Confrontation (an obstacle arises that cannot be ignored or overcome)
- Revelation (new information arises that necessitates a change of goals)

MODELING

1. The teacher records the resulting scene information, demonstrating how to fill out the chart on the board or the overhead transparency.

   The teacher should point out to students that the easiest way to determine where one scene ends and another begins is to look for the Decision, since the "Decision=Purpose" equation is what links the scenes of a story together.

2. Students are instructed to copy the information from the board into their notes.

GUIDED PRACTICE

1. Students are organized into pairs, and each pair is assigned one of the preselected stories or excerpts to work with.

2. The pairs of students now work to identify and list all the scenes and partial scenes in the story or excerpt, making a note of what has been left out of each partial scene (that is, which of the five parts labeled on the chart).

3. Pairs of students who worked on the same story or excerpt form groups of four or six to compare their lists and discuss why the author might have decided not to include all five parts of every scene.

SUGGESTION

For grade 9 and 10 classes, especially if they contain auditory and kinesthetic learners, try creating story puzzles.

Make a photocopy of a short story that you're sure your students have never read. Cut the photocopy into scenes, place the scenes inside a manila envelope, and let the students work with partners to reassemble the pieces. When they're done, ask them to explain their reasons for putting the scenes in this particular order.

4. In whole-class discussion, students share any conclusions drawn by their groups. At the end of this discussion, it should be apparent to students that the missing scene parts would have been repetitive or boring, or would otherwise have slowed down the story. Students should also have drawn conclusions regarding the following:

- the proportion of scenes peaking with Achievement in the story *(There shouldn't be many—in a scene on the Rising Action, achievement of purpose brings the story to a temporary halt.)*
- whether these scenes tend to be complete or partial *(They'll be partial, some as short as a single sentence.)*

- whether there is a correlation between the above information and how interesting the story is for the reader *(There is. Keeping the story moving along and preventing the main character from achieving his or her goals are the best ways to hold the reader's interest.)*

5. The teacher explains to the class that the parts of a scene that determine how fast or slow the scene will be are the Action and Reaction.

I have had success using the analogy of Alice in Wonderland—*eating from one side of the mushroom made her smaller, while eating from the other side made her larger. Similarly, if a scene has more Action than Reaction, it will be a faster-paced scene. If it has more Reaction than Action, it will be a slower-moving scene.*

SUGGESTION

Here is an activity that enables students to prove to themselves that the ratio of Action to Reaction determines the pacing of a scene:

1. Identify two stories from the anthology or excerpts from the novel, one clearly fast-paced and the other clearly slow-paced.
2. Students pair up with working partners. One member of each pair will work on the fast-paced story or excerpt and the other on the slow-paced story or excerpt.
3. Each student selects two or three scenes from his or her text and counts the actual lines of text given to Action and Reaction in each scene. When done, pairs of students compare notes and report their findings in a whole-class discussion.

PRACTICE

1. Each student now receives a copy of the SCENE DEVELOPMENT chart and chooses a short story or novel excerpt from the preselected list.

2. Each student, working independently, reads his or her chosen text, finding and charting four scenes.

PRODUCT

1. Students assemble in groups of four or five to share the information they have charted and discuss one of the following questions:

- On a scale of one to five, where one is hardly moving and five is supersonic, rate the overall speed of the story or excerpt you've just charted. Which scenes have sped up the story and which have slowed it down?
- Should every story be fast-paced, or do some types of stories require a more leisurely telling? Give reasons for your answer.

2. Following the time allotted for discussion, each student can do one of the following:

- write a first-draft opinion paragraph based on a discussion question
- choose a scene from his or her selected story and revise it to change the pace (from fast to slow, from slow to fast)
- select a partial scene which is missing its Reaction and write a paragraph describing what is going on in the character's mind at that point
- working with a partner, script and dramatize two original scenes, one slow-paced and one fast-paced

3. If there is time, students can reassemble in their discussion groups and share their products with the rest of their group.

PART 2: STORY STRUCTURE

INTRODUCTION

1. The teacher puts a STORY OUTLINE chart on the board or screen and labels it while reviewing with the class the parts of a short story:

   • the Story Change, Problem, or Challenge (sometimes called the story event or inciting incident). This is the plot event that disrupts the main character's life and launches the
   • Rising Action, a series of scenes that build dramatically to the
   • Climax—a final Confrontation, Achievement, or Revelation, providing the emotional high point of the story—followed by the
   • Denouement (literally means "unraveling," the relaxation after the climax). The dust settles and we see whether the main character has achieved his or her story goal and what s/he thinks about it.

2. The teacher reminds the class that any story is a series of scenes, and where a scene fits on the chart is determined by what it does and how much dramatic tension it contains:

   If it is about the main character's life before the Change, Problem, or Challenge occurs, then it belongs at the beginning of the story (unless it is a flashback, which can go anywhere).
   If it contains the Change/Problem/Challenge that launches the story, then it is the Inciting Incident.
   If it shows the main character trying unsuccessfully to solve the Problem or deal with the Change or Challenge, then it belongs on the Rising Action.
   If it shows the main character finally solving the Problem, overcoming the Challenge, or accepting the Change, then it contains the story Climax.
   If it happens after the main character has achieved (or failed to achieve) his or her story goal, then it is part of the Denouement.

MODELING

1. The teacher reads aloud to the class a short-short story that begins with a well-defined Change, Problem, or Challenge.

2. Together, the teacher and class discuss and identify the sequence of scenes. The teacher plots them on the STORY OUTLINE chart on the board or overhead transparency, pointing out how each scene on the Rising Action brings the main character one step closer to the Climax.

GUIDED PRACTICE

1. Each student receives a copy of the STORY OUTLINE chart (double-sided) and is assigned one of the preselected short stories or novel excerpts to read and chart.

   At the teacher's discretion, students may all work with the same story or excerpt or with different ones. In either case, discussion with a partner during this step of the assignment is encouraged.

SUGGESTION

   1. THINK. Each student works independently for some period of time to complete his or her chart.
   2. PAIR. Students partner up to compare and refine their charts.
   3. SHARE. Students volunteer information from their charts in a whole-class discussion.

PRACTICE

Each student now turns over the STORY OUTLINE chart and selects a second story or excerpt from the teacher's list to read and analyze, working independently.

PRODUCT

1. Students assemble in groups of four or five to share the information they have charted and discuss one of the following questions:

   • How satisfying to the reader is the Climax of your selected story? Give reasons for your answer.
   • Which of the stories you've charted is the most effectively organized? In what way?
   • If you were the author of the story you've charted, what changes if any would you make to its structure, and why?

2. Following the time allotted for discussion, each student can do one of the following:

   • write a first-draft opinion paragraph based on a discussion question
   • rewrite the ending of one of the short stories so that the main character's Achievement (or Confrontation or Revelation) in the Climax is changed to one of the other two types of peaks
   • script and perform a monologue by the main character of the story, based on either the Inciting Incident or the Denouement

3. If there is time, students can reassemble in their discussion groups and share their products with the rest of their group.

EXTENSION FOR SENIOR CLASSES

1. The teacher explains to the class the nature of Dramatic Tension.

   Dramatic Tension is a type of suspense created in a story as the main character's chances of winning go down while the stakes keep going up. In other words, as the story progresses, the main character stands to lose more and more if s/he is ultimately unsuccessful in achieving the story goal.

   > *For example, a star college athlete struggles with an injury that only he knows about. He is determined not to be benched because he has learned that a Major League scout will be attending the final game of the season. The more he plays, the worse his injury becomes and the more likely it is that he'll be benched before that crucial final game. Dramatic Tension is running high, but then something happens that kicks it up another notch: The athlete discovers that his best friend has borrowed money from a loan shark to place a bet that the star will score the winning point in the final game. Now, not only must the athlete play that game, he also has to be the one to win it.*

2. For this activity, students can revisit the charts already made or select a new story or excerpt from the teacher's list to read and analyze.

   Working with the information on the STORY OUTLINE chart, each student adds two pieces of information to each scene:

   • How have the protagonist's chances of success worsened?
   • How have the stakes risen?

3. Students then form pairs or small groups and compare their results to determine which of their stories or excerpts develops the highest level of Dramatic Tension.

4. This evaluation can be used as the basis for a whole-class discussion and subsequent multiparagraph response. *(See Studying Fiction Assignment 13.)*

STORY OUTLINE CHART

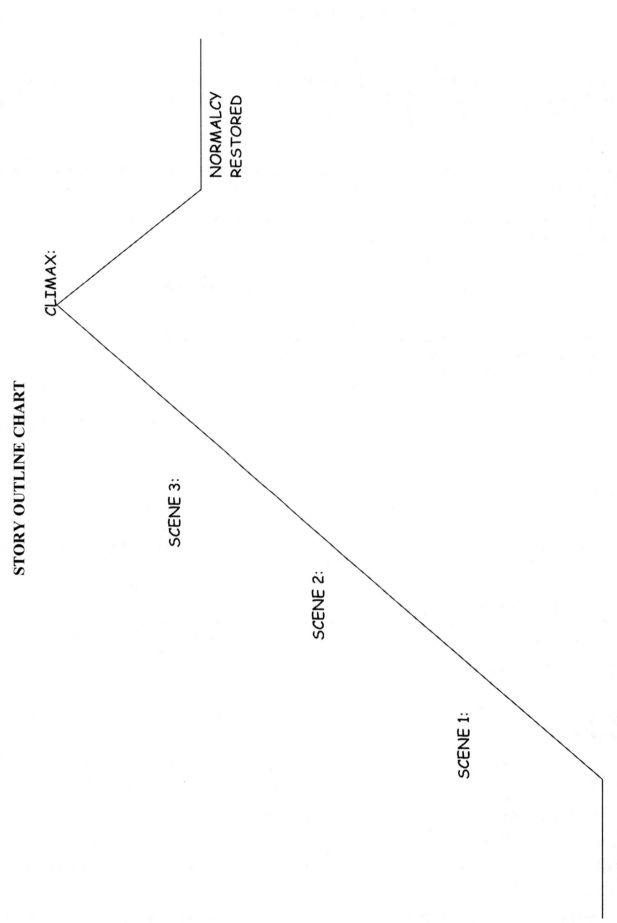

CLIMAX:

NORMALCY RESTORED

SCENE 3:

SCENE 2:

SCENE 1:

CHANGE, PROBLEM OR CHALLENGE:

SCENE STRUCTURE CHART

PEAK:

REACTION:

DECISION:

ACTION TAKEN:

PURPOSE:

SCENE DEVELOPMENT CHART

SCENE NUMBER	GOAL (purpose)	ACTION TAKEN TO ACHIEVE IT (antagonists encountered)	OUTCOME OF SCENE (type of peak)	REACTION (thoughts, feelings)	DECISION (next goal)
1					
2					
3					
4					

SCENE STRUCTURE CHART: EXEMPLAR

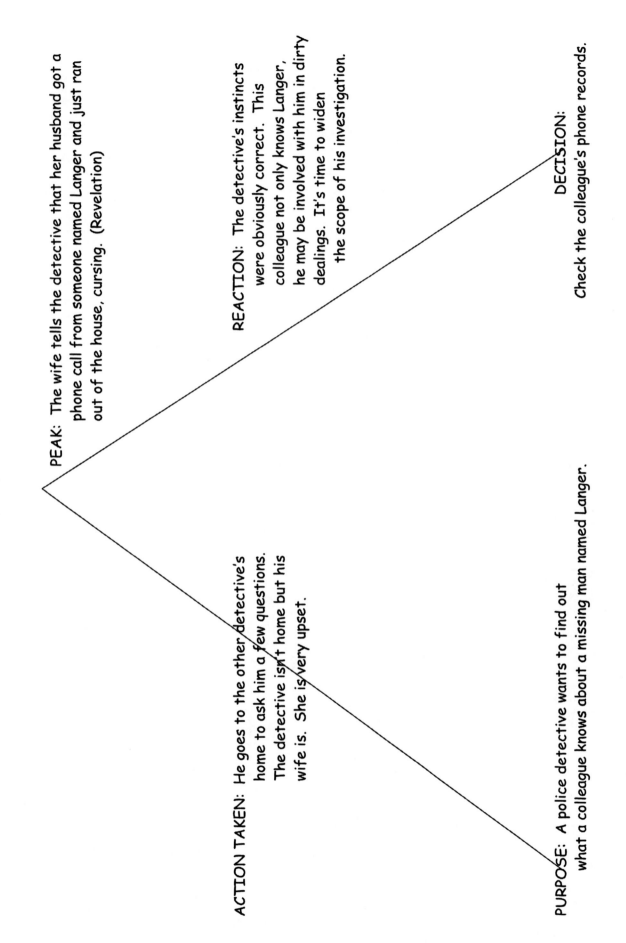

PEAK: The wife tells the detective that her husband got a
phone call from someone named Langer and just ran
out of the house, cursing. (Revelation)

REACTION: The detective's instincts
were obviously correct. This
colleague not only knows Langer,
he may be involved with him in dirty
dealings. It's time to widen
the scope of his investigation.

ACTION TAKEN: He goes to the other detective's
home to ask him a few questions.
The detective isn't home but his
wife is. She is very upset.

DECISION:
Check the colleague's phone records.

PURPOSE: A police detective wants to find out
what a colleague knows about a missing man named Langer.

Studying Fiction Assignment 5

Experience the Sensory Detail (Imagery) of the Story

✍ YOU WILL NEED

- Three selected descriptive scenes or passages from (short) stories on overhead transparencies, each chosen to illustrate one of the purposes for including sensory details in a story (see MODELING, below)
- An overhead projector
- A class set of an anthology of short stories
- 1 short story chosen from the anthology, containing a variety of sensory details (for GUIDED PRACTICE)

PLUS

- A list of 5–7 stories from the anthology, each containing at least one vividly descriptive passage with a variety of sensory details

OR

- 5 or 6 selected 2–4 page excerpts from a novel under study, each containing at least one vividly descriptive passage with a variety of sensory details

---

PURPOSE

Students practice identifying the various types of sensory details and learn what makes imagery an effective storytelling tool.

INTRODUCTION

1. The teacher begins by reviewing with the class what is meant by sensory detail (aka imagery): *descriptions of sights, smells, sounds, tastes, and skin sensations.*

2. The teacher then explains that we process reality and orient ourselves through our senses. To illustrate, the teacher asks students for examples of the five types of sensory details one might find at a municipal swimming pool. *(For instance, the students might mention the smell of chlorine in the air, the taste of it in the water, the sound of splashing, the sight of people in swimsuits, the feel of humidity in the air and of slippery wet tiles underfoot, etc.)*

MODELING

1. The teacher then shows and reads aloud the first descriptive scene or passage on the overhead screen.

2. Students are asked to pick out examples of sensory details from the passage. As students respond, the teacher begins making a list of examples on the board, modeling the format s/he wishes the class to use when extracting quotations from printed material and pointing out that quoted examples of imagery need to be complete. For example:

> *"Two squirrels had begun chattering angrily at each other from neighboring trees."* (p. 3, para. 2)

3. When the list contains at least five examples of sensory details, the teacher asks the class what effect is achieved by the use of these particular details. Discussion should yield at least one of the following three purposes:

- to create a sense of reality for the reader (verisimilitude)
- to establish a particular mood in a setting
- to reveal a point-of-view character's state of mind

4. The teacher writes the students' answer(s) on the board, then repeats the previous step with the two remaining sample passages and completes the list of purposes on the board.

Allow time for students to copy these into their notebooks before proceeding.

SUGGESTION

To help students understand the list of purposes, you may wish to use the following explanations:

Creating verisimilitude: This word comes from two Latin words, *veritas* (truth) and *similis* (resembling, same as). Authors want their readers to feel as though the settings being described in a story could be real places. In real life, we experience places and events with all of our senses; therefore, *to help a reader imagine being inside the story and living it along with the main character, an author needs to appeal to as many of the five senses as possible.*

Establishing mood: We've all been in places that we would describe by stating how they made us feel. An old, abandoned house is spooky or scary because of the way it feels and smells and looks and sounds. For the same reasons, a hockey game is exciting and a fishing trip relaxing. *When an author wants the reader to share what the main character is feeling, s/he will select which sensory details to include in a description, thus creating the desired mood in a story.*

Revealing a character's state of mind: What a character notices or fails to notice about a setting tells the reader a great deal about what's going on inside the character's head. A young man who walks out his back door after learning that he has won the lottery will see roses and a lush green lawn; the same man in the same place after learning that his fiancée has run away with another man will see only thorns and weeds and an hour of mowing ahead of him. *One way for an author to show the reader how a character is feeling or what s/he is thinking is by choosing the appropriate sensory details to include in a descriptive passage.*

GUIDED PRACTICE

1. Students are directed to the selected story from the anthology (or are given a copy of the story on a handout) and are instructed to read it through once on their own.

2. Students who have finished reading form groups of three or four and work together to find descriptive passages, identify the sensory details in each one, and determine what might have been the author's purpose(s) for including them.

SUGGESTION

Four-Corners Placemat. After reading through the story once, students get into groups of four.

1. Each group is given a sheet of chart paper with a circle drawn in the middle and straight lines extending from the circle to the edges or corners of the page, creating four equal-sized areas for jot notes.

2. Each member of the group then works individually, perhaps on a different part of the story, for some period of time, making notes on his or her quarter of the placemat.
3. The entire group can then pool and discuss their findings, using the center of the placemat to record their general conclusions before sharing them in whole-class discussion.

3. Each student group selects a spokesperson to share its findings with the rest of the class in whole-class discussion.

PRACTICE

Working independently, each student selects his or her own short story or novel excerpt from the teacher's list and proceeds to read, identify passages of description, and make lists of sensory details.

PRODUCT

1. Students assemble in groups of four or five to share their lists and their conclusions regarding the author's use of imagery, and to discuss one of the following questions:

   • Of the five human senses represented, which one appears to be most important to your selected story or excerpt? Give reasons for your answer.
   • Choose a passage in which the imagery is used to provide insights into the thoughts or feelings of the main or point-of-view character. What does the reader learn about this character from the passage?
   • If you were the author of the story or excerpt you just read, would you have put in more sensory detail? Less? Explain why.

2. Following the time allotted for discussion, each student can do one of the following:

   • write a first-draft opinion paragraph, based on a discussion question
   • choose a scene from his or her selected short story and rewrite it, using sensory details to change the mood of the scene or reveal a different aspect of the point-of-view character
   • rewrite a scene from the point of view of a different character, changing the sensory details to match the new character's state of mind

3. If there is time, students can reassemble in their discussion groups to share their finished work with the rest of the group.

EXTENSION FOR SENIOR CLASSES

🖎 YOU WILL NEED

• SFR 9–FOCUSED IMAGERY CREATES SUBTEXT, on an overhead transparency
• An overhead projector
• A selected descriptive passage containing focused imagery, on an overhead transparency
• Three to five selected descriptive passages, either from different short stories in the class anthology or from the novel being studied (half a class set, photocopied)

1. The teacher puts the FOCUSED IMAGERY sheet up on the screen and uses it to explain the meaning of the terms *focused imagery* and *subtext* to the class (see handout). Together, teacher and students brainstorm various categories of focused imagery and these are listed on the board. *(Some examples might include sports imagery, music imagery, war imagery, animal imagery, and so on.)*

2. The exemplar passage is then put up on the screen. As the teacher and students in whole class identify all the examples of imagery, the teacher uses colored markers to underline or highlight each one. At the same time, a student places a check mark beside the category on the board for each example that fits into it. *(New categories can be added as needed during the whole class analysis.)*

3. Based on the number of check marks beside each category, students can work in small groups to discuss whether there is focused imagery in the scene and what subtext the author was trying to communicate to the reader. Groups then share their findings with the rest of the class.

4. After whole-class sharing, students pair up. Each pair receives a copy of the handout with selected descriptive passages and then selects or is assigned one of the passages to work on, as follows:

    1. Identify and list all the examples of imagery in your selected or assigned passage.

    2. Determine whether the imagery is focused.

   IF IT IS FOCUSED:

   • Identify the category of imagery (music, war, clothing, animal, and so forth).
   • Determine the subtext it has been used to create and what purpose it serves.
   • Describe the role of each imagery detail in creating the subtext.

   IF IT IS NOT FOCUSED:

   • Discuss the probable thoughts and feelings of the point-of-view character in the passage.
   • Identify a category of imagery that would be appropriate for this passage.
   • Make a list of imagery details from the category that could be added to create a subtext in this passage.

SUGGESTION

A Word Web. Each pair of students is given a blank sheet of paper with a circle in the center. The type or category of imagery is written in the circle, and the web of imagery details is then built outward to the edges of the page.

Pairs of students who are analyzing a pattern of focused imagery can build a web of quotations from the passage being studied.

Pairs of students who are creating a pattern of focused imagery can build a web of their own ideas.

5. The students form three to five groups, each focusing on one of the passages studied. Within each group, pairs of students share their findings or products with the rest of the group.

6. Following the time allotted for sharing, each student can write a first-draft analytical response about the effectiveness of the imagery or imagery pattern in his or her selected passage. *(See Studying Fiction Assignment 13.)*

FOCUSED IMAGERY CREATES SUBTEXT

A subtext is like a coded message within a story, written in the language of Imagery.

EXAMPLE

A teenaged character lives with his invalid mother in a small town. They are very poor and he has no friends his own age because he must spend so much time caring for his mother. He never complains about this, but as he walks down the main street, his surroundings are described using a lot of cemetery imagery: windows shaped like tombstones, people's whispering voices drifting past him, a smell of freshly turned earth pervading the air, and so on. Clearly, the character feels like a ghost, doomed to haunt this little community for eternity.

When a character is purposely or unconsciously repressing an emotion, the author may create a subtext to reveal the character's true feelings.

EXAMPLE

In the movie *The Sixth Sense*, filmmaker M. Night Shyamalan deliberately uses the color red to "label" scenes that contain hints to the viewer that the main character, played by Bruce Willis, is dead but doesn't realize it. In one scene, he grasps the red knob on the door leading to his office in the basement of his home but the door won't open for him (because his widow has moved a piece of heavy furniture in front of it, but the character, a ghost, can't see it).

When an author (or filmmaker) wants the reader/viewer to realize that all is not as it seems, a series of connected sensory details may create a subtext to help him/her arrive at the truth.

EXAMPLE

A school dance is taking place. Not only is it happening in the school gymnasium, but the author also describes the event using a lot of sports imagery: groups of students are wearing their own "team colors" and "cheering on" a boy who is undecided about asking a girl to dance; the smell of pressure is in the air; a boy brags about getting to first base. Clearly, the author sees this as more than a social situation and wants the reader to see it that way too.

An author's personal statement about something that is happening in a story may be presented to the reader as an aside, using imagery to create a subtext.

Studying Fiction Assignment 6

Evaluate the Simile and Metaphor in the Story

(This Is a Two-Part Assignment)

✍ **YOU WILL NEED**

- SFR 10–IS IT A SIMILE? sheet (class set)
- A short-short story of 2–3 pages containing both similes and metaphors (class set, for GUIDED PRACTICE)
- SFR 11–SIMILE CHART 1, double-sided, or SFR 12–SIMILE CHART 2, double-sided (class set and a copy on an overhead transparency)
- SFR 13–METAPHOR CHART, double-sided (class set and a copy on an overhead transparency)
- An overhead projector

PLUS

- A class set of an anthology of short stories and a list of 5–7 selected stories from the anthology

OR

- 5 or 6 selected 2–4 page excerpts from a novel under study

PURPOSE

Students focus on two types of figurative language—simile and metaphor—and the contribution they make to the impact of a story.

PART 1: SIMILE

INTRODUCTION

1. The teacher hands out an IS IT A SIMILE? sheet to each student. Students form groups of four or five and proceed to work together to complete the exercise.

2. In whole class, teacher and students take up the sheet and arrive at a definition of a simile:

   a figurative (not literal) comparison, using the words "like" or "as."

3. The teacher writes the definition on the board, pointing out that a simile using "like" is often just a colorful way of replacing an adverb (Alex runs *like the wind.* = Alex runs *very fast.*) and a simile with "as" is often just a different way of saying "very" (Justin is *as tall as a tree.* = Justin is *very tall.*)

4. The teacher explains to the class that authors write stories in the hope of having an effect on the reader. Together, teacher and students recall the stories they have read or viewed and discuss the various effects a story might have. The teacher lists these on the board or on a blank overhead transparency. *(For example, a story might make the reader laugh or cry, make him or her care about a fictional character, help the reader to understand the seriousness of a situation, help him or her to share another person's feelings, help the reader to imagine what it would be like to live in a different time or place, help him or her to appreciate the importance of love in family relationships, or of having a dream, and so on.)*

The teacher points out that figures of speech such as similes and metaphors are used by authors to increase the effectiveness of stories by making them more vivid and memorable.

MODELING

1. The teacher puts a SIMILE CHART on the overhead projector and reads aloud the short-short story, stopping after the first example of a simile. Students are asked to identify the simile, and the teacher enters it under the first heading of the chart on the transparency, modeling the format she or he wishes the class to use for extracting and charting quotations. For example:

> *". . . [rap music at a wake] was as loud and unwelcome as a jackhammer on a Sunday morning . . ."* (p. 2, para. 3)

IMPORTANT: Students need to understand that a simile is a comparison and that they need to record both sides of the comparison when quoting from text.

2. The teacher and class then discuss and record information about the simile under the appropriate headings of the chart.

Two versions of the chart are provided—the teacher may choose either one or may wish to divide the class in two and use both charts.

GUIDED PRACTICE

1. The teacher hands out a copy of the short-short story to each student, along with a copy of the SIMILE CHART used in MODELING (above). Students are instructed that as they read to the end of the story, they are to identify and chart all the similes they can find (and that will fit onto one side of the page), using the same format as is shown on the overhead.

SUGGESTION

Students can partner up to complete this exercise, and then do the following:

1. Pairs can form groups of four or six to compare and discuss their charts, making any necessary changes or additions.
2. Then, in whole-class discussion, each group can select one of the similes they discussed and present it to the rest of the class.

PRACTICE

1. Each student selects a short story or novel excerpt from the teacher's list and turns the SIMILE CHART over to the blank second side.

2. Each student now reads the selected short story or excerpt and, working independently, charts all the similes s/he finds, continuing to follow the pattern established for the chart.

PRODUCT

1. Students assemble in groups of four or five to share and discuss the similes they have found and to discuss one of the following:

   • Choose the best three similes from your chart and explain why and how they are effective.
   • What might be some of the factors influencing an author's choice to use similes in a story? List them.
   • If you were the author of the story or excerpt you just read, would you have chosen these particular similes? Why or why not?

2. Following the time allotted for discussion, each student can do one of the following:

   • write a first-draft paragraph based on a discussion question
   • select a passage from his or her story which contains no similes and rewrite the passage, putting in a simile (the student must be able to explain or justify the choice of simile).
   • create a visual representation of a simile from his or her chart, showing how the figurative comparison helps to make the story more effective

3. If there is time, students can reassemble in their discussion groups and share their products with the rest of their group.

PART 2: METAPHOR

INTRODUCTION

1. The teacher writes an example of a simile on the board and asks the class what precisely is being compared. For example:

   John is as tall as a tree. *(height)*
   Sally runs like the wind. *(speed)*

   The teacher points out that besides using "like" or "as," a simile is a single-point comparison, unlike a metaphor.

2. The teacher then writes an example of a metaphor on the board:

   This city is a jungle.

   The teacher asks the class what is being compared. *(The city is compared to a jungle.)* Then, s/he asks what characteristics of a city support this comparison. *(It contains both predators and prey; tall buildings close together are like the trees in a jungle; it's very dangerous at night; and so forth.)* The teacher lists these points next to the metaphor.

3. The teacher now writes a second example on the board (or projects it onto a screen):

   Day after day, the real estate man stood patiently by the fence, fingering the paltry offer in his pocket as he watched Henry struggle to farm his pitiful piece of land.

4. The teacher asks the class what the real estate man is being compared to *(a vulture)* and what aspects of the sentence support the comparison. *(Vultures feed on carrion, and Henry's farm is dying. Vultures will keep their distance from*

a dying animal and wait patiently, like the real estate agent at the fence. When the prey is too weak to keep fighting, they swoop in and begin to feed. When Henry stops struggling, the real estate agent plans to swoop in with a ridiculously low purchase offer, thus figuratively devouring the land.) The teacher underlines these points in the example.

5. The teacher now asks the class what is the difference between these two examples. *(The first states the comparison and lets the reader think of the supporting reasons, while the second gives the supporting reasons and lets the reader think of the comparison.)* The teacher writes the word *revealed* above the first example and the word *subtle* above the second one, pointing out to the class that not every metaphor they encounter in their reading will be obvious. Sometimes, the students will have to think about it.

MODELING

1. The teacher puts the METAPHOR CHART on the overhead projector and begins reading the selected short-short story aloud, stopping after the first metaphor. The teacher asks students to identify the metaphor and records the example on the chart on the transparency, at the same time modeling the format s/he wishes students to use when extracting quotations from text. For example:

    "He hates being in the spotlight." (p. 2, para. 3)

2. Teacher and class then discuss what the comparison is and what the supporting ideas or characteristics might be, and the teacher records these in the appropriate places on the chart.

3. The teacher points out that a metaphor is a figurative device intended to affect the reader in some way. Referring back to the examples on the board, students can see that the first is intended to emphasize to the reader how dangerous the city can be, while the second paints a vivid image in the reader's mind. What might be the intent of the metaphor now being modeled on the chart? *(It may create a subtext, or give the reader a clue to how a character is feeling, for example.)* After some discussion, the teacher records the students' answer(s) in the final column of the chart.

GUIDED PRACTICE

1. Each student then receives a copy of the story, along with a copy of the METAPHOR CHART, and is instructed to continue reading the story and charting (on one side of the chart page only) each metaphor s/he finds.

2. After working independently for a set period of time, students come together in pairs or groups to discuss the metaphors they have found and help one another to complete the chart.

3. Each group can then select its favorite metaphor to present to the rest of the class. Students should be able to explain both why they like the metaphor and what makes it so effective in this story.

PRACTICE AND PRODUCT

1. Each student now chooses or is assigned a short story or novel excerpt from the teacher's list. Students are instructed to flip over the chart and record on the blank side any metaphors they find, following the same pattern as they've already practiced.

2. When done, students assemble in groups of four or five to share the metaphors they have found and discuss one of the following:

   - Select the most powerful metaphor in your story and explain what makes it so effective.
   - Select the subtlest metaphor in your story and explain it to your group.
   - Which type of metaphor—revealed or subtle—do you think works best in a short story? Give reasons for your answer.

3. Following the time allotted for discussion, each student can do one of the following:

   - write a first-draft paragraph based on a discussion question
   - choose an image or idea from his or her short story and rewrite it as a metaphor
   - visually represent one of the metaphors from his or her story

4. If there is time, students can reassemble in their discussion groups and share their products with the rest of their group.

EXTENSION FOR SENIOR CLASSES

1. The teacher can introduce the idea of extending a metaphor by returning to the example of the real estate agent and asking students what further characteristics the author might introduce in order to keep the reader visualizing this character as a vulture. *(For instance, students might mention a bald head, a beak-like nose, a tendency to be attracted with fellow agents to property owners in financial difficulty, and so on.)* These details, sprinkled throughout a story, create what is called an extended metaphor.

2. Students can be given a preselected story to read, containing an extended metaphor, and can chart this metaphor just as they did the others, with supporting details (and indicating locations in the story).

3. In small-group or whole-class discussion, students can then decide what makes an extended metaphor effective and why the author chose to create this one. Following the discussion, students can do one of the following:

   - write a first-draft explanation or analysis of the extended metaphor in the story
   - choose a story they have already read and create an extended metaphor to include in it. (The student must be able to explain why s/he chose this metaphor.)

4. If there is time, students can reassemble in their discussion groups and share their products with the rest of their group.

SFR 10

IS IT A SIMILE?

NO	YES
Mary is as busy as anyone else in the office.	Mary is as busy as a whole swarm of bees.
Justin is as tall as his father now.	Justin is as tall as a tree.
Denim is just as strong as sailcloth.	My uncle is as strong as an ox.
The approaching storm looks like a hurricane.	Mrs. Goldberg went through the room like a hurricane.
Sophia runs like her sister.	Alex runs like the wind.

Only the YES examples are similes. Can you figure out why?

_____

_____

Put the letter Y (for "yes") beside each simile below:

1. Charles looks like his father at the same age.

2. His voice grated my nerves like sandpaper.

3. Once she makes up her mind, she's like a bulldog with a bone.

4. Lucy wasn't as careful as she should have been.

5. It isn't like you to snap at perfect strangers. Is something wrong?

6. Larry is doing as well as can be expected.

7. Now your brother has just as much milk in his glass as you do.

8. They scrubbed until the entire kitchen was clean as a whistle.

9. He walked right up to the boss, bold as brass, and demanded a raise.

SIMILE CHART 1

THE SIMILE (quotation)	WHAT IS THE COMPARISON? (include both parts)	WHY IS IT EFFECTIVE? (what does it make or help the reader do?)
"The boy prowled the dark streets like a hungry tiger." (p. 11, para. 5)	*A boy who needs money to score drugs is compared to a hungry tiger, hunting prey in the jungle.*	The reader can visualize this young predator, slipping soundlessly through the shadows like a big cat—like the tiger, he's operating on instinct and the need to survive. The reader realizes how dangerous drug addiction has made him.

SFR 12

SIMILE CHART 2

THE SIMILE (quotation)	COULD ALSO HAVE BEEN (alternative comparisons)	WHY CHOOSE THIS ONE? (what makes it so effective?)
"He's slower than molasses in January."	He's slower than a turtle on crutches.	It's a vivid image—molasses is a thick syrup that hardly moves when it's warm, so the reader can just imagine how much slower it is when it's cold.

METAPHOR CHART

THE METAPHOR (quotation)	SUPPORTING POINTS/IDEAS (include both parts if using similes)	WHY IS IT EFFECTIVE? (what does it make or help the reader do?)

Studying Fiction Assignment 7

Note the Use of Language in the Story

(This Is a Two-Part Assignment)

✍ **YOU WILL NEED (FOR PART 1)**

- Two selected passages on overhead transparencies, one demonstrating formal language and one demonstrating slang, taken from stories in the class anthology or from other sources
- An overhead projector
- SFR 14–LANGUAGE REVEALS CHARACTER sheet, double-sided (class set)
- Headings from the handout written across the board

PLUS

- A class set of an anthology of short stories
- Dictionaries (at least one per group of students)
- Thesauri (one per group of students)

PLUS

- A list of 3–5 short stories from the anthology, each containing at least one passage incorporating formal or slang vocabulary

OR

- 4 or 5 selected 2–4 page excerpts from the novel under study, each containing at least one passage incorporating formal or slang vocabulary

---

PURPOSE

Students learn about the importance of word choices in story writing to emphasize mood and define characters. Students also practice using a dictionary and thesaurus to expand their vocabulary.

PART 1: LANGUAGE LEVELS

INTRODUCTION

1. The teacher writes the words *formal*, *colloquial*, and *slang* on the board and explains to the students that these are different levels of language in English, used for different types of writing and spoken by people in different situations.

Diplomats and university professors tend to use a lot of formal language; bikers and street people tend to speak mostly slang; most of us fit in the middle, using standard or colloquial speech most of the time and formal language or slang only in certain situations.

Rightly or wrongly, we tend to make assumptions about the people we meet based on the level of language we hear them use. We assume, for example, that someone who uses a lot of formal language is better educated than someone who speaks entirely in slang. That is why people who are faking it, who want others to believe that they're better educated or more important than they really are, will use as many long, formal words as possible in every situation.

2. The teacher asks the class: What are some other reasons for a person to use a lot of formal language? Students' answers are recorded on the board. *(The person could be a bookworm, "nerd" or "geek," or a sheltered aristocrat—someone who doesn't spend a lot of time with "regular" people; s/he could also be someone for whom English isn't a first language, and who is therefore unfamiliar with colloquial expressions, and so on.)*

3. The teacher now asks: What about the opposite—the person who uses a lot of slang? Again students' answers are recorded on the board. *(This could be someone who's trying hard to fit in, who is well educated and well bred but doesn't want people to think s/he is a snob; it could also be someone who's being hurtful or sarcastic, overdoing the slang to make fun or put people down, and so forth.)*

4. The teacher points out that just as a flesh-and-blood person has his or her own distinctive voice, so does a well-developed character in a story. When a character or narrator speaks, the language level s/he chooses tells us something about this person.

MODELING

1. The teacher writes the chart headings from the handout onto the board, then shows and reads aloud for the class the selected passage in which a character or narrator is speaking at a formal level. *(The teacher may also wish to paraphrase the passage for the students to ensure comprehension before beginning the discussion.)* Several of the most formal words and expressions are picked out, translated into colloquial English using a dictionary, and recorded under the appropriate chart heading on the board.

2. Together, teacher and students now identify the situation and decide whether it is appropriate for this character to be using such formal language in this situation. In whole-class discussion, students are asked what can be deduced about the character based on his or her language level, and the teacher records their expressed judgments or assumptions under the appropriate chart headings on the board.

   The teacher should take the opportunity to model as well the format s/he wishes students to use when quoting from or referring to text. For example:

   > *"He was, of course, persona non grata from that point forward."* (p. 2, para. 3)

GUIDED PRACTICE

1. The teacher now hands out copies of the LANGUAGE REVEALS CHARACTER sheet and instructs students to use only one side of the page for the next selected passage.

2. The passage in which a character or narrator is speaking at a slang level is put up on the screen and read aloud.

3. Students pair up with working partners and proceed to fill in the chart as shown on the board. As modeled earlier, students record and translate (using a dictionary) the slang words and expressions, identify the character's situation, decide whether slang is appropriate in this situation, and draw up a list of information that can be deduced about the character based on his or her speech.

SUGGESTION

After some time spent working with partners, pairs of students can get together to form groups of four or six, to share information and assist one another in completing the chart.

Following the work period, each group can select a spokesperson to share the group's findings with the rest of the class.

PRACTICE

1. Each student now selects or is assigned one of the short stories or novel excerpts on the teacher's list and turns to the blank side of the LANGUAGE REVEALS CHARACTER chart.

2. Students proceed to work independently, reading the story or excerpt, analyzing the language levels used by the characters, and filling in the chart.

PRODUCT

1. Students who worked on different stories or excerpts assemble in groups of three, four, or five to compare their charts and discuss one of the following questions:

   • Which of the characters you analyzed is the most realistic? Give reasons for your answer.
   • Which of your characters is the most likeable? Give reasons for your answer.
   • Is it essential to have dialogue in a short story? Why or why not?

2. Following the time allotted for discussion, students can do one of the following:

   • write a first-draft opinion piece based on a discussion question
   • select a passage of dialogue and rewrite it, referring to a thesaurus to change the language levels used by the characters involved
   • create a crossword puzzle using the formal or slang terms found in their selected story (all clues must be in colloquial English)
   • dramatize a scene of dialogue from one of the stories or novel excerpts, using the language levels to help create the characters involved

3. If there is time, students can reassemble in their discussion groups to share their products with the rest of the group.

PART 2: DENOTATION AND CONNOTATION

✍ **YOU WILL NEED**

- Sample passages on an overhead transparency, excerpted from stories in the class anthology and showing at least 3 examples each of the use of words with positive and negative connotations
- Blank sheets of paper (class set)
- Dictionaries (half a class set)
- Thesauri (one per 4 or 5 students)
- SFR 15–WORD CONNOTATIONS worksheet (class set)

PLUS

- A class set of an anthology of short stories and a list of 3 to 5 short stories from the anthology, containing examples of the use of words with positive or negative connotations

OR

- 3 to 5 selected 2-4 page excerpts from the novel under study, containing examples of the use of words with positive or negative connotations

INTRODUCTION

1. The teacher writes the words *denotation* and *connotation* on the board, then explains to the class that every word has two sides to it, like a coin. On the one side is the dictionary definition of the word—the denotation.

2. The teacher looks up and reads aloud to the class the definition of the word *honey*, then writes this information on the board, pointing out that this is what the word *honey* denotes. But the teacher's spouse called him or her by that name last night—so does that mean the teacher's spouse thinks s/he is a sticky golden syrup produced by bees? *(Of course, not! It just means the spouse thinks the teacher is sweet.)* Sweetness is something that we automatically associate with honey—and it's a pleasant taste, so it's what we call a *positive connotation*.

3. The teacher explains that a connotation is an idea that has become attached to a word over time and now travels along with it everywhere it goes, like baggage. There are positive and negative connotations, but there are also some words that are neutral when being used literally and only acquire connotations when used figuratively. *(For example, the expression "spare tire.")*

When we wish to insult someone, we deliberately choose words with very negative connotations, such as filth, dirt, slime, scum, snake, weasel, worm, and so forth. These words are hurtful precisely because of all the ugly baggage associated with them.

MODELING

1. On a blank overhead transparency or in the middle of the board, the teacher prints the word *castle*.

2. Teacher and students then brainstorm all the things we associate with this word and the teacher adds them to the word web. *(This may include royalty, wealth, fairy tales with happy endings, endurance, protection, social status, power, nobility, privilege, culture, and sayings such as "A man's home is his castle.")*

3. Above the word web, the teacher writes the following: *The word "castle" adds a note of romance and fantasy wherever it's used because of all the fairy-tale connotations it brings with it: royalty, wealth, and happily-ever-afters.*

GUIDED PRACTICE

1. The teacher points out that an author can influence the way the reader feels about the characters, events, and settings in a story by choosing words with specific connotations.

2. The sample passages are projected onto the overhead screen and students are asked to pick out three examples of words with positive connotations and three with negative connotations. These are then written in two lists on the board.

3. Each student receives a blank sheet of paper and is assigned one of the words on the board. Students proceed to build word webs around their assigned word, as was modeled earlier.

SUGGESTION

1. Numbered heads. Students number off from one to six around the room. Each number corresponds to one of the words on the board. Students work independently on their word webs for five to ten minutes.

2. Numbered groups. Then, all the students working on each of the words come together in focus groups. Group members share what they've done and help one another to complete the word web. Each group selects a spokesperson to present its work to the rest of the class.

4. Following the work period, the teacher and students discuss the effect on the story excerpt of each of the six words on the board and formulate a statement of impact for each one, similar to the statement modeled by the teacher earlier.

PRACTICE

1. Dictionaries and thesauri are given out. Each student selects or is assigned one of the short stories or novel excerpts selected by the teacher and receives a copy of the WORD CONNOTATIONS worksheet.

2. Working independently, each student proceeds to read his or her chosen short story or excerpt, identify words with positive and negative connotations, and fill in the worksheet.

   Students should use the dictionaries and thesauri to determine what the denotation and neutral version of each identified word would be.

3. Each student then selects a word from his or her list that has particularly strong connotations (that is, many things and ideas associated with it) and creates a word web on the back of the worksheet.

4. Finally, the student uses the word web to formulate and write out a statement of impact, describing how the use of this word or phrase makes the story or scene more effective.

PRODUCT

1. Students who worked on the same story or excerpt get together in groups to share their findings and discuss one of the following questions:

   • What might be the factors influencing an author's decision to use connotative language in a short story? List them.
   • Which words have the greatest impact on the effectiveness of this story? Explain why.
   • Is it possible to write a story without using any connotative language at all? Why or why not?

2. Following the time allotted for discussion, students can do one of the following:

   - write a first-draft opinion piece based on a discussion question
   - select a scene from one of the short stories and rewrite it, using or changing connotative language to alter its mood and impact
   - using a thesaurus and dictionary, choose two alternatives, one positive and one negative, for a neutral word that appears in the story and create a visual representation of the difference one of them would make to the story

3. If there is time, students can reassemble in their discussion groups to share their products with the rest of their group.

EXTENSION FOR SENIOR CLASSES

1. The teacher explains to the students that words with positive or negative connotations are often used by authors to convey a speaker's attitude in a piece of writing—toward the subject matter, toward the reader, and toward himself or herself. These attitudes are referred to in literature as *tone*.

2. The teacher puts up on the overhead screen the first few lines of Alfred Lord Tennyson's poem, "Ulysses."

   > *It little profits that an idle king,*
   > *By this still hearth, upon this barren crag,*
   > *Matched with an aged wife, I mete and dole*
   > *Unequal laws unto a savage race,*
   > *Who hoard, and sleep, and feed, and know not me.*

3. In whole-class discussion, the connotative words in the excerpt are identified and highlighted. Students should notice the large number of words with negative connotations. How do they think the speaker, Ulysses, is feeling at this point in the poem? *(He sounds very frustrated and unhappy.)* How can one tell? *(He has nothing to do, there's no fire in his fireplace, his kingdom is a sterile piece of rock, his wife is an old woman—he feels trapped and useless here.)* When he refers to his subjects and countrymen as "a savage race, who hoard and sleep and feed," what is he saying without actually using the words? *(He can't relate to them at all—they're like a lesser species.)* What, then, is the tone of this piece of poetry? *(It is lonely and frustrated.)*

4. On a blank overhead transparency, the teacher draws a word web in reverse, arranging the highlighted words in the poetry excerpt around an empty central circle.

5. In whole-class discussion, teacher and students then brainstorm words that describe Ulysses's attitudes, as evidenced by the words he uses to describe his life. These attitude words are written in the central circle on the overhead transparency. *(Students may come up with frustrated, disgusted, lonely, dissatisfied, restless, and the like.)*

6. Students are then organized into pairs or small groups. Each pair or group is assigned to read and analyze one of the specific passages from the novel excerpts or anthology selections in which connotative language has been used.

7. Students make a list of the connotative words in their assigned passage, then use them to create a reverse word web, with a list of "tone words" in the central circle, as already practiced. Student pairs can join to form groups of four or six for further discussion and sharing of their word webs.

8. Following this activity, students can do one of the following:

   - write a first-draft paragraph describing the use of connotative language to create tone in one of the short stories or novel excerpts
   - select a passage from a short story or novel excerpt already read and rewrite it, using connotative language to create a tone appropriate to the story or scene
   - write and deliver an original monologue, using connotative language to express a character's attitude toward himself or herself

9. If there is time, students can reassemble in their groups to share their products with the other group members.

LANGUAGE REVEALS CHARACTER

SLANG OR FORMAL EXPRESSION USED	COLLOQUIAL VERSION	APPROPRIATE IN THIS SITUATION? (why?)	WHAT THIS REVEALS ABOUT CHARACTER

WORD CONNOTATIONS

WORD OR EXPRESSION (neutral version) (positive or negative?)	CONNOTATIONS	THINGS OR IDEAS ASSOCIATED WITH IT
Mansion (house) (positive)	wealth and power	large size, many rooms, many servants, well-maintained building and grounds, high social standing, political clout

Studying Fiction Assignment 8
Analyze the Main Characters in the Story

✍ **YOU WILL NEED**

- SFR 16–DIMENSIONS OF LIFE chart, double-sided (class set)
- A copy of the blank chart on an overhead transparency
- An overhead projector
- Headings from the handout written across the board
- SFR 17–BASIC AND SECONDARY MOTIVATIONS CHART (class set)
- A short-short story of 2–3 pages (for INTRODUCTION, below)

PLUS

- A class set of an anthology of short stories and a list of 5–7 short stories from the anthology, each containing a human antagonist

OR

- 5 or 6 selected 2–4 page excerpts from the novel under study, each containing a human antagonist

---

PURPOSE

Students examine the role and nature of the protagonist and antagonist of a story and learn about the strategies used by authors to bring these characters to life for the reader.

INTRODUCTION

1. The teacher reviews with the class the parts of a Dramatic Conflict:

    Protagonist (*Who?*)
    Goal (*wants to do What?*)
    Motivation (*Why?*)
    Antagonist(s) (*What's in the way?*)

2. In whole-class discussion, students are asked to recall and identify human protagonist/antagonist pairings from movies and TV shows they have seen. From these, the class should be able to arrive at the following definitions:

    Protagonist—the character who is determined to accomplish something
    Antagonist—a character who is determined to stop him or her

3. The teacher now plays devil's advocate and points out that when James Bond is sent on a mission, it's to stop some villain from conquering the world. Does that mean the villain is the protagonist and Bond is the antagonist? (*No, of course not!*) Then how can the reader or viewer know which character is which?

4. In whole-class discussion, the teacher and students arrive at the identifying characteristics of a protagonist, which the teacher writes on the board and the students copy into their notes:

   The protagonist is:

   - *the character whose goal drives (is most important in) the story*
   - *the character the reader is supposed to care about and cheer for*
   - *usually the first character introduced or discussed in the story*
   - *usually the point-of-view character*
   - *the character who has learned and/or changed by the end of the story*

5. The teacher then reads aloud the selected short-short story. In whole-class discussion, students identify the protagonist of the story and measure him or her against the criteria listed on the board.

   The teacher should point out to students that not all protagonists will fulfill all of the criteria; however, the more criteria the character fits, the stronger that protagonist will be.

6. The teacher then introduces a discussion of the three Dimensions of Life by writing the following headings across the board and explaining them to the class: *Physical, Emotional, Psychological.*

SUGGESTION

Here is a way to explain the Dimensions of Life to a class:

A dimension is not the same as a description. A description is the author TELLING the reader about a character; when a character has dimension, the character SHOWS himself or herself to the reader.

The *Physical Dimension* provides evidence that a character has physical reality, occupies space, owns things that take up space as well, and has a physical impact on his or her surroundings (that is, on the setting). For example, a character who is a carpenter by trade and a huge hockey fan will demonstrate his or her physical dimension by keeping a workshop full of tools in the garage and cluttering up the rest of the house with sports gear and memorabilia.

The *Emotional Dimension* provides evidence that a character experiences recognizable human feelings. Characters demonstrate their emotional dimension by speech (the words spoken as well as the vocal qualities), by gesture, by facial expression, by body language, and by changes in any of these. For example, a character's eyes widen in horror, voices are raised in anger, shoulders slump to show despair, or lips purse with disapproval.

The *Psychological Dimension* provides evidence that a character thinks and reasons. Characters reveal their thoughts to the reader in one of two ways—either in dialogue or in internal monologue. Anything else is the author TELLING the reader (that is, describing what is happening inside a character's head, as opposed to letting the character show us him/herself).

GUIDED PRACTICE

1. The class is organized into three expert groups, each focusing on one of the three dimensions of the protagonist.

2. The teacher puts a copy of the DIMENSIONS OF LIFE chart on the overhead projector and points out that the students will have to listen for both descriptive and dimensional details in order to fill in the chart.

3. As the teacher rereads the short-short story aloud, pausing after each scene or paragraph, members of each group listen carefully for details that fit into their area of focus and jot them down.

   If there is time, expert groups can assemble to share and discuss their findings before the whole-class discussion.

4. The teacher and students together discuss and record, under the appropriate chart headings on the overhead transparency, all the details the students noticed while listening to the story. While doing this, the teacher should also model the format s/he wishes students to use when quoting or referring to examples from the text. For example:

   The clumsy detective trips over a stack of books and knocks them all over the floor. (p. 2, para. 4)

PRACTICE 1: PROTAGONIST

1. Each student receives a copy of the DIMENSIONS OF LIFE chart and selects or is assigned a short story or novel excerpt from the preselected list.

   Students should be instructed to record their findings on only one side of the page.

2. Each student proceeds to read his or her text and work independently to chart the descriptions and dimensions of the protagonist, as practiced earlier.

PRODUCT 1: PROTAGONIST

1. Students assemble in groups of four or five to share their findings and discuss one of the following:

   • On a scale of one to five, where one is very weak and five is very strong, rate the protagonist of your short story or novel. Give reasons for your evaluation.
   • On a scale of one to five, where one is very unlikable and five is very likable, rate the protagonist of your short story or novel. Give reasons for your evaluation.
   • On a scale of one to five, where one is very unrealistic and five is very realistic, rate the protagonist of your short story or novel. Give reasons for your evaluation.

2. Following the time allotted for discussion, each student can do one of the following:

   • write a first-draft opinion paragraph based on a discussion question
   • create a visual representation of a protagonist's Dimensions of Life
   • write and illustrate an instruction pamphlet, titled, "So You Want to Be a Protagonist?"
   • write an original scene in which a character demonstrates all three Dimensions of Life

3. If there is time, students can reassemble in their discussion groups and share their work with the rest of their group.

PRACTICE 2: ANTAGONIST

1. Students are instructed to flip over their DIMENSIONS OF LIFE chart and work with the blank second copy on the back. Students may work with the same story or excerpt as before or be assigned a different one.

2. The teacher explains that this time, students will be looking closely at the antagonist of the story and recording on the chart any description and dimension details they find.

3. Working independently, each student proceeds to read his or her short story or novel excerpt and chart the descriptions and dimensions of the antagonist.

PRODUCT 2: ANTAGONIST

1. Students assemble in groups of four or five to share their findings and discuss one of the following:

   • In what ways do the protagonist and antagonist of your story or excerpt balance each other? How important is it that they do so? Give reasons for your answer.
   • Did you like the protagonist and dislike the antagonist from the very beginning of the story or excerpt? Why or why not?
   • On a scale of one to five, where one is very unsuccessful and five is very successful, rate the short story or excerpt you just read. How important is a multidimensional antagonist to ensuring the success of a story? Give reasons for your answer.

2. Following the time allotted for discussion, each student can do one of the following:

   • write a first-draft paragraph based on a discussion question
   • create a visual representation of the conflict between the protagonist and the antagonist (being sure not to change the events of the story)
   • summarize the story or excerpt, writing from the point of view of the antagonist
   • choose a scene from one of the stories or excerpts and rewrite it, supplying any previously missing Dimensions of Life to the antagonist

3. If there is time, students can reassemble in their discussion groups and share their work with the rest of their group.

EXTENSION FOR SENIOR CLASSES

1. The teacher introduces the discussion by asking the students to visualize a scenario:

   A man comes racing out of an apartment building, carrying a bouquet of roses in his hand. He dashes across the road, dodging traffic, and hurries down the entrance to the subway.

   The teacher and students together brainstorm possible reasons for the man's behavior, and the teacher lists them on the board or on a blank overhead transparency, phrasing each one as a fear, a need, or a desire. *(For example, he needs to tell someone he loves her before she boards a train and leaves him forever. Or, he just found his fiancée in bed with his best friend and he wants to destroy the flowers the friend gave her by tossing them under a train. Or, he works for a florist. He forgot to deliver the roses earlier in the day and he's terrified of losing his job if he screws up again. And so on.)*

2. Taking each idea in turn, the teacher asks the class: Can this need or desire or fear be satisfied at any point in the foreseeable future? If the answer is yes, the teacher moves on. If the answer is no, the teacher circles the idea before moving on. At the end, the teacher explains that each circled idea is a Basic Motivation, and each of the others is a Secondary Motivation.

3. The teacher explains that every individual has some basic need, fear, or desire that can never be allayed or satisfied. Because it will not go away, it drives a person to behave in certain ways and influences every decision s/he makes in life. Many people are unaware of their own Basic Motivations and, if asked the reason for their actions, will reply by giving Secondary Motivations instead. For example:

   A student who desperately needs to be liked has taken up smoking in order to have something in common with his or her peers. If asked why s/he smokes, the student will probably answer that it makes him or her look cool or feel more grown up.

Authors create realistic characters by giving them both Basic Motivations and Secondary Motivations that can be analyzed by examining their behavior.

4. The teacher then writes the following headings across the board: *Character's Actions, Reason(s) Given, Probable Basic Motivation.*

5. Students listen carefully as the teacher rereads the short-short story introduced earlier in the assignment. Together, teacher and students discuss the behavior of the main character in the story, and the teacher records the appropriate information under the headings on the board, modeling the way s/he wishes students to record a quotation from or reference to text in the first column of the chart.

6. When several lines of the chart have been filled, students discuss and determine what the probable Basic Motivation of the character is, phrased as a fear, need, or desire. *(For example: a fear of being abandoned, a need to be needed, a thirst for power.)*

7. With this knowledge in hand, the teacher and students complete the chart, identifying how the character's Basic Motivation influences everything she or he does in the story.

8. Each student now receives a copy of the BASIC AND SECONDARY MOTIVATIONS chart. Students may revisit a story or novel excerpt already read or choose a different one from the teacher's preselected list.

9. Working independently, students proceed to read their stories or excerpts and chart the behaviors and motivations of the main character.

10. Students assemble in groups of four or five to share and discuss their findings. These can be focus groups whose members have all analyzed the same character or jigsaw groups in which every student has worked with a different short story or excerpt. In any case, each group considers the following questions:

    • What is the basic motivation of the main character on your chart and how does it operate to influence his or her choices and decisions?
    • Is a story more interesting or less interesting if the main character is aware of his or her Basic Motivations? Give reasons for your answer.

11. Following the discussion, students can write a first-draft analysis of a main character from one of the short stories or novel excerpts, using the references and quotations on the chart to support their conclusions. If there is time, students can reassemble in their discussion groups to share their work with the rest of the group.

THE DIMENSIONS OF LIFE

The character is _____

PHYSICAL DESCRIPTION The character's appearance.	EMOTIONAL DESCRIPTION The character's feelings.	PSYCHOLOGICAL DESCRIPTION The character's thoughts.
PHYSICAL DIMENSION The character influencing his or her surroundings.	EMOTIONAL DIMENSION The character demonstrating his or her feelings.	PSYCHOLOGICAL DIMENSION The character revealing his or her thoughts in monologue or dialogue.

BASIC AND SECONDARY MOTIVATIONS

MAIN CHARACTER'S ACTIONS OR CHOICES (refer to or quote from text)	SECONDARY MOTIVATION (reason given by character)	PROBABLE BASIC MOTIVATION (phrased as a fear, desire, or need)
1.		
2.		
3.		
4.		
5.		
6.		
7.		
8.		
9.		

Studying Fiction Assignment 9

Appreciate the Humor in the Story

✍ **YOU WILL NEED**

- SFR 18–THREE KINDS OF HUMOR handout, double-sided (2 class sets)
- 3 humorous video clips from different eras (e.g., Abbott and Costello, a *M*A*S*H* episode, and an *Ice Age* movie)
- A TV and VCR/DVD player
- A selected humorous short-short story (200–1200 words)

PLUS

- A class set of an anthology and a list of 3–5 preselected humorous stories from the anthology

OR

- 3–5 selected humorous scenes from a novel under study

PURPOSE

Students analyze the techniques that create humor in a story and the role of humor in effective storytelling.

INTRODUCTION AND MODELING

1. The teacher asks the class to brainstorm answers to the question: *What makes you laugh? Tell us about something you laughed at yesterday or today.* A student secretary can help to record all the responses on the board. (There should be at least ten to fifteen different ones.)

2. The teacher finds an example of physical humor on the board and uses it to begin creating a three-column chart on a different board. The teacher then challenges the students to look over their responses and come up with a second and third category of humor (that is, verbal and character). That information is used to complete the framework of the chart.

3. Students are invited to come work at the board in small groups, classifying all the brainstormed items under one of the three headings and filling in the chart.

4. The teacher asks what conclusions can be drawn from this exercise. *(Students might explain that different people laugh at different things, that most people tend to laugh when something unexpected happens, and so on.)*

5. The teacher wonders aloud whether something that was funny fifty or one hundred years ago would still be laughed at today. *Does humor have a "shelf life"? Let's see . . .*

GUIDED PRACTICE

1. Each student receives a copy of the THREE KINDS OF HUMOR handout. The teacher explains that the students will be watching three video clips, and every time they smile or laugh at something on the screen, they are to do their best to record it on the chart under the appropriate heading (using only one side of the page).

2. The teacher then plays the three video clips, in order from oldest to most recent, allowing time in between for students to finish jotting down their thoughts and observations.

3. In whole-class discussion, students share the information on their charts and determine from the number of items listed in each category which kind of humor seems to "age" the best. *(Generally, it's physical humor.)*

4. The teacher then points out that each of these scenes had to be scripted, which means an author had to imagine and write the humor before the viewer could see and hear it.

   The humor in fiction is also often written in such a way that the reader can visualize as well as hear it.

5. The students are instructed to turn over their sheets and work with the blank chart on the second side. The teacher explains that s/he will be reading a short-short story to the class. As was done for the video clips, students will be visualizing what they hear and recording examples of the three kinds of humor on their charts.

6. The teacher reads aloud the short-short story, pausing periodically to permit students to finish jotting down their thoughts and observations on their charts.

7. Students can get into groups of three or four to compare the information on their charts and try to determine which kind of humor comes through most effectively in writing.

PRACTICE

1. Each student receives a second copy of the THREE KINDS OF HUMOR chart and selects or is assigned a humorous short story or novel excerpt to read.

2. Working independently, each student reads the story or scene and records examples of the three kinds of humor on his or her chart.

PRODUCT

1. Students assemble in groups of four or five to share their favorite examples of humor and to discuss one of the following questions:

   • Which kind of humor is dominant in your assigned story or excerpt? How effectively did the author utilize it to tell the story?
   • How does humor help the author to tell the story more effectively?

2. Following the time allotted for discussion, each student can do one of the following:

   • write a first-draft opinion paragraph based on one of the questions
   • create a humorous public service radio announcement
   • draw a cartoon illustrating a particularly humorous moment from his or her assigned story or excerpt
   • dramatize a humorous scene from one of the stories or novel excerpts

3. If there is time, students can reassemble in their discussion groups and share their products with the rest of their group.

SUGGESTION

3-2-1. The teacher selects important points that each student needs to have learned from the small-group discussion and asks students to write them down—and possibly hand them in—as per the following example:

Three new things that I learned about humor today
Two purposes for putting humor into a story
One thing about humor that I would like to say to the author of this story

EXTENSION FOR SENIOR STUDENTS

1. The teacher explains that *satire* is to literature as a caricature is to a portrait. A caricature exaggerates certain features of a person's face to create a humorous image. In the same way, satire uses exaggeration and provides a way for literature and the media to poke fun at certain aspects of society.

   When a film caricatures another film, or when a novel caricatures another novel, that isn't a satire—it's a *parody*. When a film caricatures the entire film industry, however, that is a satire. When a novel caricatures the entire publishing industry, that, too, is a satire. Parodies are meant to be laughed at; satires are meant to be knowingly smiled at.

2. The teacher can illustrate the difference by showing clips from two films or providing excerpts from two stories and letting students compare the levels of humor in them. Here are some suggestions:

FILM PARODIES	FILM SATIRES
Young Frankenstein, Blazing Saddles, or *Spaceballs* *Shaun of the Dead*	*Wag the Dog* *Get Shorty*
LITERARY PARODIES	LITERARY SATIRES
Pride and Prejudice and Zombies (Seth Grahame-Smith) James Thurber's parody of "Little Red Riding Hood" (or any fairy tale parody)	"A Modest Proposal" (Jonathan Swift) *Catch-22* (Joseph Heller)

3. Without knowing which is the parody and which is the satire, students can read/view and chart both film clips or both story excerpts. Pairs of students can then compare and discuss their charts to try to identify which clip or excerpt is the satire and which is the parody.

4. This determination can serve as the basis for a whole class discussion and subsequent product. Students can do one of the following:

   • write a first-draft multiparagraph comparison of the two film clips or novel excerpts
   • choose a serious film and make a list of details that could be exaggerated to turn it into a parody

- watch several episodes of a satirical TV program (for example, *The Office*) and plan and write a paragraph explaining what is being satirized and how
- write their own short parody or satire, using the humor strategies studied in this module

5. Students can form groups of four or five and share their completed products with the rest of the group.

THREE KINDS OF HUMOR

PHYSICAL HUMOR (slapstick, situational)	VERBAL HUMOR (sarcasm, play on words, punning)	CHARACTER HUMOR (the klutz, the hypochondriac, etc.)

Studying Fiction Assignment 10

Explore the Setting of the Story

PURPOSE

Students look at the techniques used by authors to create interesting settings and the importance of setting details to the mood of a story.

INTRODUCTION

1. The teacher asks the class to brainstorm answers to the question: How do you know where you are? (Or, to put it another way, if you had been suddenly teleported to this location without being told where you were going, what details would let you know that you were in a school?) As student answers are recorded on the board, they are grouped under the following headings: visual details, sounds, smells, and textures.

2. The teacher points out that sensory details are often used by characters in a story to figure out where they (or where other characters) are. For example:

   - A blind character knows that he is on a moving train because . . .
   - The police know that a kidnapper has phoned in the ransom demand from somewhere near a construction site because . . .
   - A character knows that she is not waking up in her own bedroom because . . .

MODELING

1. The teacher puts the blank DETAILS REVEAL SETTING chart on the overhead projector and reads aloud to the class the selected short story or novel excerpt.

2. Together, teacher and students identify the various kinds of sensory detail provided. The teacher records the information on the top part of the chart, modeling for students the way s/he wants them to format quotations from text. For example:

". . . a strange yellow cast to the air in the room . . ." (p. 2, para. 2)

SUGGESTION

Before reading the story or excerpt, divide the class into four expert groups, each responsible for picking out and jotting down examples of one of the categories of sensory detail in the text.

Before the whole-class discussion, give the expert groups a couple of minutes to compare notes and ensure that they have a complete list of examples.

3. The teacher then points out that authors consciously select the setting details to be provided to the reader, depending on the following:

   • The point-of-view character. He or she may be blind, for example, or hearing-impaired, depressed, or distracted, and this would influence what the character is able to notice.
   • The role that is being played by the setting in the story. It may be an antagonist in the Dramatic Conflict, making certain details more important than others.
   • Whether it's a familiar or unfamiliar setting for the character. People tend to notice things that are unfamiliar or out of place.

   This information is written on the board for students to copy into their notes.

4. Teacher and students now consider the chart that they filled in together on the overhead transparency and discuss which of the three factors might have played a part in determining which setting details were included in the story or excerpt just read. Their conclusions are filled in under the appropriate heading along the bottom of the chart.

GUIDED PRACTICE

1. Each student receives a double-sided copy of the DETAILS REVEAL SETTING chart and chooses or is assigned one of the selected short stories or novel excerpts.

2. Each student proceeds to read and chart his or her text, using only one side of the handout. The teacher circulates, assisting students where necessary.

PRACTICE

Each student now chooses a second short story or novel excerpt and proceeds to read and chart it on the second side of the handout.

PRODUCT

1. Students assemble in groups of four or five to share their work and discuss one of the following questions:

   • Which of the settings charted by your group is the most effectively described? Give reasons for your answer.
   • How important is it for a story to have a fully described setting?
   • Which is better for a story, a real-life setting or an invented one? Why?

2. Following the time allotted for discussion, each student can do one of the following:

   • write a first-draft opinion paragraph based on a discussion question
   • create a travel brochure for an imagined place, using plenty of sensory details to describe it
   • create a multisensory representation of one of the settings described in his or her selected stories or excerpts

3. If there is time, students can reassemble in their discussion groups and share their products with the rest of their group.

EXTENSION FOR SENIOR STUDENTS

1. The teacher points out to the class that authors have a variety of ways to use setting in a story. One of the most important jobs for a setting is to reveal things about a character to the reader.

2. The teacher then asks:

   How can you tell by looking at someone's bedroom . . .
   . . . that the person who sleeps there is a young child?
   . . . that the person who sleeps there is really into science fiction?
   . . . that the person who sleeps there is a student?

   What can you deduce about a character whose favorite hangout is . . .
   . . . the local amusement park?
   . . . a movie theater?
   . . . a park bench beside a pond?
   . . . the local airport?

   And, what can you deduce about a character who enters a setting and . . .
   . . . sees only ugliness, nothing beautiful at all?
   . . . sees only things that s/he must work to change or repair?
   . . . wishes s/he were somewhere else?
   . . . is immediately angry or fearful?

3. The teacher then hands out copies of the SETTING REVEALS CHARACTER chart and instructs students that they will be recording on the top half of the chart descriptive details from one of the short stories or novel excerpts, and on the bottom half of the chart their own conclusions drawn about the character.

4. Each student chooses one of the selected short stories or novel excerpts and proceeds to fill in the chart, working independently.

5. Students can then assemble in pairs or small groups to discuss and compare their charts. This discussion can serve as the basis for a product. Students can do one of the following:

   • write a first-draft analysis of a character from one of the short stories or novel excerpts, based entirely on evidence provided by the setting

- choose a setting from another story already studied and draw up a list of details that could be added to make it reveal more about the character involved
- write an original scene in which the setting (or the character's reaction to it) reveals information about a main character

6. If time permits, students can form groups of four or five and share their completed products with the rest of the group.

DETAILS REVEAL SETTING

This setting is _____

VISUAL DETAILS	SOUNDS	SMELLS	TEXTURES

Why were these details chosen by the author?

SETTING REVEALS CHARACTER

This character is _____

WHERE THE CHARACTER LIVES OR WORKS	WHERE THE CHARACTER GOES TO RELAX	HOW THE CHARACTER REACTS TO NEW SETTINGS
WHAT THIS REVEALS ABOUT THE CHARACTER	WHAT THIS REVEALS ABOUT THE CHARACTER	WHAT THIS REVEALS ABOUT THE CHARACTER

Studying Fiction Assignment 11
Rate the Opening of the Story

✍ YOU WILL NEED

- An opening scene from a story the class has not already studied
- Opening scene criteria on the board (in INTRODUCTION)
- SFR 21–WHAT WE LEARN chart, double-sided (class set)
- Headings from the WHAT WE LEARN chart on a transparency
- Overhead projector and markers

PLUS

- A class set of an anthology of short stories and a list of 5–7 selected stories from the anthology

OR

- The opening and closing scenes of a novel not currently being studied and the opening and closing scenes of a novel currently being studied

---

PURPOSE

Students identify the characteristics of a well-written story opening and practice evaluating the effectiveness of the first scene of a variety of story types.

INTRODUCTION

1. The teacher asks the class to think about a film or TV show they watched recently that grabbed their attention and drew them into the story right from the beginning. What happened in the opening scene of that story?

   Class discussion should include at least the following criteria, which the teacher records on the board:

   - a main character is introduced
   - the Dramatic Conflict is introduced
   - the setting is established (time and place)
   - important background information is provided
   - the curiosity of the reader or viewer is aroused

2. Looking more closely at the last criterion on the board, the teacher points out that in order for the other four criteria to be fulfilled, the reader has to actually read the opening scene of a story. In other words, the opening scene must "hook the reader" from the beginning. In whole class, the teacher and students brainstorm ways in which this can be accomplished, and the teacher records these on the board as well.

The second list should include the following:

- a mystery that raises questions in the mind of the reader or viewer
- a provocative statement by a character—a challenge, a threat, a promise
- a provocative situation that makes the reader or viewer want to get involved
- begin in the middle of the action
- throw a sudden, unexplained change into the opening scene
- a point-of-view character addresses the reader or viewer directly
- introduce a wacky, fascinating, or unconventional character

Students are given three to five minutes to copy the two lists into their notebooks.

MODELING

1. The teacher reads aloud the opening scene from a story the students have not read.

2. The headings from the WHAT WE LEARN chart are put up on the screen, and the teacher and students discuss and record under each of the headings all the information that is presented in this opening scene.

3. Referring to the list of "hooking" strategies on the board, the teacher and students then identify the strategies the author used in the opening scene just read and briefly discuss how effective they are.

4. Finally, the teacher asks students to rate this opening scene on a scale of one *(I nearly dozed off.)* to ten *(I HAVE to read the rest of this story!)*.

SUGGESTION

A Value Line. The teacher can draw a line on the board or can create a line on a classroom wall using string or masking tape. One end of the line is marked as 1 and the other end as 10. Each student is then given a sticker to place at the spot on the value line that represents the rating or score that s/he would give to the story opening.

GUIDED PRACTICE

1. Each student receives a copy of the WHAT WE LEARN chart and is assigned either a short story from the teacher's list or the opening scene of a novel already studied.

2. Working independently, each student then proceeds to read and analyze the opening scene, as modeled earlier. *Information is to be entered on only one side of the handout.*

   The teacher circulates, offering encouragement and assistance as needed.

3. Students who have finished can pair up with partners who have read the same story to compare their analyses and offer each other constructive suggestions for improvement.

PRACTICE

Each student now flips over the WHAT WE LEARN chart to the blank side of the page and selects either a different story from the teacher's list or the opening scene of the novel currently being studied to read and analyze, recording information as already practiced.

PRODUCT

1. Students assemble in groups of four or five to share their work and discuss one of the following questions:

   - Which of the story openings did the most effective job of "hooking" your attention? Give reasons for your answer.
   - Which is more important to an effective opening scene: the information it provides or the "hooking" strategy used to grab the attention of the reader or viewer? Explain your answer.
   - Do some of the "hooking" strategies tend to lend themselves to particular types of stories? To particular types of readers or viewers? Why do you think this might be so?

2. Following the time allotted for discussion, each student can do one of the following:

   - write a first-draft opinion paragraph based on a discussion question
   - rewrite the beginning of a story already studied to include a "hooking" strategy not already used
   - create a trailer or radio ad for the movie version of a story under study, including at least three "hooking" strategies from the list

3. If time permits, students can reassemble in their discussion groups to share their products with the rest of the group.

EXTENSION FOR SENIOR CLASSES

1. The concluding scene of a story is just as important as the opening scene. The teacher asks students to recall a time when they were dissatisfied with the final scene of a film and asks the class: What made the scene unsatisfying for the viewer?

2. The resulting discussion should include at least the following points, which the teacher records on the board:

   - loose ends not tied up—questions still left in the viewer's mind
   - main character does not achieve emotional closure—actual goal still not achieved
   - conclusion is drawn out—shows the viewer too much of what follows the Climax
   - mood is ominous or uncertain—viewer gets the feeling the story isn't really over
   - ending includes an unpleasant twist or surprise
   - nobody has learned anything or changed by the end of the film

3. The teacher now turns each of these negative points into a positive statement (for example, all loose ends are tied up, the main character achieves emotional closure, and so on), recording the list under the heading, *Elements of an Effective Story Closing*. Students are asked to extend the list with further points that occur to them, and these are added as well. Students are given three to five minutes to copy the final list into their notebooks.

4. The teacher reads aloud the closing scene of a story or novel whose opening scene the class has already analyzed.

5. Students form groups of four or five to discuss the effectiveness of the closing scene, using the list of criteria in their notebooks. Each group then assigns the scene a score from one *(This wasn't an ending at all!)* to ten *(Great ending—find me another story by this author!)*

   These findings are shared in whole class discussion.

6. Each student now works independently to analyze and rate the closing scene of either a third short story from the teacher's list (one the student did not read in the main part of the assignment) or the novel most recently studied by the class.

7. Students assemble in groups of four or five to share their findings and discuss one of the following questions:

   - Do the visual and print media have different definitions of a "satisfactory ending"? Give reasons and illustrative examples to support your answer.
   - How could the ending of the story you just read have been made even more effective?
   - Is there a relationship between the opening and closing scenes of the story you just read? Explain your answer.

8. Following the time allotted for discussion, each student can do one of the following:

   - write a first-draft opinion paragraph based on a discussion question
   - rewrite the closing of a story already read to make it more satisfying for the reader
   - write the first draft of a summary of the opening and closing scenes of the story currently being studied, as they would appear in a film

9. If time permits, students can reassemble in their discussion groups to share their products with the rest of the group.

WHAT WE LEARN
(FROM THE OPENING SCENE OF A STORY)

ABOUT THE MAIN CHARACTER (protagonist or antagonist)	ABOUT THE PLOT (conflict)	ABOUT THE SETTING (time, place, society)	ABOUT THE PAST (important background information)

Studying Fiction Assignment 12
Evaluate the Story

✍ **YOU WILL NEED**

- SFR 22–STORY EVALUATION sheet, double-sided (class set)
- A short-short story 2-4 pages long (class set, to be used in GUIDED PRACTICE)

PLUS

- A class set of an anthology and a list of 4 to 6 selected short stories from the anthology

OR

- Copies of a novel recently studied (1 per student)

PURPOSE

Students determine the characteristics of a well-written story and practice using these criteria to evaluate works of fiction.

INTRODUCTION

1. The teacher hands out a copy of the STORY EVALUATION sheet to each student.

2. Teacher and students briefly discuss each of the criteria that they will be applying to the literature under study.

   NOTE TO TEACHER: The criteria that you select for this assignment may depend on which assignments the class has already done. Feel free to modify the evaluation sheet, adding and deleting material to make it suit the particular needs of each class.

GUIDED PRACTICE

1. Students assemble in groups of three or four. Each student receives a copy of the selected short-short story to read.

2. Students read the short-short story, then work in their groups to discuss and evaluate it according to the criteria on the STORY EVALUATION sheet.

3. Each student fills out one side only of his or her personal copy of the sheet to reflect the group's discussion. The teacher circulates, offering encouragement and assistance as needed.

4. In whole class, the students share their findings and arrive at an overall score for the story.

PRACTICE

1. Students are now instructed to flip over their evaluation sheets to the blank second side.

2. Working independently, each student uses the criteria on the chart to evaluate either an assigned short story from the teacher's list or the novel recently studied in class.

3. Each student then fills out the chart and assigns a numerical score to the work being evaluated.

PRODUCT

1. Students who have read and evaluated the same story assemble in groups of four or five to compare their findings and discuss one of the following:

   • Which part of the story would you say is the strongest, according to the criteria on the evaluation sheet? Which part is the weakest? Give reasons for your assessment.
   • Identify an area of the evaluation in which group members' opinions on the story differed. Why is this so?
   • If you were going to adapt this story into a film, which part or parts would you keep, and which would you change? Give reasons for your decisions.

2. Following the time allotted for discussion, each student can do one of the following:

   • write a first-draft opinion paragraph based on a discussion question
   • write the first draft of a letter to the author, commenting on the effectiveness of his or her story
   • outline an original short story, sharing one important element with the story just analyzed (character, setting, theme, and so on)

3. If time permits, students can reassemble in their discussion groups to share their products with the rest of the group.

EXTENSION FOR SENIOR CLASSES

The analysis and discussion in the main part of the assignment can lead to the writing of a response or a literary essay.

Detailed lesson plans are available in Studying Fiction Assignment 13, "Write a Literary Response," and in Writing the Literary Essay.

STORY EVALUATION SHEET

SCORING: 5 = OUTSTANDING 4 = GOOD 3 = SO-SO

2 = PRETTY WEAK 1 = VERY POOR

HAS THIS AUTHOR EFFECTIVELY:

1. opened the story with a scene that introduces a main character, launches the plot, establishes a believable setting, provides the necessary background information, and "hooks" the reader's interest right away?	5	4	3	2	1
2. created an interesting setting that supports the unfolding of the story?	5	4	3	2	1
3. developed a strong and sympathetic main character?	5	4	3	2	1
4. constructed the story around a strong and gripping dramatic conflict?	5	4	3	2	1
5. written a tale that flows from scene to scene?	5	4	3	2	1
6. built suspense into the story, to hold the reader's interest?	5	4	3	2	1
7. used action and dialogue to keep the story moving at a good pace?	5	4	3	2	1
8. brought the story to a logical and exciting climax?	5	4	3	2	1
9. provided an emotionally satisfying ending to the story?	5	4	3	2	1
10. created a well-written, interesting story for the reader?	5	4	3	2	1

TOTAL =   **/50**

COMMENTS:

Studying Fiction Assignment 13
Write a Literary Response

✍ YOU WILL NEED

- A short-short story that the class has not already read (class set)
- A blank overhead transparency
- Overhead projector and markers
- SFR 23–WRITING A RESPONSE sheet (class set)
- SFR 24–WRITING AN ANALYTICAL RESPONSE sheet (class set)
- The appropriate peer-editing and assessment checklists from among the following:
  - SFR 25–PROOFREAD WITH A PARTNER: DIALECTICAL RESPONSE CHECKLIST (class set)
  - SFR 26–PROOFREAD WITH A PARTNER: PERSONAL RESPONSE CHECKLIST (class set)
  - SFR 27–PROOFREAD WITH A PARTNER: ANALYTICAL RESPONSE CHECKLIST (class set)
  - SFR 28–ASSESSMENT CHECKLIST: DIALECTICAL RESPONSE (half a class set)
  - SFR 29–ASSESSMENT CHECKLIST: PERSONAL RESPONSE (half a class set)
  - SFR 30–ASSESSMENT CHECKLIST: ANALYTICAL RESPONSE (half a class set)
                            PLUS
- A class set of an anthology and a list of short stories already studied from the anthology
                            OR
- A novel that the class is currently studying or has just finished and a list of selected 2–4 page excerpts from the novel

---

PURPOSE

Students practice writing three different kinds of responses to fiction: dialectical, personal, and analytical.

INTRODUCTION

The teacher explains to the class that there are many different ways that a reader can respond to a work of fiction, including putting the book down and not picking it back up again. In this writing assignment, however, students are going to be learning and practicing how to create a response that can be shared with others.

NOTE TO THE TEACHER: There are three types of response in this assignment. In order of increasing difficulty, they are a dialectical response, a personal response, and an analytical response. Select the one(s) that would best suit the needs, abilities, and interests of your students.

MODELING 1: DIALECTICAL RESPONSE

1. The teacher explains to the class that the simplest form of response is the dialectical or "double entry" journal in which the reader records his or her strong immediate impressions of the text while reading it.

2. The blank transparency is put on the overhead projector. With a marker, the teacher draws a vertical line down the middle of the transparency, creating two columns of equal width. The teacher then prints a header at the top of each column: *Quotation* and *Response*.

3. Each student receives a copy of the short-short story and follows along as the teacher begins reading it aloud.

   The teacher stops after reading an interesting sentence or phrase and explains why it seemed to jump off the page: *the vivid description painted a picture in his or her mind, or the metaphor was especially powerful, or this character reminded the teacher of someone s/he used to know, and so on.*

4. The teacher then copies the sentence or phrase into the left-hand column of the transparency, modeling the correct format for extracting and citing quotations from text, and records his or her response to the text in the right-hand column, elaborating with some detail the explanation given to the class a moment earlier.

GUIDED PRACTICE 1: DIALECTICAL RESPONSE

1. The teacher now instructs the students to each take a clean sheet of lined paper, fold it vertically in half, and print the headings *Quotation* and *Response* at the tops of the resulting two columns.

2. Working independently, each student finishes reading the short-short story, recording his or her immediate responses in the form of a dialectical journal, as modeled by the teacher.

   Students should be instructed to select and respond to at least three separate quotations, filling one side of the page. The teacher circulates, offering encouragement and assistance as needed. *(Allow up to twenty minutes for this exercise.)*

3. Students form groups of four or five to share and compare their responses and offer one another constructive suggestions for improvement. *(Allow up to five minutes.)*

PRACTICE 1: DIALECTICAL RESPONSE

1. Each student now chooses either a short story already studied or a selected excerpt from the novel.

2. The student divides another clean sheet of lined paper in half lengthwise and creates a dialectical journal, filling at least one side of the page with correctly formatted quotations and detailed personal responses. *(Allow up to thirty minutes.)*

PRODUCT 1: DIALECTICAL RESPONSE

1. Each student receives a copy of the peer-editing sheet (SFR 25–DIALECTICAL RESPONSE CHECKLIST). The teacher goes over each item with the class to ensure that students understand what they will be expected to produce.

2. *Homework:* That night, each student reads over the peer-editing sheet and his or her dialectical journal, expanding the responses with additional detail if necessary before recopying the journal onto a fresh sheet of paper. The student also checks to ensure that each quotation in the completed draft is correctly copied, formatted, and cited.

3. The finished product may be turned in for formative or summative assessment.

(See "Completing the Final Draft, All Responses," below.)

MODELING AND GUIDED PRACTICE 2: PERSONAL RESPONSE

1. The teacher points out to the class that a written personal response is much more than just saying whether or not one likes the story. The reader also has to be able to explain WHY s/he feels that way, WHAT about the story is effective or ineffective, and HOW the story connects to the reader's own life.

2. The blank transparency is put on the overhead projector. With a marker, the teacher divides the transparency into four sections and labels them: *Plot, Characters, Setting,* and *Theme.* The teacher explains that while reading the story, s/he is going to use this "placemat" to record his or her immediate strong impressions and interesting quotations.

3. Each student receives a copy of the short-short story and follows along as the teacher begins reading it aloud.

4. The teacher stops after reading an interesting sentence or phrase and explains how s/he is feeling right now and why. *(The teacher might feel surprised because the plot has taken a sudden unexpected turn, or sad because s/he identifies with the main character and can feel the character's loss, and so on.)*

5. The teacher then copies the sentence or phrase onto the appropriate section of the placemat on the transparency, modeling the correct format for extracting and citing quotations from text. The teacher proceeds to record his or her response to the quotation in point form just below it, elaborating with some detail the explanation s/he gave the class a moment earlier.

6. Students are instructed to take out a clean sheet of paper and create their own four-section placemat. Working in groups of four, students are to continue reading the short-short story, monitoring and discussing their reactions to the plot, characters, setting, and theme, and recording the relevant quotations on their personal placemats. The teacher circulates, offering encouragement and assistance where needed. *(Allow up to twenty-five minutes for this exercise.)*

7. Each student now receives a copy of the WRITING A RESPONSE sheet, and the teacher and class go over it together, finding and discussing the questions that relate to the quotation and reaction recorded on the exemplar placemat. The teacher expands the recorded material, adding further detail and explanation to answer the question or questions as the whole-class discussion progresses.

8. The teacher explains that what they have just done is the PLANNING stage. Now they have to create the OUTLINE for their response.

   The teacher begins the process by picking the prompt question from the handout that generated the greatest amount of animated discussion. The response is going to be the answer to that question.

PRACTICE 2: PERSONAL RESPONSE

1. Students are instructed to choose one of the studied short stories or novel excerpts to work with.

2. Working independently, each student takes a clean sheet of paper, creates a new placemat, and follows the steps modeled and practiced earlier to PLAN his or her personal response.

3. Each student then considers the list of prompt questions, makes further detailed notes, and finally selects the prompt question that relates most strongly and directly to his or her reactions to the text. The student's response is going to answer this question.

4. If time permits, students can pair up and compare notes. Partners can offer each other constructive suggestions for improvement.

5. *Homework*: That night, each student goes over his or her notes and uses a colored marker to highlight the material—points, explanations, and quotations—that will be included in the finished response. The student copies the prompt question and the highlighted portions of the notes onto a fresh sheet of paper.

PRODUCT 2: PERSONAL RESPONSE

1. Working independently in class, each student divides up his or her notes and quotations from the night before into paragraphs and proceeds to write a first draft of his or her personal response in sentence and paragraph form.

2. Students now pair up with new partners and read each other's responses. Reading partners may offer suggestions for improved wording and organization of ideas but should not actually make changes to the other author's work.

3. *Homework*: That night, each student reads over his or her draft response and makes any necessary changes or improvements before recopying the response onto a fresh sheet of paper.

4. The finished product may be turned in for formative or summative assessment.

   (See "Completing the Final Draft, All Responses," below.)

MODELING 3: ANALYTICAL RESPONSE

1. The teacher hands out copies of WRITING AN ANALYTICAL RESPONSE to the class and goes over it with the students, discussing it item by item to ensure that the process is understood.

   The teacher should point out to the students that an analytical response is a piece of formal writing, unlike either the dialectical journal or the personal response, and that it is important that the rules on the handout be followed.

2. A blank transparency is put on the overhead projector. The teacher explains that while reading the story, s/he is going to use a marker to make notes and record his or her immediate strong impressions along with interesting quotations.

3. Each student receives a copy of the short-short story and follows along as the teacher reads aloud, modeling Steps 1 and 2 from the handout and writing out notes on the overhead transparency.

   By reading over the notes, the teacher and class should be able to determine the focus of the analysis.

PRACTICE 3: ANALYTICAL RESPONSE

1. Working independently, each student chooses a short story or novel excerpt and completes Steps 1 and 2 from the handout, as modeled by the teacher. The teacher circulates, offering encouragement and assistance as needed.

2. Students are then instructed to go on, following Steps 3, 4, and 5 on the handout.

3. Students who complete the planning phase in class can pair up to share and discuss their written outlines (Step 5). Partners can make constructive suggestions for improving the wording of the focus statement and the order in which the supporting points and quotations are presented.

PRODUCT 3: ANALYTICAL RESPONSE

1. Working independently, each student writes a first draft of his or her response, following the instructions in Step 6 on the handout.

   NOTE TO THE TEACHER: In a response to an excerpted scene from a story, the opening paragraph will need to establish the context of the scene within the story (that is, where it takes place and what has just happened). For example,

   > *This scene follows the first real one-on-one confrontation between the protagonist and main antagonist of the story. Thrown together on a school field trip to the museum, they have spent most of the afternoon sniping at each other. When a scheme to have the protagonist left behind backfires, the school bus leaves without either of them aboard, forcing them to call home and ask to be picked up.*

2. *Homework*: At home, each student completes the first draft of his or her response. The student then reads over the draft to check that there are no missing or extra words and to ensure that the instructions on the handout have been followed.

3. The finished product may be turned in for formative or summative assessment.

   (See "Completing the Final Draft, All Responses," below.)

COMPLETING THE FINAL DRAFT, ALL RESPONSES

INTRODUCTION

1. Each student receives a copy of the PROOFREAD WITH A PARTNER checklist and the teacher and class go over it together, discussing each item to ensure that students understand the expectations.

   Students also need to understand the following, which the teacher may wish to write on the board in condensed form as a reminder:

   • *Student authors are the owners of their writing and take final responsibility for the completeness and correctness of the work that is handed in for marking.*
   • *Peer-editing partners are not to make corrections or changes to other authors' work. They may point out words to be checked for spelling or suggest improvements to wording, punctuation, and so on, but the author is the one who actually makes revisions to the text.*

PRACTICE

1. Students pair up with a new working partner (different from all previous pairings) and designate themselves Author A and Author B.

2. Together, both partners work on Author A's response, reading it aloud and discussing the criteria on the PROOF-READ WITH A PARTNER checklist. Author A reads with a pencil in hand, making changes and improvements to his or her own work. As each item on the checklist has been discussed, Author A's editing partner checks it off in the left-hand column of Author A's sheet.

3. The process is then repeated for Author B's response. The teacher circulates meanwhile, offering encouragement and assistance as needed.

FINAL PRODUCT

1. Each student receives a copy of the ASSESSMENT CHECKLIST and the teacher goes over it with the class, discussing each item to ensure that students understand the criteria that will be used to evaluate their work.

   NOTE TO THE TEACHER: The peer-editing and assessment checklists supplied here have been used successfully in my classes. You may wish to shorten, reword, simplify, or reformat either or both of these checklists to suit the needs of your own classes, at all grade levels. Please feel free to do so.

2. *Homework*: That night, each student goes over his or her edited draft once more, making final changes and improvements and checking off items on the PROOFREAD WITH A PARTNER checklist (right-hand column) as they are completed. The student also refers to the ASSESSMENT CHECKLIST to ensure that all the evaluation criteria have been met.

3. Before the due date specified for the response, the student types or prints out a clean final draft of the response. The student also gathers all the elements required for the submission package and assembles them as specified by the teacher. For example:

   Final draft response on top, with student name, course code, and submission date on the first page, THEN
   Assessment checklist, THEN
   Edited rough draft with peer-editing checklist behind it, THEN
   Planning materials, including notes, outline, etc.

   The submission package is then stapled together, ready to be handed in for evaluation on the due date.

WRITING A RESPONSE

WHAT IS A RESPONSE?

A response is a thoughtful and organized reaction to a piece of artwork or literature. In high school, students are asked to write two different kinds of essay-style responses.

A PERSONAL RESPONSE

A personal response is just what its name suggests—your personal reaction to the essay or story that you have just read. But it has to be a *thoughtful* reaction. "Wow, this is a great story!" is just the beginning of your response. You now have to do the following:

THINK ABOUT THE WORK

- Why is this a great (or not-so-great) story? What parts of it were really effective, which were ineffective, and why?
- Does it remind you of other stories you've read or viewed? How?
- How realistic are the characters in the story? Why?
- How does the setting contribute to the effectiveness of the story?
- What message do you think the author wants the reader to get from reading this story?

RELATE THE WORK TO YOURSELF

- Which parts of the story did you like, and why?
- Which parts didn't you like? Why?
- Which characters did you like or dislike? Why?
- How did the end of the story make you feel? Why?
- Does this story remind you of anything that has happened to anyone you know? Or of something similar that happened to you when you were younger?
- If you could rewrite any part of this story, what part would it be? How would you make it different? Why?
- If you could speak with the author of this story, what would you like to say to him or her? Why?

PICK A QUOTATION FROM THE WORK AND RELATE IT TO YOURSELF

- Why did you choose this quotation? How does it relate to your feelings or your life?
- What do you think is the main idea of this quotation? Why do you think the author included it in the story?

The teacher will tell you when assigning the response how long he or she wants it to be and whether you are to base it on a quotation or on the entire story.

(continued on other side)

A FORMAL RESPONSE

A formal response is also called an "analytical response." Unlike the personal response, it isn't about your personal feelings or memories triggered by the piece of literature. It's about the things that make the work *work*. A formal response lets you show the teacher your critical thinking skills.

THE WRITING PROCESS

Whether it is personal or formal, any piece of writing that is to be turned in for marking must be put through the writing process:

PLANNING (sometimes called prewriting) is the stage of gathering information and organizing it. You might use a chart, a web, a concept map, or a Venn diagram to put your impressions or supported opinions in order. Then you must **OUTLINE THE RESPONSE**, either using a template supplied by your teacher or laying out the information in some arrangement or sequence that makes it meaningful for the reader.

Write out your **FIRST DRAFT**. It does not have to be perfect. Just get the information down on the page in sentence and paragraph form, being sure you haven't left anything out.

Now **REVISE THE FIRST DRAFT**. Make sure it has a beginning, a middle, and an end and that everything in it is on topic and in the most effective order. Does anything else need to be added? Should something be left out? Would it read better if you rearranged parts of it? Check the rubric to ensure that you've included everything the teacher will be looking for when he or she marks your response. That is what revising is about—format and completion. When you're done, recopy the entire response as your **SECOND DRAFT**.

EDIT AND POLISH THE SECOND DRAFT. Now you're looking for:

- sentences that are incomplete or don't make sense
- words that have been left out or need to be left out
- words that have been incorrectly spelled (don't rely on your computer's spellchecker—it can't tell the difference between "again" and "a gain," but you can!)
- verb tenses that don't make sense
- symbols (&) or abbreviations (etc.) that need to be written out in full
- commas, apostrophes, and capital letters that are missing or out of place

When you're sure the response is as grammatically correct as you can make it, copy it out one last time as your **FINAL DRAFT.** Be sure to attach your marking rubric, Works Cited page, or whatever else your teacher has requested as part of the submission package.

WRITING AN ANALYTICAL RESPONSE

An analytical response is not an essay, and it isn't a personal response—it's somewhere in between.

- It has no thesis statement and no formal introduction. However, there has to be a thread running through it, holding it all together.
- It is written in the third person (avoiding all use of "I," "you," "we," or any form thereof).
- It assumes a critical viewpoint and maintains the same perspective throughout.
- It is written entirely in the present tense, in proper sentence and paragraph format. It avoids slang, contractions, abbreviations, and symbols, just like a formal essay.
- Unlike a formal literary essay, it may take a humorous tone.

Here are the steps to follow when preparing an analytical response to a piece of writing. Be sure not to skip any!

1. Perform a close reading of the text and make plenty of notes in the margins and on separate pieces of paper. Authors make conscious decisions about what to include in their writing and how to express it. Notice everything that is there (and what is NOT stated as well). Go paragraph by paragraph and sentence by sentence and pick everything apart, pulling as much meaning out of the text as you can.

2. Now that you fully understand the text, decide what your critical approach is going to be. Which of the following will you be focusing on in your analysis?

   - a literary device that runs like a thread through the text, pulling it all together (for example, a structural metaphor or a series of rhetorical questions)
   - a gap, lie, or inconsistency that undermines the unity of the piece
   - the author's "personal agenda" served by writing the piece
   - a theme that is reflected in the characters, plot, setting, or writing style
   - an echo of another, much older story (for instance, biblical references, mythology, or a fairy tale)
   - gender-based discrepancies in the text (such as stereotypes or one gender dominating or excluding the other)
   - a power imbalance or power struggle (perhaps between rich and poor or educated and uneducated)
   - relationships between/among the characters

3. Return to your notes and the original text, and identify two or three points or quotations that relate strongly to the focus you've chosen for your response. Copy them out in a list. They will form the backbone of your analysis.

(continued on other side)

4. Now turn your attention to each of the points or quotations in turn and begin analyzing in depth by thinking about and answering the following questions, making detailed notes as you go.

   - Why do you think the author chose to include this in the work?
   - Why would s/he consider it important?
   - What does this say about (the focus of your response)?
   - How does this enhance or reflect or reinforce (the focus of your response)?
   - How does it relate to the other points or quotations you've chosen?
   - What is the effect of this on the main character, the speaker, or the other characters in the piece?
   - To what extent do their reactions and interactions enhance, reflect, or reinforce (the focus of your response)?
   - What is the effect on the reader? (In general, not just the effect on you—this is not a personal response.)

5. If you have thought deeply about the piece and made detailed notes, you should now have something insightful and meaningful to say about it. Express this as a written statement in your notes. Then, based on your answers to the analytical questions in Step 4, decide on the best order in which to present your two or three points and which strong examples (quotations) from your notes will support each one. Write this information out to serve as the outline for your response.

6. Begin writing your first draft, using the DFAR pattern.

   - D—In the first paragraph, Define and Discuss the focus of the analysis and come to a Decision about it. This is not a thesis statement, but it provides a unifying purpose for your response.
   - F, A, R—In each of the following paragraphs, Find an example, Analyze it, and Relate it back to the decision at the end of the first paragraph.
   - Give each of your important points or quotations its own paragraph.
   - Make sure you're not just identifying and explaining examples (although that is a good place to start). Go deeper and explain how the example connects with the critical focus of your response. Discuss what makes each example effectively support your decision statement. Show the reader that you've given this story a close examination and a lot of thought.
   - You don't need to have a concluding paragraph as long as your response ends on a completed thought.

7. Now put your completed first draft through the rest of the writing process: revise, edit, proofread, polish, and create a final draft for submission.

REVISE, EDIT, AND PROOFREAD WITH A PARTNER
DIALECTICAL RESPONSE CHECKLIST

Author's Name: _____

Editing Partner's Name: _____

Checked by Partner	EDITING AND PROOFREADING CRITERIA	Improved by Author
	The response has a descriptive title.	
	The response is organized on the page in two columns of equal width, headed "Quotation" and "Response."	
	The student has selected at least three different quotations to copy into the left-hand column.	
	Each quotation has been accurately copied from the text. There are no words left out and no spelling errors.	
	Each quotation has been correctly formatted and cited.	
	The student has responded to each of the selected quotations individually.	
	Each response is personal and thoughtful, fully describing the effect the quotation had on the responding reader.	
	Each response is detailed and specific rather than general.	
	Each response is written out in complete and correctly punctuated sentences.	
	The grammar and spelling have been checked and corrected if necessary.	

TO BE COMPLETED BY THE EDITING PARTNER:

One thing I especially enjoyed about reading this response was

_____

One thing that I think would improve this response is

_____

Remember to attach this checklist (filled out) to the back of your edited draft when assembling your package for submission.

REVISE, EDIT, AND PROOFREAD WITH A PARTNER
PERSONAL RESPONSE CHECKLIST

Author's Name: _____

Editing Partner's Name: _____

Checked by Partner	EDITING AND PROOFREADING CRITERIA	Improved by Author
	The response has been given an interesting, descriptive title. ("Personal Response" is not going to do it.)	
	The response has been written out in complete sentence and paragraph form. (No jot notes or point-form lists.)	
	The response follows the instructions given by the teacher: It is the correct length and is based on either the entire story or the specified number of quotations.	
	The response begins with the answer to a specific prompt question from the list on the handout.	
	The response is a thoughtful personal reaction to a piece of writing. It provides a detailed explanation for each statement the reader makes about the text: the "why," the "what," and the "how."	
	The response is well organized. Paragraphs have been put in the most effective order.	
	The response has coherence. Sentences and paragraphs are linked together so the writing flows from the opening to the closing sentence.	
	Each quotation used in the response has been correctly copied, formatted, and cited, as demonstrated by the teacher in class.	
	The language used in the response is not slangy. All words are written out in full. When referring to the story, the responder has used the present tense. The author of the text is never referred to by first name only.	
	The grammar, spelling, and punctuation have been checked and corrected if necessary. There are no sentence fragments, run-on sentences, or confusing pronoun references in the text.	

Remember to attach this checklist (filled out) to the back of your edited draft when assembling your package for submission.

REVISE, EDIT, AND PROOFREAD WITH A PARTNER
ANALYTICAL RESPONSE CHECKLIST

Author's Name: _____

Editing Partner's Name: _____

Checked by Partner	EDITING AND PROOFREADING CRITERIA	Improved by Author
	The response has been given an interesting, descriptive title.	
	The first paragraph *defines* and *discusses* a thread that runs through the text and that will become the focus of the analysis.	
	The response is based on a *decision* the responder has made about the thread that runs through the text.	
	The statement expressing this *decision* appears at the end of the introductory paragraph.	
	Each quotation chosen to illustrate the *decision* is analyzed in detail and is contained in its own paragraph.	
	The selected quotations strongly support the *decision* expressed in the first paragraph.	
	Each quotation in the response is correctly copied, formatted, and cited, as demonstrated by the teacher in class. Each quotation is smoothly integrated into the text of the response.	
	Each analytical paragraph concludes by relating the analysis to the *decision* at the end of the introductory paragraph. The response concludes with a completed thought.	
	The language used in the response is formal, not slangy. "I," "we," and "you" have been avoided. There are no contractions, abbreviations, or symbols in the text. The present tense is used throughout. The author is never referred to by first name only.	
	The grammar, spelling, and punctuation have been checked and corrected if necessary. There are no sentence fragments, run-on sentences, or ambiguous pronoun references in the text.	

Remember to attach this checklist (filled out) to the back of your edited draft when assembling your package for submission.

SFR 28

ASSESSMENT CHECKLIST: DIALECTICAL RESPONSE

Student's Name: _____

ASSESSMENT CRITERIA

Knowledge/Understanding   /10

- Student's responses demonstrate a thoughtful, age-appropriate understanding of the chosen quotations.
- Student's work shows clear understanding of the form and purpose of a dialectical response—that is, the page is correctly organized and the selected quotations are responded to rather than summarized or explained.

Thinking   /10

- Student's choice of quotations reflects a logical awareness of the greater meaning of the text.
- Student's responses demonstrate an appropriately sophisticated level of thinking.

Comments:

ASSESSMENT CHECKLIST: DIALECTICAL RESPONSE

Student's Name: _____

ASSESSMENT CRITERIA

Knowledge/Understanding   /10

- Student's responses demonstrate a thoughtful, age-appropriate understanding of the chosen quotations.
- Student's work shows clear understanding of the form and purpose of a dialectical response—that is, the page is correctly organized and the selected quotations are responded to rather than summarized or explained.

Thinking   /10

- Student's choice of quotations reflects a logical awareness of the greater meaning of the text.
- Student's responses demonstrate an appropriately sophisticated level of thinking.

Comments:

ASSESSMENT CHECKLIST: PERSONAL RESPONSE

Student's Name: _____

ASSESSMENT CRITERIA

Knowledge/Understanding   /10

- Student demonstrates *insightful understanding* of the text being responded to and is able to make *interesting and thoughtful comments* about it.
- Student shows clear understanding of the *form of a personal response*—that is, the work under discussion is responded to rather than summarized or explained; student has written a response, not an essay.

Thinking   /10

- The writing is *well organized*. Ideas have been placed in the most effective order and linked together to create coherence.
- Student's comments demonstrate an *appropriately sophisticated level of thinking*. Example quotations are thoughtfully considered and firmly related to the responder's life and emotions.

Comments:

ASSESSMENT CHECKLIST: PERSONAL RESPONSE

Student's Name: _____

ASSESSMENT CRITERIA

Knowledge/Understanding   /10

- Student demonstrates *insightful understanding* of the text being responded to and is able to make *interesting and thoughtful comments* about it.
- Student shows clear understanding of the *form of a personal response*—that is, the work under discussion is responded to rather than summarized or explained; student has written a response, not an essay.

Thinking   /10

- The writing is *well organized*. Ideas have been placed in the most effective order and linked together to create coherence.
- Student's comments demonstrate an *appropriately sophisticated level of thinking*. Example quotations are thoughtfully considered and firmly related to the responder's life and emotions.

Comments:

ASSESSMENT CHECKLIST: ANALYTICAL RESPONSE

Student's Name: _____

ASSESSMENT CRITERIA

Knowledge/Understanding   /10

- Student demonstrates *insightful understanding* of the text chosen for analysis and is able to make *interesting and specific comments* about it.
- Student demonstrates clear understanding of the chosen *critical focus*.
- Student shows clear understanding of *the form of an analytical response*—that is, the work under discussion is analyzed rather than summarized or explained; student has written a response, not an essay.

Thinking   /10

- The writing is well organized. Response is *clearly focused* on the identified thread running through the text and all quoted examples are strongly related to it.
- Student's analysis demonstrates an *appropriately sophisticated level of thinking*. Examples are thoughtfully examined, then solidly tied together.

Comments:

ASSESSMENT CHECKLIST: ANALYTICAL RESPONSE

Student's Name: _____

ASSESSMENT CRITERIA

Knowledge/Understanding   /10

- Student demonstrates *insightful understanding* of the text chosen for analysis and is able to make *interesting and specific comments* about it.
- Student demonstrates clear understanding of the chosen *critical focus*.
- Student shows clear understanding of *the form of an analytical response*—that is, the work under discussion is analyzed rather than summarized or explained; student has written a response, not an essay.

Thinking   /10

- The writing is well organized. Response is *clearly focused* on the identified thread running through the text and all quoted examples are strongly related to it.
- Student's analysis demonstrates an *appropriately sophisticated level of thinking*. Examples are thoughtfully examined, then solidly tied together.

Comments:

Literary Criticism 101

An Introduction to Critical Viewpoints

This mini-unit is designed to introduce students to an analytical process that they can use with success through their high school years and beyond—and on more than just works of literature. The unit is eminently adaptable and has been successfully taught to (and enjoyed by) students in grades 9, 10, 11, and 12.

Here are some suggested modifications that will enable you to implement Literary Criticism 101 in all of your English classes:

1. *Change the time frame.* The time allowances shown in this unit are what I have found to be average requirements for a grade 11 or 12 class. Grade 9 or 10 classes may need more time to digest the concepts and complete the work. Advanced Placement (AP) or Pre-AP students may barrel through it in much less time. Your students may need more time with some parts of the unit and less time with others. That's fine—give them whatever time they require.

2. *Change the number of critical viewpoints.* Six are provided, ranging in difficulty from simple to advanced. Grade 12 students should be able to handle all six of them, but for a grade 9 or 10 class, you might want to select just two or three (I recommend neo-Marxist and gender-based criticism especially) on which to focus. For a pre–Advanced Placement course, you may want to begin with two viewpoints, then repeat the unit, adding two more each time.

3. *Change the practice assignment media.* Critical viewpoints are lenses that can be trained on just about anything: a news article, a television show, a video game, sports event coverage, any kind of advertising, song lyrics, as well as works of literature. Before students dive into essays or poetry, let them practice focusing their lenses on various other media. Depending on the class, you might even try a reverse assignment, using several published letters to the editor in response to a particular event or a "hot issue." Students can read and discuss the letters and determine each writer's critical viewpoint.

4. *Change the basis for analysis.* Syntax is the focus supplied in the mini-unit, but it has been successfully taught with an emphasis on diction, imagery, and figurative comparisons, among other literary and rhetorical devices. Based on the literature your class is studying, you may want students to take a close look at the use of simile and metaphor in a poem, or comparison and contrast in an essay. In that case, use the mini-unit as a template, substituting the desired writing strategy in place of syntax. You can find relevant student materials elsewhere in this program or employ existing resources of your own.

5. *Change the summative assignment.* Not every student in every class needs to write a complete analytical response during class time. For a grade 9 class, a paragraph answering an effectiveness question might be sufficient. I have used this mini-unit to begin preparing students to write three essay-length responses in two hours on the Advanced Placement English Literature exam. I have also used it to teach grade 10 students how to compare two short poems. Instead of one long response from a single critical viewpoint, you may want students to write three short responses from three different viewpoints. In general, providing a menu of assignments at several levels of difficulty is an effective way to differentiate the unit for students of varying interests and abilities. Some students may even wish to devise their own assignment. For example, a talented young man in one of my grade 12 classes once stepped into a

studied author's shoes, scripting and delivering a spirited (and entertaining) rebuttal to the critics of the author's era, turning their own critical viewpoints against them.

Flexibility is key to the students' enjoyment of this mini-unit and, ultimately, of literature. You will find that it is key to your own enjoyment as well. Have fun helping your students to develop their critical faculties and analytical thinking skills!

AIMS AND OBJECTIVES OF THIS MODULE

Aims:

Students shall have opportunities to:

1. become aware of themselves as critical readers and realize the worth and validity of their perceptions, interpretations, and expressed opinions;

2. become proficient in the mechanics of written language and in the use of spoken and written language to think, learn, and communicate;

3. understand the role that language, literature, and the media play in the exploration of intellectual issues and in the establishment of personal and societal values; and

4. develop critical skills and use them to analyze and respond to the products of various media.

Objectives:

Through this module, students will be encouraged to:

1. become better communicators of their own observations and interpretations;

2. gain a deeper understanding of the ways in which literature and media products are purposefully composed and organized to have an effect on the reader or viewer;

3. develop a better understanding of themselves and others;

4. hone and channel their analytical skills by assuming a variety of critical viewpoints;

5. practice effective teamwork through group discussion and cooperative writing activities; and

6. follow a structured process to produce a piece of analytical writing.

Literary Criticism 101

An Introduction to Critical Viewpoints

✍ YOU WILL NEED (FOR DAY 1)

- A small painting or "mystery gadget"
- LCR 1 to LCR 6–CRITICAL VIEWPOINTS handout package (class set)
- LCR 7–CRITICAL VIEWPOINTS OVERVIEW chart (class set)

DAY 1: INTRODUCTION

1. The teacher shows the class the painting and explains that the teacher's spouse brought it home from an auction and absolutely loves it; looking at the painting helps him or her to relax. Meanwhile, looking at the painting sets the teacher's teeth on edge. So who is right about the painting, the teacher or the teacher's spouse?

   After some class discussion, a student will eventually point out that both can be right, since art is subjective.

   Wait for the answer you want—the second you supply it, the students' minds will snap shut.

   In a predominantly male class, the teacher may wish to use a "mystery gadget" from a hardware store or building supplies outlet—that is, something whose function is not immediately apparent. The teacher explains that s/he found it while cleaning out the basement and asks the class what it could possibly be used for. In whole-class discussion, students brainstorm a variety of uses for the device.

   Do not reveal the "right" answer. The point of this exercise is to get students to realize that there are many different—and valid—ways to approach a question, a situation, or a creative product.

2. The teacher points out that there are multiple ways of looking at anything, especially things like art, music, and literature. Literary criticism is based on the individual approach. When a large enough number of critics—a "critical mass," if you like—regularly take the same approach, then a "school of critical thought" is born. (The word *school* here relates to the phrase "a school of fish"—which is just a bunch of fish all traveling in the same direction.)

3. Each student now receives a copy of the CRITICAL VIEWPOINTS handout package. The teacher explains that there are many different critical schools of thought, but in this course the class will be learning about just six of them—chosen because they are the most commonly used and the most easily understood, requiring little or no additional research on the student's part. *(However, a bibliography is provided at the end of this module as a starting point for any student who wishes to delve deeper into a particular critical viewpoint.)*

4. The teacher gives the class a tour of the handout package, pointing out that for each critical viewpoint, there is a summary, a list of "look fors," and (very important) a list of writing and discussion prompts. Students need to understand that these viewpoints act as lenses, permitting the critical reader to focus on certain aspects of the work being analyzed.

The viewpoints are like tools in a carpenter's kit—the more kinds of tools there are in the kit, the better the job the carpenter will be able to do.

TEACHING TIP

If you need to explain the term "ideology" (from the handout package) to your class, here's a quick and easy way to do it:

An *idea* is a notion that suddenly occurs to you: "That red hat is really attractive."

An *ideal* is an image of perfection that you try to achieve: "I'd like to fill my closet with red hats just like that one."

An *ideology* creates an us-or-them attitude: "Anyone who doesn't like red hats is no friend of mine."

5. The students number off to form focus groups, one per critical viewpoint in the handout package. (The teacher will need to make a note of which students are in each group.) Each group of students now reads and discusses their assigned critical viewpoint and answers the question at the bottom of the page, listing examples of works that lend themselves to this particular approach. *(Give them about ten minutes for this part of the activity.)*

6. In whole class, each group briefly summarizes (in one or two minutes) its assigned viewpoint for the benefit of the other groups and provides any examples group members have come up with.

7. Each student now receives a copy of the CRITICAL VIEWPOINT OVERVIEW chart, summarizing all six viewpoints, and the teacher goes over it with the class. This will be students' quick reference for future assignments.

8. Based on the preceding discussion, each student decides which three viewpoints s/he would like to explore in more depth in the remaining assignments in this module. A slip of paper listing these is the student's "ticket out the door."

Students may need to be reminded to put their names on these ballots. At the teacher's discretion, they may also be instructed NOT to choose the viewpoint they've just explored in their focus groups.

TEACHER'S HOMEWORK: Compile all the ballots into a chart, organizing students' choices around three assignments, being careful to balance the numbers in each viewpoint group for each assignment.

The sheets in the CRITICAL VIEWPOINTS handout package are provided here, along with the overview sheet.

CRITICAL VIEWPOINTS 1
FORMALISM/STRUCTURALISM (NEW CRITICISM)

BASIC PRINCIPLES

- Assumes that the piece of literature works well (that is, form and content reinforce each other; language, structure, and literary devices together make up a unified and logical whole).
- Purpose of analysis is to discover *why* and *how* this is so.
- Focus is on the formal elements of a work, without regard for anything outside of the text (such as the author's personality or the historical context of the writing). Emphasis is on *how* ideas are conveyed, not on the merit of the ideas themselves.
- Demands a close reading of the work—line by line and sometimes word by word.

WHAT YOU SHOULD LOOK FOR

- oppositions (black/white, right/wrong, push/pull, and so on) that are resolved, creating unity in the text
- the organizing principle (usually a theme but may be a literary device such as irony) that brings the opposites together, thus creating a unified structure

FORMALIST CRITICISM: WRITING AND DISCUSSION PROMPTS

- What do you notice about the larger elements of the work, such as plot, characterization, and narrative technique?
- What do you notice about the stylistic elements of the work, such as diction, irony, paradox, metaphor, and symbol?
- How do the various elements of the work (plot, character, point of view, setting, tone, diction, images, symbols, and so forth) mirror or echo its content (that is, its theme or meaning)?
- How are individual elements related to the work as a whole?
- What is the effect of the work on the reader and how is that effect accomplished?
- What is the organizing principle? How is the structure of the work unified?

WORKS YOU HAVE READ, SEEN, OR CREATED
THAT LEND THEMSELVES TO FORMALIST CRITICISM

CRITICAL VIEWPOINTS 2
MYTHOPOEIC/ARCHETYPAL CRITICISM

BASIC PRINCIPLES

- Assumes that every literary text is related to the entire body of literature, based on the inclusion of archetypal (that is, earliest or most influential) structures or patterns.
- Draws on the knowledge of many different fields, especially comparative religion, history, and psychology to assist in establishing these connections.
- Focuses on archetypal characters, situations, images, and symbols that appear in literature throughout history.
- Demands a close and careful reading of the text.
- Emphasis is on making connections between this text and other, earlier texts, such as mythology, folklore, legends, and fairy tales.

WHAT YOU SHOULD LOOK FOR

- symbols and universal recurring patterns (the hero's journey, transformation, or a quest)
- specific or metaphorical references to myths or archetypal characters, situations, images, and symbols (for example, the sun described as a flaming chariot)
- links to or echoes of other major works of literature, mythologies, legends, and folk tales

MYTHOPOEIC/ARCHETYPAL CRITICISM: WRITING AND DISCUSSION PROMPTS

- What journey does the protagonist undertake and how does it relate to other journeys in literature, myth, or legend?
- What archetypal characters, images, and symbols (such as water as a source of life, the fairy godmother, etc.) do you notice in this work of literature?
- What transformation (such as innocence to experience or youth to old age) does the protagonist undergo? Is it actual or metaphorical? What are its causes?

WORKS YOU HAVE READ, SEEN, OR CREATED
THAT LEND THEMSELVES TO MYTHOPOEIC CRITICISM

CRITICAL VIEWPOINTS 3
NEO-MARXIST CRITICISM

BASIC PRINCIPLES

- Assumes that literature is the reflection of a struggle between the powerful and the oppressed in society and that it will try to "win over" the reader to one side or the other.
- Focuses on power (sexual, social, economic, political, etc.) and how it operates.
- Analysis is conducted with regard to both the struggle and the outcome of the struggle—that is, either a *revolution* (overturning of the established order) or the *destruction* of both sides.
- Demands an objective, unbiased reading of the text, despite the ideology inherently expressed.

WHAT YOU SHOULD LOOK FOR

- how the work supports the dominant social class and whether injustices in the social order are highlighted
- whether the author and characters are aware that they are being oppressed and to what extent the oppressed assist their oppressors in keeping them down
- how the text works to persuade the reader to take sides in the power struggle depicted
- how the literary work itself might contribute to the struggle against socioeconomic oppression

NEO-MARXIST CRITICISM: WRITING AND DISCUSSION PROMPTS

- What or whose ideology is evident in the text? How do you know?
- Who has power (and what kind is it) in the text? How does this influence people and events? How does it change from the beginning to the end of the text?
- What dominant social ideals are supported or opposed in the text?
- To what degree do the characters believe in and live by the rules set by the powerful class or classes in their society? Why? How do you know?
- At what point or points do characters recognize that they are being oppressed?
- How do they respond? What limits their options for changing their situation?
- What will be the probable outcome of the power struggle represented in the text?

WORKS YOU HAVE READ, SEEN, OR CREATED
THAT LEND THEMSELVES TO NEO-MARXIST CRITICISM

CRITICAL VIEWPOINTS 4
GENDER-BASED CRITICISM

BASIC PRINCIPLES

- Assumes that males and females write, read, and perceive literature differently because of the ways in which they have been conditioned by society to think of themselves.
- Assumes that literature reflects many unexamined gender-based assumptions that need to be revisited and re-evaluated.
- Focuses (like the neo-Marxist approach) on the powerful and the oppressed, and the social injustices that create and maintain these two groups.
- Demands an objective, unbiased reading of the text, regardless of the reader's own gender and existing ideology.
- May be combined with any or all other critical approaches.

WHAT YOU SHOULD LOOK FOR

- how women are represented in male-written texts and vice versa
- how male-female relationships are portrayed—that is, who has the power and why, and whether these relationships lead to growth or conflict
- how men and women tend to write about or represent their own experiences
- gender-based assumptions or expectations of various eras and how they can point to an interpretation of a work

GENDER-BASED CRITICISM: WRITING AND DISCUSSION PROMPTS

- How are the form, content, and theme of the work influenced by the author's gender?
- How are men and women represented in this work? What stereotypes can you identify?
- Does this work support or does it rebel against traditional ideas regarding male and female roles in society, the degree of sexuality permitted, and so on? How is this shown?
- What is the protagonist's attitude toward the opposite-gender characters in the text? How is this shown, and how does it affect the reader's level of sympathy with him or her?
- In a story of conflict between men and women, whose version of the truth do you believe? Why?
- How do or did the social and historic conditions portrayed influence the lives, roles, and desires of the women (as opposed to the men) in the text?
- How do the women in this work obtain and exercise their power (differently than the men)? With what consequences?

WORKS YOU HAVE READ, SEEN, OR CREATED
THAT LEND THEMSELVES TO GENDER-BASED CRITICISM

CRITICAL VIEWPOINTS 5
DECONSTRUCTIONIST CRITICISM

BASIC PRINCIPLES

- Assumes that the literary work is not unified, but rather full of oppositions and (self-) contradictions waiting to be revealed.
- Assumes that both the author and the language s/he is using are unstable "works in progress," being shaped on a daily basis by outside forces.
- Focuses on the struggle and contradictions in the text, on the multiple possible meanings and interpretations, on unresolved oppositions, and on gaps and falsehoods.
- The purpose of analysis is to demonstrate that this text is NOT working well and explain why.
- Demands a close, careful reading of the text.

WHAT YOU SHOULD LOOK FOR

- oppositions (black/white, male/female, natural/unnatural) that remain unresolved—generally, one side will dominate or exclude the other
- someone's ideology or agenda concealed in the text, and whether the author supports it or is resisting it
- power dynamics in the world of the text and in the real world—that is, how and why the work was published, chosen for study, and so on, and who profits from it
- gaps in the text, as well as contradictions and falsehoods that get the text into trouble
- the voice(s) heard in the text (and the ones that aren't)

DECONSTRUCTIONIST CRITICISM: WRITING AND DISCUSSION PROMPTS

- Do you see contradictory "truths" in this text? How are they being supported?
- Who speaks in this text, and who is silent? Why?
- From whose perspective is the story told? Why?
- How does the author's choice of point of view influence the meaning that the reader can draw from the text?
- With which character do you identify in this story? Why? How might this affect your interpretation of its meaning?
- What social factors in your own life might influence the way you interpret or respond to the text?
- Who is represented in this text, and how? Who is not represented, and why?

WORKS YOU HAVE READ, SEEN, OR CREATED
THAT LEND THEMSELVES TO DECONSTRUCTIONIST CRITICISM

CRITICAL VIEWPOINTS 6
PSYCHOLOGICAL CRITICISM

BASIC PRINCIPLES

- Assumes that it is possible to gain insight into the workings of an author's mind by examining the various aspects of his/her writing—taking a "clinical" approach to literature.
- Assumes that a work of literature can provide a "window into the soul" of both its creator and humanity in general.
- Focuses on the speeches, actions and interactions of characters, as well as on the author's creative choices regarding setting, mood, plot, and theme.
- Demands careful and thoughtful reading of the text in order to detect subtext.
- Demands objectivity on the part of the reader.

WHAT YOU SHOULD LOOK FOR

- characters' basic motivations and probable background as shown by their behavior and interactions with other characters and with the setting chosen for the text
- symptoms of mental or emotional disturbance shown by the characters in the text
- indications of emotional extremes in the setting and mood of a literary work

PSYCHOLOGICAL CRITICISM: WRITING AND DISCUSSION PROMPTS

- What do the interactions of the characters in the story reveal about each of the personalities involved?
- What conclusions could you draw from looking at the relationships between characters in this text? How well or poorly do they understand one another? Why?
- What mood is established by the setting in this story? Provide examples.
- What evidence do you see of mental or emotional problems (for example, low self-esteem, guilt, codependency, and so on) in the thoughts, speech, or actions of the characters?
- How do the setting and situations reflect, perpetuate, or intensify the characters' mental or emotional problems?
- What is the basic need, fear, or desire that drives each of the characters in this text? How does s/he strive to satisfy or avoid it? How does s/he repress or channel it?
- How do the characters' dreams reveal their underlying needs, fears, and desires?

WORKS YOU HAVE READ, SEEN, OR CREATED
THAT LEND THEMSELVES TO PSYCHOLOGICAL CRITICISM

CRITICAL VIEWPOINTS: AN OVERVIEW

CRITICAL VIEWPOINT	FOCUSES ON	BASIS FOR ANALYSIS
Formalist/Structuralist (New Criticism)	Oppositions that are resolved through a unifying principle (usually a theme), making the work well structured and unified.	Plot events, character development/revelation, symbolism, irony, metaphor, imagery, setting, comparison, and so forth.
Deconstructionist	Oppositions that bring about unresolvable conflict, preventing unity and/or actively leading to confusion.	Gaps, inconsistencies, contradictions, falsehoods, the multiple meaning of words, multiple possible interpretations.
Neo-Marxist	Class struggle between oppressor and oppressed, which can only result in revolution or mutual destruction.	Power imbalances (all kinds), ideologies, social forces, awareness (or lack of awareness) of oppression.
Gender-Based	How girls/women or men/boys are (mis)represented and discriminated against in literature and the publishing industry.	How women are portrayed in men's writing and vice versa, relationships and power imbalances, what men and women are expected/allowed to do in the society portrayed in the literary work.
Mythopoeic	Connections to and echoes of the entire body of literature and storytelling; archetypes, symbols, transformations, and heroic quests and journeys.	Archetypal characters, situations, and journeys; transformations; archetypal symbols and images.
Psychological	The state of mind of the author of, and/or characters in, the literary work.	How things, people, and events are described; characters' actions, reactions, dreams, words, and thoughts (in dramatic monologue); how characters relate to other people, things, and settings in the literary work.

✍️ **YOU WILL NEED (FOR DAYS 2 AND 3)**

• Group assignments chart on a handout (class set)
• A magazine advertisement (exemplar)
• A brief analysis of the exemplar ad from each of the six critical viewpoints (may be read aloud from written notes or delivered from memory)
• 12 to 18 print magazine advertisements in clear sheet protectors
• A selected short essay that lends itself to analysis from all of the critical viewpoints being studied (class set)

DAY 2: ASSIGNMENT 1 (Analyze Magazine Ads)

1. The teacher explains to the class that today they will have an opportunity to practice applying the critical viewpoints to the analysis of a series of magazine ads. The exemplar ad is shown around the classroom. The teacher then proceeds to model the assignment by analyzing the ad aloud for the class, using each of the six critical viewpoints in turn.

2. Each student receives a copy of the group assignments handout and refers to it to see which critical viewpoint group s/he will be in for Assignment 1. The teacher assigns locations in the room to each of the six expert groups and students move to their designated spots.

3. Each expert group receives an ad to analyze, applying the group's designated critical viewpoint and using the prompts on the relevant information sheet to guide the group discussion. *Each student in the group should be instructed to make his or her own personal notes on each ad.*

4. The teacher places the remaining ads on a table or desk in the center of the room, accessible to all the expert groups. As each group completes its analysis of an ad, a group member can trade it for another from the collection. Students are given until the end of the period to analyze as many ads as they can.

DAY 3: ASSIGNMENTS 1 AND 2 (Analyze A Short Essay)

1. Each expert group comes to the front of the room, selects its favorite magazine ad from the pile, and presents its analysis of the ad to the rest of the class, from its designated critical viewpoint. *(These presentations should take no longer than five minutes each, or about twenty to thirty minutes in total.)*

   At the teacher's discretion, these presentations may be diagnostically assessed and/or followed by a metacognitive discussion revolving around the students' level of comfort as they used the "lenses" from their toolkits to analyze a media product. *(What were the hardest and easiest parts of the assignment? How did working in a group make things easier or more difficult? How did using the lens of a critical viewpoint change the way you looked at each of the ads? How will you be looking at the advertising media from now on?)*

2. The teacher then introduces the short essay analysis assignment by defining "close reading" for the class:

   Close reading means performing a slow and thorough examination of a piece of text, going sentence by sentence and at times even word by word in order to draw as much meaning as possible out of it.

3. The teacher points out that close reading and critical analysis go hand-in-hand. The following analogy may help your students to understand this concept better:

When a sports team manager and his coaching staff sit down after a game and watch it again on tape, they're analyzing it. Analysis means asking and answering questions. When the manager and coaches walk into the viewing room after the game, they already have their questions formulated: they want to know why *they won or lost the game and* how *they can either keep on winning or improve in order to beat these opponents the next time they meet them on the court or field. The coaches may watch the same game several times, picking apart the details of each play, in order to find the answers to these questions.*

The teacher explains that when a student sits down to reread and analyze a piece of text, s/he should already have questions formulated as well. The particular questions will depend on the critical viewpoint the student has decided to use.

4. Students are directed to their copy of the group assignments chart to see which critical viewpoint they will be applying for the next activity and then to the information sheet about that critical viewpoint. In critical analysis, the questions generally begin with how, why, and to what extent or with what result. The teacher asks: *How many of the writing and discussion prompts on your information sheet begin that way?*

5. The teacher hands out the selected short essay to the class and models a close reading of the first few paragraphs, making connections with all six of the critical viewpoints. This demonstration should include such reading strategies as "talking to the text," self-monitoring for comprehension, and rereading for clarification.

6. The students form their six expert groups for Assignment 2 and each group continues to read and analyze the essay until the end of the period.

Each group member should be instructed to make his or her own personal notes based on the group discussion.

✍ YOU WILL NEED (FOR DAY 4)

- LCR 8–WRITING THE ANALYTICAL RESPONSE handout (class set)
  OR
- SFR 24–WRITING THE ANALYTICAL RESPONSE handout (class set)
- Supplementary reading essays or articles; 3 different titles, totaling 1 class set (optional)

DAY 4: ASSIGNMENT 2 (Conclusion)

1. Students continue to work on the short essay in their expert groups and make personal notes.

2. When all the groups have finished, the teacher hands out WRITING THE ANALYTICAL RESPONSE to each student and goes over it with the class. It should be emphasized that a response is not an essay and therefore does not require a formal introductory paragraph or a thesis. However, an analytical response is still a formal piece of writing, which must be written in the third person.

The teacher should also take this opportunity to model the format s/he wishes students to use for referring to or quoting from text. For example:

The speaker hears conflict everywhere he turns, especially in the so-called "peaceful surroundings of nature." (para. 2)

3. Each group then works together to plan and first-draft a group analytical response to the essay, using the group's assigned critical viewpoint.

At the teacher's discretion, these responses may be collected for formative assessment or shared with the members of another group, who can offer suggestions for improvement. The teacher might also want to keep the best ones to use as exemplars for the next time this unit is taught.

4. (OPTIONAL) Grade 12 students can be introduced to the concept of study groups to make large nonfiction reading assignments more manageable. *(This is good preparation for handling the workload at college or university.)*

Students form groups of six, and each group receives two copies each of three different essays or articles about literary criticism. Within each "study group," the reading load is distributed so that each student only has to read and make notes on one-half of an article but will then teach its contents to the rest of the group. This becomes the class homework assignment, due on DAY 9.

NOTE TO THE TEACHER: There are suggested sources for articles in the bibliography following this module. Particularly recommended are "The Quest Hero" by W. H. Auden and anything by Northrop Frye, which would be very helpful for understanding the mythopoeic critical viewpoint.

WRITING AN ANALYTICAL RESPONSE

An analytical response is not an essay, and it isn't a personal response—it's somewhere in between.

- It has no thesis statement and no formal introduction. However, there has to be a thread running through it, holding it all together.
- It is written in the third person (avoiding all use of "I," "you," "we," or any form thereof).
- It assumes a critical viewpoint and maintains the same perspective throughout.
- It is written entirely in the present tense, in proper sentence and paragraph format. It avoids slang, contractions, abbreviations, and symbols, just like a formal essay.
- Unlike a formal literary essay, it may take a humorous tone.

Here are the steps to follow when preparing an analytical response to a piece of writing. Be sure not to skip any!

1. *Before assuming a critical viewpoint, perform a close reading of the text and make copious notes in the margins and on separate pieces of paper.* Authors make conscious decisions about what to include in their writing and how to express it. Notice everything that is there (and what is NOT stated as well). Go paragraph by paragraph and sentence by sentence and pick everything apart, pulling as much meaning out of the text as you can.

2. Now that you fully understand the text, *pull a critical viewpoint out of your toolkit and place it between you and the page.* Take note of what "leaps off the page" at you and record it, thus creating a second and more focused set of notes.

3. Look at the second set of notes you've made and apply the criteria of your selected critical viewpoint. *Find the thread that will run through your response:*

   - If you are a formalist critic, it will be a theme or a literary device that everything in the piece refers or relates to. This is the unifying principle that resolves a contrast or opposition, making the writing work well.
   - If you are a neo-Marxist critic, it will be a power struggle that ends in a revolution or in total destruction.
   - If you are a deconstructionist critic, it will be a gap, lie, or inconsistency that undermines the unity of the piece by preventing an opposition from being resolved.
   - If you are a psychological critic, it will be a basic motivation—a powerful need, desire, fear, hatred, or love—that influences every choice and reaction by a character or an author.
   - If you are a gender-based critic, it will be an imbalance of power between the sexes that is reflected in multiple aspects of the writing.
   - If you are a mythopoeic critic, it will be an archetypal symbol, quest, or transformation (magical or otherwise) that powerfully affects the main character, recalling other, older stories to the reader's mind.

(continued on other side)

4. Return to your notes and the original text, and *identify two or three points or quotations that relate strongly to the unifying thread of your response*. Although you may refer in your response to any relevant observations that you've made, these few will form the backbone of your detailed analysis.

5. Now turn your attention to each of the points or quotations in turn and *begin analyzing in depth by thinking about and answering at least some of the following questions*:

   - Why did the author choose to include this in the work?
   - Why did he or she consider it important?
   - What does this say about (the thread of your response)?
   - How does this enhance, reflect, or reinforce (the thread of your response)?
   - How does it relate to the other points or quotations you've chosen?
   - What is the effect of this on the main character, the speaker, or other characters in the piece?
   - To what extent do their reactions and interactions enhance, reflect, or reinforce (the thread of your response)?
   - What is the effect on the reader? (Be general, not specific—it isn't a personal response.)

6. If you have thought deeply about the piece, you now have something insightful and meaningful to say. Based on the answers to your analytical questions, *decide in which order to present your points and which supplementary examples from your notes will support each one*.

7. *Begin writing your first draft*:

   - In the first paragraph, do NOT name your critical viewpoint. Instead, name the work and the author and briefly describe the unifying thread that will run through the entire response.
   - Give each of your important points or quotations its own paragraph.
   - Make sure you're not just identifying and explaining examples—go below the surface and make in-depth connections. Show the reader that you've given this a close examination and a lot of thought. Be sure to relate the discussion back to the unifying thread you identified in the first paragraph.
   - You don't need to have a concluding paragraph as long as your response ends on a completed thought.

✍ **YOU WILL NEED (FOR DAYS 5, 6, 7, AND 8)**

• A package of 6 selected short essays (class set)

                                    OR

• A class set of an anthology and a list of 6 essays selected from it
• LCR 9–CLAUSES DETERMINE SENTENCE PATTERNS handout (class set)
• LCR 10–SYNTACTICAL EFFECTS handout (class set)
• LCR 11–SYNTAX PRACTICE chart (class set)

DAY 5: ASSIGNMENT 3 (The Essay Six-Pack)

1. Students refer to their group assignment sheets and form their expert groups for Assignment 3, gathering in the classroom locations designated by the teacher.

2. Each student receives a copy of either the anthology and list of titles or the short essay package. Each expert group now reads, discusses, and thoroughly analyzes all the essays in the package, applying its assigned critical viewpoint as each group member records his or her own personal notes on a separate sheet of paper.

   NOTE TO TEACHER: If you plan to collect these packages at the end of the unit for reuse by other classes, then students will need to be reminded not to highlight, underline, or write on the essays in the six-pack.

3. Homework: Each student completes whatever part of the analysis his or her group was unable to finish during class time.

DAY 6: ASSIGNMENT 3 (Continued)

1. The expert groups jigsaw, so that each new group contains at least one person from each of the six critical viewpoint groups.

2. Each student takes two sheets of blank paper and divides up the space into six labeled note-making areas, one for each of the essays in the six-pack.

3. Each jigsaw group member now shares what his or her expert group discussed on the previous class day about each of the essays while groupmates record personal jot notes in the relevant spaces on their "placemats."

DAY 7: INTRODUCTION TO ASSIGNMENT 3 FOCUS

1. The teacher defines the term *syntax* for the students and records the definition on the board:

   Syntax refers to the way that words are put together to create meaning and emphasis.

2. Each student receives a copy of the CLAUSES DETERMINE SENTENCE PATTERNS handout. The teacher and students then go over the handout and complete the exercise together.

   NOTE TO TEACHER: Depending on the interests and abilities of your class, you may wish to go right back to basics and review the parts of a sentence—subject, predicate, transitive/intransitive/copula verbs, direct/indirect objects, and subjective completions—before tackling the concept of independent and subordinate clauses. To plan a mini-unit on syntax, see Studying Poetry, Part 6 (Timed Writing Practice), elsewhere in this book.

3. The teacher explains that an awareness of syntax is essential to any critical analysis of literature and introduces students to the acronym PLOTS:

> P is for sentence PATTERNS
> L is for sentence LENGTHS
> O is for sentence ORGANIZATION
> T is for sentence TYPES
> S is for a SHIFT in any of the above (from short to long, from statement to question, and so on)

4. The teacher distributes copies of the SYNTACTICAL EFFECTS handout and goes over it with the students, defining and clarifying as necessary.

Grade 12 students who are doing the study group assignment should be reminded about their homework for day 9.

DAY 8: ASSIGNMENT 3 (Continued)

1. Each person in each group now becomes a specialist in one of the six essays, either by choice or by numbering off.

2. The groups jigsaw once more to form six new groups, each focusing on a different one of the essays.

3. The teacher hands out copies of the SYNTAX PRACTICE chart and explains that students will work in their new groups to fill in the middle column of their chart by finding and recording examples of the use of syntax from their assigned or chosen essay.

   Each student will then work independently to respond to the effectiveness question on the sheet and fill in the right-hand column of the chart using the lens of his or her current critical viewpoint. The question to be answered is written on the board:

   How does this example make the essay more effective?

4. The teacher explains that what makes a piece of writing *effective* is that it has *an effect* on the reader. In this case, the reader is a student looking at the text from a particular critical viewpoint, and this means that the effect will be filtered through a lens. *(Just as a happy person sees the rose's petals and an unhappy person sees the thorns, a reader's perceptions are colored by his or her personal—or critical—point of view.)*

   The teacher then models for students the best way to answer an effectiveness question by describing first what the example does, and then what it helps the reader to do. You may wish to provide an example from the essay chosen for day 3 and 4, or use the exemplar below:

   > *The anger that rose up inside me then was a force of nature. Wave after wave crashed over me, spilling me head over heels. Rudderless, oarless, all I could do was submit to the storm.*

   > This metaphor compares a man at the mercy of his own rage to a tiny boat caught in a storm at sea. *(That is what the example does.)* The reader can visualize the boat being battered relentlessly by the wind and the water, and can thus appreciate how powerful the man's anger is and how helpless and overwhelmed it makes him feel. *(That is what the example helps the reader to do.)*
   >   NOTE: *The above example was viewed through the lens of formalist criticism.*

5. Students proceed to complete the assignment as outlined by the teacher in Step 3. In whole class, teacher and students then share and discuss the assignment and the students' findings.

CLAUSES DETERMINE SENTENCE PATTERNS

A clause is a group of words containing a subject and a verb. There are two kinds of clauses: IN-DEPENDENT CLAUSES and SUBORDINATE CLAUSES.

An INDEPENDENT CLAUSE is able to stand on its own, and when it does, it is called a SIMPLE SENTENCE:

> Sharzad has caught a big fish.
> We cannot go to the restaurant today.

When two independent clauses are joined by a COORDINATING CONJUNCTION or equivalent punctuation, the result is called a COMPOUND SENTENCE:

> Sharzad has caught a big fish *and* she plans to cook it for dinner.
> Sharzad has caught a big fish; she plans to cook it for dinner.
> We cannot go to the restaurant today *but* perhaps we'll go tomorrow.
> We cannot go to the restaurant today—perhaps we'll go tomorrow.

When two independent clauses are joined by a SUBORDINATING CONJUNCTION, one of them remains the independent clause and the other becomes the subordinate clause. The result is called a COMPLEX SENTENCE:

> Sharzad has caught a big fish *that* she plans to cook for dinner.
> We cannot go to the restaurant today *because* my father is feeling ill.

Subordinate clauses do the same work as nouns, adjectives, and adverbs, depending on the conjunction that has been used.

An ADVERBIAL CLAUSE answers the questions *why*, *where*, *when*, and *how*.

> *Since you feel so strongly about this*, we will consider your request.
> Cats are so independent! They go *wherever they please*.
> We'll discuss this *after your mother gets home from her meeting*.
> Protect these library books *as if they were your own*.

An ADJECTIVE CLAUSE answers the questions *which* or *what* kind. The conjunction WHICH, WHO, WHOSE, WHOM, or THAT becomes the subject or object of the subordinate clause and is called a RELATIVE PRONOUN.

> So this is the young man *who has stolen my niece's heart*!
> Who needs a boat *that won't stay afloat*?

A NOUN CLAUSE answers the question *what*. It can be the subject or object of a sentence, or the object of a preposition.

I like that he's such a hard worker.
(Subject: I)
(Transitive verb: like)
(Direct object of verb: that he's such a hard worker)

Whether or not you chose this path is unimportant.
(Subject: whether or not you chose this path)
(Copula verb: is)
(Subjective completion: unimportant)

A sentence can be SIMPLE, COMPOUND, COMPLEX, or COMPOUND-COMPLEX, depending on how the author has put it together:

Jill is getting married this week. (simple)
Jill is getting married this week, and I am her maid of honor. (compound)
Jill is getting married this week because her fiancé's unit is being shipped out next Wednesday. (complex)
Jill is getting married this week because her fiancé is being shipped out next Wednesday, and I am her maid of honor. (compound-complex)

EXERCISE: Identify and label each clause in the following sentences, then state what type of sentence it is (simple, compound, complex, or compound-complex):

1. Oh, what a tangled web we weave, when first we practice to deceive!

2. If you hurry, I'll give you a ride to the mall before I run my errands.

3. The woman who just entered the room and the man who just left it have been looking for each other since the movie began.

4. Su-Yin wants to study for her test, but Carl would rather play video games.

5. How many times have I told you not to leave your dirty clothes on the floor?

SYNTACTICAL EFFECTS

SENTENCE TYPES

- Sentences may be declarative (statements), interrogative (questions), or exclamatory.
- Shifting sentence types has the effect of (re)focusing the reader's attention.
- Varying sentence types holds the reader's interest.
- Interrogative and exclamatory sentences are used sparingly in essays and for specific rhetorical effect.

Rhetorical Question
- makes the reader think
  - stronger than a statement for making a point
  - may be used to redirect the reader to an author's next point (like a subject heading in a textbook)
  - allows author to express a second (possibly dissenting) viewpoint —to play "devil's advocate"
  - may or may not be answered by the author, depending on how it is used

Exclamation
- conveys a burst of strong emotion—"Oh, good grief!"
  - especially effective when following or surrounded by factual or logical text —"wakes up" the reader
  - emphasizes some aspect of the topic under discussion: "What a quagmire this was turning out to be!"

SENTENCE LENGTHS

- Varying sentence lengths holds the reader's interest.

Short sentence
- often used by authors to present a key idea (the "short, pithy statement")
  - used in series, will speed the pace of a passage but also chop it up, creating or heightening tension
  - used in dialogue or first-person writing, may indicate emotional tension (for instance, a series of short questions beginning "what if" to convey anxiety)
  - lightens the writing style

Long sentence
- slows the pace of a passage
  - adds weight to the writing style
  - provides a measured, thoughtful delivery of information (scholarly, authoritative tone)
  - may be used in the form of a run-on sentence to convey excitement or mitate a speaking style

(continued on other side)

SENTENCE ORGANIZATION

The end of a sentence is the position of greatest emphasis; the beginning of a sentence is the position of second-greatest emphasis. Authors will purposely arrange the words and parts of their sentences in order to emphasize key thoughts or ideas.

Periodic sentences —meaning is incomplete until the end of the sentence.
(e.g., Through the meadow and into the woods, to search for gold we go.)

Loose sentences —meaning is provided at the beginning of the sentence.
(e.g., We're going treasure hunting in the forest beyond the fields.)

Natural order —subject, verb, predicate (subject is important but the predicate is more important)
(e.g., The prize goes to the winner.)

Inverted order —predicate, verb, subject (subject is most important)
(e.g., To the winner goes the prize.)

Similarly, in a list or series, authors will often arrange items in order:

Climactic order
• from least to most, lowest to highest
• builds drama, tension, suspense
• may be applied to individual words, phrases, clauses

Anticlimactic order
• from most to least, highest to lowest
• generally found in humorous or satirical writing
• may be applied to words, phrases, clauses

SENTENCE PATTERNS

• Sentences may be simple, compound, complex, or compound-complex.
• Varying sentence patterns makes a text more interesting to read.
• Sentence patterns become rhetorically important when they:
    • physically reflect the content of the text (for example, a series of compound sentences used to weigh the pros and cons of an issue);
    • occur with frequency in a passage (for example, an entire paragraph of simple sentences);
    • indicate the speaker's attitude or recreate his or her voice (For example, a five-year-old narrator will speak mainly in simple sentences; so will a speaker who is reluctantly or impatiently explaining something. A university professor, however, or someone who is trying to sound very intelligent will probably use entire strings of compound-complex sentences.).

SYNTAX PRACTICE SHEET

Working with a partner or in a group, choose ONE of the short essays in the six-pack to analyze for syntax.

In your selected essay, find one example of each syntactical feature indicated on the grid. Quote the example by copying it onto the grid in the middle column.

For each example, answer the question, "How does the author's use of this syntactical device contribute to the overall effectiveness of the essay?" Write your answer in point form in the right-hand column of the grid.

HINT: When answering an "effectiveness" question, state (a) what the example does and (b) what it helps the reader or listener to do.

Syntactical Device	Example from Text	How It Enhances the Essay's Effectiveness
Rhetorical question OR Exclamation		
Sentence fragment(s) OR Run-on sentence		
A shift in sentence length (from long to short or from short to long)		
A periodic sentence		
Climactic or anticlimactic order		
Shift in sentence pattern (from simple to compound or from compound-complex to simple)		

✍ **YOU WILL NEED (FOR DAYS 9, 10, AND 11)**

• LCR 12–HOW TO READ A LITERARY QUESTION (class set, optional)
• LCR 13–THE SCIENCE OF LITERARY ANALYSIS (class set, optional)
• LCR 14/14A–THE SCIENCE OF CRITICAL ANALYSIS, double-sided, blank and exemplar (class set; optional)
• LCR 15–IN-CLASS ANALYTICAL RESPONSE ASSIGNMENT SHEET (class set)
• LCR 16–IN-CLASS RESPONSE ASSESSMENT SHEET (half a class set, cut in half)

DAY 9: OPTIONAL ACTIVITY (Introduce Summative Assignment)

1. (OPTIONAL: Study Groups activity) Students get into their study groups and take turns reporting on their assigned portion of the reading to the rest of the group. Groupmates should be able to ask questions to clarify their own understanding. All students should make extensive personal notes.

2. In whole class, the assignment is discussed metacognitively: *How hard was it? How valuable was it? How has it changed the way you view the critical viewpoints you are using for literary analysis?*

3. The teacher and class recap the unit so far, reviewing the concept of "close reading" and the process of writing an analytical response from a critical viewpoint.

4. The teacher now introduces tomorrow's in-class written assignment: each student will choose one of the critical viewpoints and one of the six essays in the package and will write an analytical response based on the discussions of the past five days. Students will have two days to complete this assignment, which will be handed in for summative assessment.

HOMEWORK FOR TONIGHT: Decide which essay and which critical viewpoint to use for this assignment. Review all the handouts given so far, especially the one on writing an analytical response, and create a single page of jot notes to be used (along with the essay itself) in completing the first draft of the response.

In other words, students are to conduct the analysis for homework so that they can write a first draft of the response in class the next day.

NOTE TO TEACHER: *Alternative Steps 1 and 2 are suggested here to enrich the unit for students in AP or pre-AP classes, or who are otherwise identified as being capable of handling more challenging work.*

How to Read a Literary Question

1. The teacher and class recap how to answer an effectiveness question about a literary or rhetorical device used in a text: *identify the device and quote the example, tell what the example does, then describe what it helps the reader to do.* For example:

    Q: Find an example of metaphor in the first stanza and explain how it enhances the effectiveness of the poem.

    A: *(Identify and quote:)* An example of metaphor in this poem is "goldfish pirouetting across the glittering scene at the bottom of their bowl" in lines 3 and 4. *(Tell what the example does:)* The goldfish are compared to a chorus of dancing ballerinas on a stage. *(Describe what it helps the reader to do:)* This metaphor paints a picture in the reader's mind, helping him or her to visualize the fish all moving gracefully in circles around the sparkling sand and figurines at the bottom of their bowl.

    The teacher should point out to students that if they tell what the device does instead of what the example does, then they will not be answering the question, and it is very important when writing a test or an exam to answer the question that has been asked.

2. Each student receives a copy of the HOW TO READ A LITERARY QUESTION handout. Teacher and students go through the handout together, discussing which of the critical viewpoints would be the best fit for each of the key verbs and example questions provided on the sheet.

The Science of Literary Analysis

1. The teacher points out that there are different levels of literary analysis, depending on the kind of question that forms the basis for the analysis, and reminds students of the example of the sports team manager and coaches reviewing a game video. The teacher then writes or reveals the following pairs of questions on the board:

> *How many strikes and how many balls did (a particular pitcher) throw in each inning?*
> *How has this game affected each player's batting average?*
>
> *What new hitting (or pitching) strategies did we see from the other team this time out?*
> *How did our outfield performance differ this time from previous games we've played?*
>
> *What could we have done to neutralize the other team's hitting strategy?*
> *What do our players need to practice for next time?*

Students are then asked: *Which set of questions can be answered with a single viewing of the game video? Which set requires the coaches to make comparisons? Which set demands that the coaches use their imaginations as well as their judgment?*

2. The teacher hands out copies of THE SCIENCE OF LITERARY ANALYSIS, and teacher and class go over the sheet together, classifying each set of questions on the board under one of the headings on the chart *(functional, associative, thematic)*.

Students can then pair up with working partners and perform the same classification exercise using the discussion questions on the information sheet for their current critical viewpoint.

The Science of Critical Analysis

1. The teacher points out that there are different levels of literary analysis, depending on the kind of question that forms the basis for the analysis, and reminds students of the example of the sports team coaches reviewing a game video. The questions they are trying to answer require them to do more than just watch the screen. To determine why their team won or lost the game, they must compare the plays executed by the two teams; and to figure out how to ensure a win the next time, they have to use both their imagination and their judgment.

The teacher writes three words on the board: *Functional, Associative,* and *Thematic,* and explains the differences among them:

Functional analysis is superficial, requiring the lowest level of thinking skills—the reader is an observer, finding answers within the text by simply paying attention while reading.

Associative analysis is comparative—the reader finds answers by making connections—between elements of the text, between the subject text and other texts, and between the text and real life.

Thematic analysis is the deepest, requiring the highest level of thinking skills—the reader finds answers within his or her own mind by imagining scenarios and making judgments based on the text.

2. To illustrate, the teacher hands out THE SCIENCE OF CRITICAL ANALYSIS chart, directing students first to the completed exemplar (based on Sophocles's play *Oedipus Rex*). Teacher and students together go over this chart, discussing the differences among the questions that led to their being classified as functional, associative or thematic.

Each student now pairs up with a partner from the same critical viewpoint expert group (Assignment 3). Each pair selects an essay from the six-pack and proceeds to compose three analytical questions (one of each type) for the line of the chart dedicated to their critical viewpoint.

DAY 10: IN-CLASS WRITTEN RESPONSE (First Draft)

1. Students arrive with their essay package and single page of notes and begin working independently on the first draft of the analytical response.

   The teacher hands out the assessment sheet, which is to be used as a guide and must be handed in with the student's work at the end of the period.

   The teacher should emphasize to students that this is an in-class writing assignment and that they are not to take any part of it out of the classroom.

   The teacher may wish to supply foolscap paper to ensure that all writing is done in class on this assignment.

2. At the end of the period, the teacher hands out paper clips so that students can clip their work together when handing it in.

DAY 11: IN-CLASS WRITTEN RESPONSE (Completion)

1. Students take their seats and resume working on their analytical response once their work from the previous day is returned to them.

2. When finished, each student staples his or her work into a package with the good copy on top and hands it in for summative assessment (Knowledge and Thinking).

   At the teacher's discretion, students' work may be photocopied and the photocopy returned to the student for additional editing and polishing. The resulting final draft can then be printed out and resubmitted for a further evaluation in a different achievement category (Communication and/or Application).

HOW TO READ A LITERARY QUESTION

A well-framed question will have three parts:
>a *key verb* and *object* that tell you what you are to do, and
>one or more *limiting factors* that narrow the question and make it more specific.

THE KEY VERB

The key verb is the most important part of a literary question. Here are some of the most commonly used verbs that you may encounter:

STATE: means to tell, as clearly and concisely as possible.

(Example: State two reasons for the protagonist's growing anger in this story.)

EXPLAIN: means to tell about something, providing enough detail to make it logical and understandable to another person.

(Example: Explain the point being made by the author in paragraph 3 of the essay.)

EVALUATE: means to rate something on a scale, giving reasons to support your judgement.

(Example: Evaluate the effectiveness of the metaphor in the first stanza of this poem.)

DESCRIBE: means to talk about something in some detail.

(Example: Describe how the setting of this story participates in the unfolding of the plot.)

DEFEND: means to support a position using quotations and/or specific references from one or more particular works.

(Example: Defend the publication of this essay on the front page of a daily newspaper.)

COMPARE: means to list or talk about specific examples of similarities and differences.

(Example: Compare the language used to express the speaker's attitude towards himself in the opening stanzas of these two poems.)

CONTRAST: means to list or talk about specific examples of the differences between items.

(Example: Contrast the ways in which these two story excerpts describe girls.)

EXAMINE: means to look closely and critically at the various parts of something.
(or ANALYZE) The focus you are expected to take will be given to you as part of the question: How, Why, To what extent, With what result.

(Example: Examine the relationship between the protagonist and antagonist in this novel. How does it affect the decisions they make?)

DISCUSS: means to formulate a thesis and support it using examples from the text.

(Example: Discuss the role played by travel in the lives of two characters in the novel.)

**Note: If the question has two key verbs – for example, "Identify and explain . . ." – remember to do both.)

THE OBJECT

The object of a question is its focusing factor. You don't just explain—you explain the author's methods. You don't just examine—you examine a character's attitude. To ensure that you are answering the question that is asked, you need to read the question carefully. To ensure that you're answering it fully, you need to make note of the focusing factor. Are you being asked to explain more than one method? Will you have to define or explain the character's attitude before you can analyze it? Together with the limiting factor, the object of the question will tell you exactly how much work you need to do.

LIMITING FACTORS

Limiting factors are included in literary questions to narrow a task and make it more specific and therefore more manageable. Remember that you have to answer the question that is asked. If the question specifies the first three paragraphs, then that is where you must focus your attention and find your supporting examples. If you're asked to support a discussion with examples of simile and metaphor, then those are the devices you should be looking for, ignoring everything else. Pay special attention to the limiting factor of a literary question, as it can save you a great deal of time and effort.

THE SCIENCE OF LITERARY ANALYSIS

Type of Analysis:	FUNCTIONAL	ASSOCIATIVE	THEMATIC
Descriptor:	Superficial	Comparative	Close or deep
Similar to a crime scene investigator who:	Weighs, measures, determines composition of evidence	Determines source and origin of evidence, how it got to crime scene	Uses evidence to create a crime scenario
Considers:	Where elements are placed and how they function (separately and together)	How elements relate and compare to one another and to the real world	How elements acquire meaning from being connected to the reader's own life experiences, attitudes, and ideas
Reader is:	an aware and knowledgeable observer	a connection maker	a meaning maker a puzzle solver
Example questions to ask and answer: Why? How? With what result or effect? To what extent?	What makes this scene the turning point of the play? Why does Oedipus react so violently to Teiresias's statement?	In what way or ways is King Oedipus similar to Gloucester in *King Lear?* Explain the effectiveness of the metaphor in line 3.	What is accomplished by the use of dramatic irony in this scene? What is the symbolic value of Mount Kithairon in the play?
Answer is found:	in the text being studied	in other texts and in the outside world	in the reader's thoughts, imagination, and memories
Literary techniques and devices that inform this type of analysis:	story structure, plot, character, setting, (poetic) rhyme schemes, rhythms, pacing, repetition, alliteration, word placement	comparison and contrast, metaphor, simile, personification, imagery, juxtaposition, mirroring (How does X reflect Y?)	allusion, irony, symbolism, imagery patterns, word connotations, subtexts

THE SCIENCE OF CRITICAL ANALYSIS

Type of Analysis:	FUNCTIONAL	ASSOCIATIVE	THEMATIC
Questions from a GENDER-BASED viewpoint:			
Questions from a DECONSTRUCTIONIST viewpoint:			
Questions from a FORMALIST viewpoint:			
Questions from a NEO-MARXIST viewpoint:			
Questions from a MYTHOPOEIC viewpoint:			
Questions from a PSYCHOLOGICAL viewpoint:			

THE SCIENCE OF CRITICAL ANALYSIS

Type of Analysis:	FUNCTIONAL	ASSOCIATIVE	THEMATIC
Questions from a GENDER-BASED viewpoint:	How are women portrayed in this play?	How do Jocasta's words and actions reflect the status of women in ancient Greece?	What is the symbolic value of Oedipus's stabbing out his eyes with Jocasta's brooch?
Questions from a DECONSTRUCTIONIST viewpoint:	Explain the role played by untruth in the destruction of the Theban royal family.	How are the interests of the ancient Greek religious establishment served by this play?	What is accomplished in this play by putting mortals in unwinnable situations?
Questions from a FORMALIST viewpoint:	How are good and evil represented in this play? Who are the villains and who is the hero?	To what extent is Antigone like her father?	How do the Odes of the Chorus reinforce the deeper meaning of the play?
Questions from a NEO-MARXIST viewpoint:	Who are the oppressors in this play, and who are the oppressed?	At what point does power transfer from the oppressor to the oppressed in this play?	To what extent does the fall of Oedipus represent an overthrow of the established order?
Questions from a MYTHOPOEIC viewpoint:	Describe the journey that Oedipus must take in the course of this play.	Relate Oedipus's quest for enlightenment to another epic quest studied in the course.	Justify the transformation that takes place in Oedipus at the end of the play.
Questions from a PSYCHOLOGICAL viewpoint:	How does Oedipus's state of mind change from the beginning of the play to the end?	To what extent could Oedipus be said to suffer from post-traumatic stress at the end of the play?	Explain the irony of Oedipus's blinding himself as self-punishment at the end of the play.

IN-CLASS ANALYTICAL RESPONSE

DATE:

CRITICAL VIEWPOINT: Your choice—ONE of the six discussed in class

SOURCE MATERIAL: Your choice—ONE of the six short essays in your package

LENGTH: 250 words minimum (no maximum)

FORMAT:
> Hand-written neatly on every other line of white paper.
> Editing using the spaces between the lines is encouraged.
> Product to be evaluated must be written in dark blue or black ink.
> Student's name and a page number must appear at the top of every page.
> Response is to be written in correct sentence and paragraph form.

TIME ALLOWED: One class period for first draft
> One class period for producing good copy

MATERIALS ALLOWED: English to English dictionary (paper only)
> Thesaurus (paper only)
> One page of handwritten notes

SUBMISSION PACKAGE:
> Draft of response to be evaluated PLUS
> Any rough drafts or notes produced in class

ASSESSMENT CRITERIA:

Knowledge/Understanding: /10
Student demonstrates clear understanding of the critical viewpoint selected, of the short essay being analyzed, and of the form of a critical response (i.e., analysis, not summary; response, not an essay).

Thinking: /10
Student demonstrates an appropriately sophisticated level of thinking and makes effective use of specific references to the work to support critical comments.

IN-CLASS ANALYTICAL RESPONSE

Student's Name: _____

ASSESSMENT CRITERIA:

Knowledge/Understanding   /10

- Student demonstrates *insightful understanding* of the essay chosen for analysis and is able to make *interesting and specific comments* about it.
- Student demonstrates clear understanding of the chosen critical viewpoint.
- Student shows clear understanding of the form of an analytical response—that is, the work under discussion is analyzed rather than summarized or explained; student has written a response, not an essay.

Thinking   /10

- Response is *clearly focused*. A critical viewpoint has been used to identify the thread running through the essay and all quoted examples are strongly related to it.
- Student's analysis demonstrates an *appropriately sophisticated level of thinking*. Examples are thoughtfully examined, then solidly tied together.

Comments:

IN-CLASS ANALYTICAL RESPONSE

Student's Name: _____

ASSESSMENT CRITERIA:

Knowledge/Understanding   /10

- Student demonstrates *insightful understanding* of the essay chosen for analysis and is able to make *interesting and specific comments* about it.
- Student demonstrates clear understanding of the chosen critical viewpoint.
- Student shows clear understanding of the form of an analytical response—that is, the work under discussion is analyzed rather than summarized or explained; student has written a response, not an essay.

Thinking   /10

- Response is *clearly focused*. A critical viewpoint has been used to identify the thread running through the essay and all quoted examples are strongly related to it.
- Student's analysis demonstrates an *appropriately sophisticated level of thinking*. Examples are thoughtfully examined, then solidly tied together.

Comments:

A Bibliography: Critical Viewpoints

NOTE TO TEACHERS: Some of these sources I have personally read, while others I heard about from teaching colleagues or found listed at the back of other works. Northrop Frye's *The Educated Imagination* was actually part of my English course for college-bound students in grade 12, and the students handled it quite competently. In addition to Frye, Cleanth Brooks and W. H. Auden are both accessible for senior-grade students, and colleagues have recommended both Eagleton and Lynn (listed in the "General Sources" section) as well.

FORMALIST/STRUCTURALIST (NEW) CRITICISM

Brooks, Cleanth, and Robert Penn Warren, *Understanding Fiction.* New York: Appleton-Century-Crofts, 1959.
Richards, I. A. *Practical Criticism: A Study of Literary Judgment.* London: Kegan Paul, 1929.

MYTHOPOEIC CRITICISM

Auden, W. H. "The Quest Hero." *Perspectives in Contemporary Criticism.* Ed. Sheldon N. Grebstein. New York: Harper & Row, 1968.
Frye, Northrop. *Anatomy of Criticism: Four Essays.* Princeton University Press, 1957.
———. *The Educated Imagination.* Toronto: House of Anansi Press, 1963.

NEO-MARXIST CRITICISM

Bennett, Tony. *Outside Literature.* London: Routledge, 1990.
Bonnycastle, S. *In Search of Authority: An Introductory Guide to Literary Theory.* 2nd ed. Peterborough, Ontario: Broadview Press, 1996.
Eagleton, Terry. *Criticism and Ideology: A Study in Marxist Literary Theory.* London: Verso, 1976.

GENDER-BASED CRITICISM

Belsey, Catherine. "Constructing the Subject: Deconstructing the Text." *Feminist Criticism and Social Change: Sex, Class and Race in Literature and Culture.* Eds. Judith Newton and Deborah Rosenfelt. New York: Methuen, 1985.
Ellman, Mary. "Phallic Criticism." *Thinking about Women.* New York: Harcourt, Brace & Jovanovich, 1968.
Fetterley, Judith. *The Resisting Reader: a Feminist Approach to American Fiction.* Bloomington: University Press, 1978.
Gilbert, Sandra, and Susan Gubar. *The Madwoman in the Attic: The Woman Writer and the Nineteenth-Century Literary Imagination.* New Haven, CT: Yale University Press, 1979.
Millet, Kate. *Sexual Politics.* New York: Avon, 1971.
Showalter, Elaine. *A Literature of Their Own: British Women Novelists from Bronte to Lessing.* Princeton, NJ: Princeton University Press, 1977.

DECONSTRUCTIVE CRITICISM

Derrida, Jacques. *Acts of Literature.* New York: Routledge, 1992.
Morrison, Toni. *Playing in the Dark: Whiteness and the Literary Imagination.* Harvard University Press, 1992.

PSYCHOLOGICAL CRITICISM

Eagleton, Terry. "Psychoanalysis." *Literary Theory: An Introduction.* Minneapolis: University of Minnesota Press, 1983. 151–93.
Gay, Peter, ed. *The Freud Reader.* New York: Norton, 1989.
Holland, Norman. *Holland's Guide to Psychoanalytic Psychology and Literature-and-Psychology.* New York: Oxford University Press, 1990.
Jones, Judy, and William Wilson. *An Incomplete Education.* New York: Ballantine, 1987.
Marshall, Donald G. "Literary Interpretation." *Introduction to Scholarship in Modern Languages and Literatures.* Ed. Joseph Gibaldi. New York: MLA, 1992. 159–82.
Meltzer, Francoise. "Unconscious." *Critical Terms for Literary Study.* Ed. Frank Lentricchia and Thomas McLaughlin. Chicago: University of Chicago Press, 1990. 147–62.
Willbern, David. "Reading after Freud." *Contemporary Literary Theory.* Ed. G. Douglas Atkins and Laura Morrow. Amherst: University of Massachusetts Press, 1989. 158–79.

GENERAL SOURCES

Eagleton, Terry. *Literary Theory: An Introduction.* Minneapolis: University of Minnesota Press, 1983.
Grebstein, Sheldon N., ed. *Perspectives in Contemporary Criticism.* New York: Harper & Row, 1968.
Lynn, Steven. *Texts and Contexts: Writing About the Literature with Critical Theory.* New York: Pearson Longman, 2010.

Writing the Literary Essay

This module of *Literacy: Made for All* is designed to help your high school students learn and practice the basics of literary essay writing.

WHAT IS A LITERARY ESSAY?

Concisely defined, a literary essay is a multiparagraph piece of formal persuasive writing that discusses another author's written text.

Now, let's unpack that definition:

Multiparagraph means that the essay is made up of an introduction, a body, and a conclusion, totaling no fewer than five paragraphs. There is no ceiling on the number of paragraphs a literary essay may contain. Typically, there will be one paragraph per argument in the body of the work. In grades 9 and 10 (ages fourteen to sixteen), it is reasonable to expect a body of three paragraphs; in the senior grades (age sixteen and up), a literary essay may put forth anywhere from three to six arguments, contained in as many paragraphs as are needed to develop them effectively.

Formal means that the student's writing conforms to an established set of rules. You may wish to turn the following list into a poster and mount it on the wall for student reference:

FORMAL ESSAYS

- are written entirely in the third person (no "I," "we," "you," or any forms thereof);
- maintain an appropriate level of language (no slang or overly colloquial expressions);
- respect the reader by using correct grammar, spelling, and punctuation throughout;
- avoid the use of contractions (can't), abbreviations (St.), and symbols (&);
- refer to authors by their last names or both names, NEVER by first name only;
- follow MLA formatting rules when quoting or paraphrasing text, and always provide both in-text references and a Works Cited or Works Consulted page; and,
- when literary, are written entirely in the present tense.

Persuasive means that the purpose of the essay is to present and then defend or support an expressed point of view. A persuasive essay is built around a statement, referred to as the *thesis*, which expresses the author's assumed viewpoint in a clear, focused, and *argumentative* fashion *(that is, it invites the reader to disagree with it)*.

Discusses means that there are two sides to the topic and the author of the essay must take one side or the other when formulating his or her thesis statement. The reader of the essay is presumed to be on the opposite side, in need of persuading. An essayist must therefore not "sit on the fence."

WHAT STUDENTS NEED TO UNDERSTAND

- There is nothing creative about writing a literary essay—its success depends on the author's logical thinking skills, as well as her or his ability to organize information, marshal arguments, and express ideas in formal, grammatical English.
- A persuasive or argumentative essay stands or falls on the strength of its thesis statement.
- As in formal debating, it is possible to mount a spirited defense of either side of an issue—the student essayist is not being evaluated on the sincerity of the arguments, merely their effectiveness at persuading the reader.

WHAT STUDENTS NEED TO PRACTICE

In order to write effective literary essays, students should practice the following:

- close reading of literary texts
- unpacking writing prompts
- formulating thesis statements
- generating and ranking arguments to support a thesis
- building argumentation
- choosing effective supporting quotations
- the writing process—preplanning, outlining, drafting, and polishing
- self- and peer-editing skills

There are seven assignments in this module, taking a class from a list of topics to a finished product for submission. Depending on the grade level, each assignment could take up to several days to complete, so unless you are planning a writing unit on this topic, it may not be necessary or even desirable to use all seven assignments with every class. You can choose the skills that you wish to emphasize at any particular time, do them in class, then let your students complete their literary essays as an out-of-class summative writing assignment.

The handouts supplied with the assignments in this module are intended as examples or starting points. You may use them as is if they suit your needs, but you are also free to adapt or modify them—or pitch them out entirely—if they do not.

In the meanwhile, have fun teaching your students to write literary essays!

The Literary Essay Assignment 1
Developing a Topic

✍ **YOU WILL NEED**

- An example topic or writing prompt (not on the practice topic or assignment handout)
- A blank overhead transparency and markers (for brainstorming)
- Overhead projector
- A list of 5 or 6 practice topics based on a literary work already studied in the course (class set)
- Board space for several groups of students to work simultaneously
- An essay assignment sheet with a menu of topics, based on the literary work currently under study (class set)

INTRODUCTION

1. The teacher begins by explaining to the students that their summative assignment for this unit of the course will be a formal literary essay, based on a selection of topics or writing prompts. *(Students may or may not have finished reading the work[s] under study at this point.)*

2. In a mini-lecture about ten minutes long, the teacher provides the necessary information about what a formal literary essay is and what it involves (from the introductory pages of this module), recording the important points on the board for students to copy into their notes.

MODELING

1. The teacher writes the example topic or writing prompt at the top of the blank overhead transparency and models the unpacking process, creating a word web on the transparency while inviting student participation in the discussion:

   (a) Read the topic carefully. Highlight or underline the key words so you know what you are being asked to do. Then brainstorm around the key words (as denoted below with an asterisk), defining what they mean when connected with this particular literary work and creating a word web or concept map.

      Example 1: Discuss the qualities of a good king with reference to the play *King Oedipus*.

   Discuss means the student will be required to take and support one side of an issue arising from the topic and the play.

   *Qualities of a good king.** What are these qualities, exactly? How are they shown? Is a good king different from a good person? If so, in what way(s)? What would a peasant consider to be the qualities of a good king, compared to the viewpoint of a soldier or nobleman?

King Oedipus. Who are the characters in this play? Which of them demonstrate good kingly qualities and which ones don't? How do they show them? Is King Oedipus (the character) a good or a bad king? Why? Who in the play might be a better king? Why?

HINT FOR TEACHER: When brainstorming, you may want to use more than one color of overhead marker to distinguish the qualities of a good king from the qualities of a good person. I've found that creating a visual contrast on the word web helps students to arrive more easily at a viable thesis question.

      Example 2: Good and evil in *Lord of the Flies*

When a topic is phrased this way, the default instruction is to *discuss*. The process is the same as for Example 1. (The key words are *good* and *evil*—the contrast is built into the topic.)

      Example 3: To what extent does justice exist in the world of this novel?

When a topic is already phrased as a question, the default instruction is still *discuss*, and the process remains the same as for Example 1. (Here the key words are *justice* and *the world of the novel*; the contrast could be between justice out of context and justice as defined by society).

(b) From the brainstorming on the transparency and the wording of the topic, formulate a thought question that your thesis statement will answer.

Examples

- To what extent is Oedipus a good king in this play?
- How do the characters in the play *King Oedipus* exemplify the qualities of a good king?
- How good is good and how evil is evil in the novel *Lord of the Flies*?
- How realistic are the portrayals of good and evil in the novel?
- Why do bad things happen to the good people in this novel?
- How does justice operate in this novel?

2. The teacher records the thesis question(s) at the bottom of the overhead transparency for use in the next assignment. The teacher should point out to students that a strong thesis question is a thought question, and thought questions generally begin with *how, why, to what extent*, and *with what result*.

GUIDED PRACTICE

1. Students number off and form groups, one per topic on the practice sheet.

2. The teacher then hands out copies of the practice sheet and assigns each group a different essay topic and a different space on the board on which to work.

3. In their groups, students practice developing their assigned topics, unpacking, brainstorming on the board, and finally formulating two questions (beginning with *how, why, with what result*, or *to what extent*) that could lead to the thesis of a literary essay.

The teacher circulates, providing encouragement and assistance where needed.

4. In whole-class discussion, each group's thesis questions are shared and constructive suggestions are offered in order to make one or both questions more thought provoking and therefore more effective as starting points for a literary essay.

PRACTICE

1. Each student now receives a copy of the essay assignment sheet. Working independently, each student proceeds to select and develop one of the topics on the sheet, following the process already practiced. *(Allow up to twenty minutes for this activity.)*

2. If there is time, students can form small groups for the sharing and discussion of their thesis questions. Groupmates can offer ideas for improving the effectiveness of one or both questions.

PRODUCT

1. That evening, each student reviews the topic development process practiced in class, redoing it if necessary to ensure that all steps have been followed in preparation for the next assignment.

2. The student then selects the thesis question that will form the basis for his or her literary essay.

   See the next page for a sample Assignment Sheet (used with my grade 12 college/university-bound classes).

KING LEAR ESSAY ASSIGNMENT

Select one of the topics below to develop into a formal literary essay of 600–1000 words (two to four pages, typed or printed out, double-spaced with one-inch margins). Take time to organize and outline your paper before writing it. *You will be including your chart and planning materials in your submission package.*

TOPICS

1. To what extent is there justice in the world of this play?

2. An element of every tragedy is a battle between good and evil. How are these forces portrayed in the play?

3. How effective is this play as a tragedy, from the perspective of a twenty-first-century audience?

Due Date for Revision, Editing, and Proofreading with Partners:

DUE DATE FOR FINAL COPY:

Marking Criteria: See attached rubric.

REMEMBER:

1. Your essay must have an argumentative thesis. Arguments are to be supported with quotations from the play. You will be expected to follow the prewriting process discussed in class.

2. *Your rough draft, showing editing and signed by an editing partner, is to be attached to the back of your good copy and submitted with it. You must also submit your chart, planning materials, and peer editing checklist as part of your package.*

3. The rubric that accompanies this sheet is to be attached to the back of your final copy, as I will be using it to evaluate your essay.

4. Your good copy must be typed or printed out, on every second line, in black ink, using a font no smaller than the print on this page. On the first page of your essay, in the upper left corner, provide your name, the course code, teacher's name, and date submitted, as specified earlier in the course. *See the first day handout titled "Submission Criteria" for further details.*

The Literary Essay Assignment 2
Organizing the Information

✍ **YOU WILL NEED**

• All the materials from Literary Essay Assignment 1

INTRODUCTION AND MODELING

1. The teacher reviews with the students the work that was done with the example essay topic in the previous assignment and puts the word web up on the screen.

2. The teacher then explains that before attempting to answer the thesis question, students must first organize the brainstormed information and ideas in the form of a chart.

3. The teacher creates a blank chart on the board. Teacher and class together decide what the headings should be for the *columns*, based on the wording of the topic and the thesis question chosen, and the teacher fills them in. For example:

   Topic: Discuss the qualities of a good king with reference to the play King Oedipus.
   Thesis question: What makes Oedipus a good or bad king (compared with others)?

Chart column headings based on topic and thesis question

What a Good King Does	Oedipus	Creon	Others

4. Together, teacher and students then decide what the headings should be for the *rows* of the chart, based on the brainstormed word web, and the teacher fills them in. For example:

Chart row headings based on brainstorming

What a Good King Does	Oedipus	Creon	Others
He does what is best for the kingdom.			
He treats his subjects fairly and justly.			
He inspires loyalty in his subjects.			
He is a role model and respects his subjects' religion and traditions.			

5. Leaving the word web on the screen for student reference, the teacher divides the class into groups of three to five students and assigns each one a row of the chart. Each group discusses how to fill in its row of the chart, from the word web and from their own knowledge of the literary work on which it is based. *(Allow five to eight minutes for this activity.)*

6. In whole class, the teacher and students then complete the chart together. *(One member can speak for each group, providing information that the teacher copies onto the master chart on the board.)*

   Students need to understand that nothing about the chart is "engraved in stone." They may make changes and additions to the criteria as the rows of the chart begin to fill. *(See example chart filled in, below.)*

7. Teacher and class together discuss the contents of the chart, identifying similarities and differences, trends and commonalities, and (most importantly) the "reasons why." Additional resulting information is added to the chart.

8. Out of this discussion should come a conclusion, which may or may not be an answer to the thesis question, but which relates to the topic and can be identified as a first-draft thesis statement. The teacher records this beside or below the chart on the board.

   For example:

Completed chart showing headings modified by discussion

What a Good King Does	Oedipus	Creon
He does what's best for the kingdom—in his own judgment—*without compromising his power and authority to rule.*	- sends Creon to Delphi to ask Apollo's advice when the city is hit by plague - promises to find and punish Laius's killer and anyone sheltering him - has a high opinion of himself (his intelligence) and his importance to Thebes—believes he is what's best for the kingdom - refuses to believe *he* could be Laius's murderer until the evidence is overwhelming - finally accepts his self-pronounced punishment	- doesn't want to be king, but he takes the throne anyway after the rest of the royal family is disgraced - knows Thebes needs a ruler, especially now
He is fair and just in his treatment of his *loyal* subjects *but will not tolerate even suspected disloyalty.*	- tells Thebans he thinks of them as his children, loses sleep when they are threatened (by plague) - quick to level accusations of treason against Teiresias and Creon when he feels threatened	- merciful; he lets Oedipus say goodbye to his daughters before he is sent into exile
He inspires trust and loyalty by his courage and leadership, *but does not shrink away from making unpopular decisions.*	- citizens remember how he destroyed the Sphinx and reserve judgment until his guilt is firmly proven	- very popular with the Thebans; royalty but not the king, he has never had to make any unpopular decisions
He appears to respect his subjects' religion and tradition *but has his own personal beliefs.*	- argues in public—committing blasphemy against Apollo and prophecy	- pious; he waits for the gods to tell him how to deal with Oedipus

First-draft thesis: Oedipus is a good king because he's not always a good person.

PRACTICE AND PRODUCT

1. Each student now turns to the word web and thesis question produced while working independently in the previous assignment. Each student proceeds to create, fill, and analyze a chart based on his or her chosen essay topic, following the procedure just modeled in whole class. Each student should complete this exercise by formulating a first-draft thesis statement. *(Allow up to thirty minutes for this activity.)*

2. If time permits, students can partner up to share and discuss first-draft thesis statements. Partners can assist by suggesting ways to strengthen each other's thesis statement.

The Literary Essay Assignment 3
Testing a Thesis

✍️ **YOU WILL NEED**

• All the materials from the previous assignments

INTRODUCTION

1. The teacher writes on the board the first-draft thesis statement based on the example essay topic and points out to the class that this is only a first draft. It will need to be tested and improved before it can become the basis for a literary essay.

2. The teacher then shares the following important information about thesis statements, recording points on the board to be copied by students into their notebooks:

   • A thesis statement is a promise to the reader that must be kept. It says, "This is what I intend to prove to you in the rest of this essay. This is what you will find if you keep reading." *This is why a thesis statement must be on topic. It must answer the question implied by the original topic, and it must answer the question arrived at following the brainstorming step of the process.*
   • The thesis statement is the source of every argument in the essay. It is by asking, "Why do I say this?" about the thesis that the author generates the supporting arguments needed for the body of the essay. *Statements of generally accepted fact do not yield arguments when this question is asked. This is why a thesis statement must be argumentative.*
   • The thesis statement must communicate clearly with the reader. It must not contain abstract words that leave its message open to interpretation. *This is why a thesis statement must be clear and focused.*

MODELING

1. The teacher draws the class's attention to the first-draft thesis on the board and models the process that students will use to test their own thesis statements against the preceding three criteria.

   (a) The teacher first asks: Is this thesis statement on topic? Teacher and class compare the thesis statement to both the example topic and the example thesis question to ensure that this thesis statement is a response to both of them. *(If it is not, teacher and students work together to improve the thesis statement until it is.)*

(b) The teacher then asks: Is this thesis statement argumentative? *(Does it invite the reader to disagree with it? Or is it a generally accepted statement of fact?)* Together, teacher and class decide whether the thesis statement on the board needs to be improved, and they then make the necessary changes to strengthen it.

(c) The teacher finally asks the students to read over the example thesis statement and decide whether the thesis is clear and focused. *(Is it specific, or does it contain a lot of abstract words that leave its meaning open to interpretation?)* Together, teacher and class decide whether further improvements are needed and revise the wording to make the thesis as clear and strong as possible.

For example:

Topic: Discuss the qualities of a good king with reference to the play King Oedipus.

Thesis question: What makes Oedipus a good king (compared with others)?

First-draft thesis: Goodness is a relative term when applied to royalty. (Too abstract.)

Improved thesis: Oedipus is a good king because he's not always a good person. (Much better focused.)

Better yet: As shown by the title character in the play King Oedipus, *the dark side of a man is what makes him fit to rule. (Much more argumentative.)*

PRACTICE AND PRODUCT

1. Students are now instructed to take out their own first-draft thesis statements and apply the three criteria to them. Students proceed to test and improve their thesis statements, writing out the "new and improved" version below the previous one. *(Allow up to five minutes for this.)*

2. If time permits, students can pair up and share their thesis statements with partners who may be able to suggest further improvements.

The Literary Essay Assignment 4
Generating Arguments

✍ **YOU WILL NEED**

All the materials from the previous assignments

INTRODUCTION

1. The teacher explains to the class what the differences are among a thesis, an argument, and an elaboration, recording important points on the board for students to copy into their notes:

   - When "Why do I say that?" is asked of a thesis statement, it generates arguments, but when the same question is asked of an argument, it generates elaboration.
   - An argument does not make specific reference to the literary work. It does not mention characters' names or particular events from a story. An argument speaks in more general terms.
   - A thesis is supported by arguments; an argument is supported by elaboration and examples.

   For example:

   Thesis: As shown by the title character in the play King Oedipus, *a man's dark side is what keeps him on the throne.*

   (Why do I say this? Because . . .)

   Argument: A good king can treat his loyal subjects with fairness and compassion, but must deal swiftly and harshly with suspected traitors.

   (Why do I say this? Because . . .)

   Elaboration: A good king understands how much power he wields and how attractive it must be to those who envy his position. Even a beloved ruler will not remain on the throne for long if he shows mercy to those who entertain thoughts of overthrowing him. He must therefore make an example of anyone he suspects of plotting treason, whether or not the accusation is justified.

MODELING

1. The teacher reintroduces the thesis and chart based on the example essay topic from Assignment 1 and, together with the class, goes through the exercise of generating arguments to support it. (See below.)

Completed chart showing headings modified by discussion

What a Good King Does	Oedipus	Creon
He does what's best for the kingdom—in his own judgment—*without compromising his power and authority to rule.*	- sends Creon to Delphi to ask Apollo's advice when the city is hit by plague - promises to find and punish Laius's killer and anyone sheltering him - has a high opinion of himself (his intelligence) and his importance to Thebes—believes he is what's best for the kingdom - refuses to believe *he* could be Laius's murderer until the evidence is overwhelming - finally accepts his self-pronounced punishment	- doesn't want to be king, but he takes the throne anyway after the rest of the royal family is disgraced - knows Thebes needs a ruler, especially now
He is fair and just in his treatment of his *loyal* subjects *but will not tolerate even suspected disloyalty.*	- tells Thebans he thinks of them as his children, loses sleep when they are threatened (by plague) - quick to level accusations of treason against Teiresias and Creon when he feels threatened	- merciful; he lets Oedipus say goodbye to his daughters before he is sent into exile
He inspires trust and loyalty by his courage and leadership, *but does not shrink away from making unpopular decisions.*	- citizens remember how he destroyed the Sphinx and reserve judgment until his guilt is firmly proven	- very popular with the Thebans; royalty but not the king, he has never had to make any unpopular decisions
He appears to respect his subjects' religion and tradition *but has his own personal beliefs.*	- argues in public—committing blasphemy against Apollo and prophecy	- pious; he waits for the gods to tell him how to deal with Oedipus

Thesis: As shown by the title character in the play King Oedipus, *a man's dark side is what keeps him on the throne.*

Why do I say this? Because . . .

Argument A: A good king may appear to make sacrifices for the good of his kingdom, but never jeopardizes his power and authority to rule.

Repeat: *Why do I say this? Because . . .*

Argument B: A good king can treat his loyal subjects with fairness and compassion, but must deal swiftly and harshly with suspected traitors.

Repeat: *Why do I say this? Because . . .*

Argument C: A good king inspires loyalty in those who follow him, but must not shrink away from making an unpopular decision.

Repeat: *Why do I say this? Because . . .*

Argument D: A good king must appear to respect his subjects' religion and traditions, even if he does not personally subscribe to them.

The teacher should point out to students that if the chart is complete and on topic, the arguments to support the thesis should be found on the rows of the chart. The arguments themselves may need some rewording, but the ideas should be there.

2. In whole class, teacher and students now look at arguments A through D and by asking "Why do I say this?" about each one, rank them in order from strongest to weakest.

   IMPORTANT: The amount and depth of elaboration that each argument suggests should be the determining factor in deciding which is the strongest and which is the weakest.

3. The teacher puts a check mark beside the three or four strongest arguments, pointing out to the students that these would be the arguments contained in the body of the essay.

PRACTICE

1. Each student takes out the chart and thesis statement s/he produced in the previous assignment and, working independently, proceeds to generate arguments to support the thesis, based on the rows of the completed chart.

2. The student reads over and ranks his or her arguments from strongest to weakest, then eliminates the weakest ones, leaving at least three strong arguments. These are recopied as a list onto a fresh sheet of paper.

   The teacher circulates, offering encouragement and assistance where needed.

3. The teacher reads aloud to the class an example of elaboration (see INTRODUCTION, above), pointing out that no matter how self-explanatory an argument may seem, it lacks persuasive power on its own. Elaboration is a necessary building block of argumentation.

4. If time permits, students can pair up with new working partners to read each other's list of arguments and make constructive suggestions for improving the wording and rankings.

PRODUCT

That night, each student first-drafts an elaboration to support each of the arguments on his or her revised list.

The Literary Essay Assignment 5
Building Argumentation

INTRODUCTION AND MODELING

1. The teacher explains to the class that they are ready to build the argumentation for their essays and outlines the structure of an argument while recording the following points on the board:

   Place each argument in its own paragraph, organized this way:

   State the argument.
   Elaborate the argument.
   Match the argument with an example from text and a supporting quotation.
   <u>Relate the argument back to the thesis.</u>

2. The teacher now puts the example of argumentation up on the screen and deconstructs it, discussing with the class how the parts of an argument go together to create coherence in an essay. For example:

   A good king can treat his loyal subjects with fairness and compassion, but must deal swiftly and harshly with suspected traitors. *A good king understands how much power he wields and how attractive it must be to those who envy his position. Even a beloved ruler will not remain on the throne for long if he shows mercy to those who entertain thoughts of overthrowing him. He must therefore make an example of anyone he suspects of plotting treason, whether the accusation is justified or not.* Long beloved by the Thebans, Oedipus rightly considers himself to be the most important person in the city of Thebes. He is outraged when the seer, Teiresias, tells him that the best thing he can do for his subjects is to give up the throne and go away. Suspecting a plot to overthrow him, Oedipus immediately levels charges of treason against the person who stands to benefit most from his abdication:

   > Must Creon, so long my friend, my most trusted friend,
   > Stalk me by stealth, and study to dispossess me
   > Of the power this city has given me—freely given—
   > Not of my asking. . . . (Sophocles 36)

153

Beloved by his subjects, Oedipus has been a just and compassionate king; however, he is well trained and reacts quickly to any perceived threat to his authority, even when the suspect is his own brother-in-law. By not losing track of his political situation, Oedipus demonstrates his fitness to rule.

3. The teacher should point out to students that the example argument is contained in a single paragraph, as each of theirs should be. This is also a good opportunity for the teacher to model for the class how they will be expected to format, punctuate, and cite a quotation taken from text.

PRACTICE

1. Students are instructed to take out their homework from the previous evening.

2. Working independently, each student reads over his or her arguments and elaborations and completes each argument by matching it up with a supporting quotation from the text and then relating it back to the thesis of his or her essay.

   This can be done in outline or point form; however, to save time and effort later on, each quotation should be copied out in full, with the embedded reference in parentheses following it.

3. Each student then puts his or her arguments in the most effective order: as in a formal debate, the strongest argument will come at the end of the body and the second strongest at the beginning. Other arguments can be organized between these two, in whatever order makes sense. Students are instructed to number their arguments in the order in which they will appear in the body of the essay. The teacher circulates, offering encouragement and assistance where needed.

4. If time permits, students can pair up with a different working partner than in previous pairings and read each other's work. The reading partner can offer constructive suggestions for improving the choice of quotations and the order of the arguments.

PRODUCT

That night, each student first-drafts the body of his or her essay, turning each argument into a paragraph and putting the paragraphs in the most effective order.

The Literary Essay Assignment 6
Writing the Introduction and Conclusion

✍ **YOU WILL NEED**

- All the materials from the previous assignments
- A note on the board or on an overhead transparency (see below)
- Example introductory and concluding paragraphs on overhead transparencies (see below)
- WLR 1–INTEGRATING QUOTATIONS worksheet (class set)

INTRODUCTION AND MODELING

1. The teacher explains to the class that they are now ready to add the opening and closing paragraphs to their essays and draws students' attention to the note on the board or on the screen:

<u>The Elements of an Essay Introduction</u>

A theme statement—a general observation about the topic or a definition of the main concept of the topic, THEN
A BRIEF explanation or elaboration of the theme statement, THEN
A harnessing sentence that identifies the literary work by title and author and links it to the topic, THEN
The thesis statement

<u>The Elements of an Essay Conclusion</u>

Restate the thesis in different words, THEN
Mention the name of the literary work, THEN
End with a provocative final statement about the topic (NOT a question)

2. The teacher goes over the note with the class, discussing each point to ensure that students understand what will be expected of them. The teacher should also point out to the class that the introduction and conclusion of an essay mirror each other's structure.

Students should be given three to five minutes to copy the note from the board or screen into their notebooks.

3. The teacher now shows the students an example introduction and conclusion, using either an exemplar from a student's writing or the example essay topic from Assignment 1. (See below.)

4. Together, teacher and students deconstruct the two paragraphs as the teacher color-codes the different parts using overhead markers.

Introductory paragraph:

What is politically good may be perceived as morally bad, and vice versa. A politician's job is not primarily to serve the public—it is to remain in office while convincing the voters that they are his first priority, whether or not that is actually the case. To accomplish this, he may decide to act immorally. If his actions get him reelected, then he may not be a good person, but he is a good politician. Similarly, a king's job is to convince his loyal subjects that they are always his first priority, while keeping himself on the throne by whatever means are necessary. In the play King Oedipus *by Sophocles, a mass-murderer who inadvertently saved a city and was made king by the grateful citizens has held onto his power for nearly twenty years. Clearly, it is Oedipus's dark side that makes him fit to rule.*

(BODY OF ESSAY)

Concluding paragraph:

Moral goodness does not make a man fit to rule a kingdom. Creon understands this. Polybus understands it too. King Oedipus has good qualities that make him a beloved ruler of Thebes, but his training as a prince of Corinth has also made him a shrewd politician. It is his political instinct that has kept his reign peaceful, and that comes to the fore when his fitness to rule is challenged. If there is one important message in the play King Oedipus, *it is that good and bad are not as opposite as people would like to think.*

5. The teacher points out to the students:

   - The concluding paragraph does not begin with "In conclusion" or any similar phrase.
   - There are no questions in the introduction or the conclusion. Essays are about making statements. Questions, even rhetorical questions, tend to weaken a formal literary essay.
   - The author has completely avoided the use of "I," "we," and "you."

PRACTICE

1. Students are instructed to take out their homework from the night before. Each student now first-drafts the introductory and concluding paragraphs of his or her essay, following the instructions copied into his or her notes.

2. If time permits, the student can read over the completed draft to check that there are no missing words or punctuation errors, and to ensure that all the required elements have been included in both the introduction and the conclusion.

3. Students pair up with a different working partner from previous pairings to read each other's introduction and conclusion. Reading partners can offer ideas for improving the wording to heighten the impact of the writing.

PRODUCT

1. The teacher now hands out the INTEGRATING QUOTATIONS sheet and goes over it with the class, discussing each item to ensure that students understand what will be expected of them.

2. That night, each student assembles the first draft of his or her essay, recopying it onto fresh sheets of paper: introduction, body paragraphs in most effective order, and concluding paragraph.

3. The student then reviews the INTEGRATING QUOTATIONS sheet and checks to ensure that each quotation in the completed draft is correctly formatted and that the punctuation and embedded reference are without error in each case.

INTEGRATING QUOTATIONS INTO YOUR LITERARY ESSAY

There are several simple rules to remember about integrating quotations into an essay:

1. Always tell the reader where the quotation came from. The following is BLOCK FORM, indented on the left side. Notice the embedded references and the lack of quotation marks around the quoted words.

> Because I would not see thy cruel nails
> Pluck out his poor old eyes; nor thy fierce sister
> In his anointed flesh stick boarish fangs. (*King Lear* 3.7.56–58)

> All writers are conventional, because all writers have the same problem of transferring their language from direct speech to the imagination. (Frye 17)

2. If all your quotations come from a single literary text that has been identified in the opening paragraph of the essay, all that is needed in the embedded reference is the page number.

> Uphill and down, across the deserts of salt or sand, through forests, into the violet depth of canyons, over crag and peak and table-topped mesa, the fence marched on and on, irresistibly the straight line, the geometrical symbol of triumphant human purpose. (94)

3. When quoting more than one line of poetry, retain the form of the poetry. Do not convert it into sentences and paragraphs. Copy it exactly as it appears on the page of your source.

4. If the quotation is one line long or less, you can incorporate it into the body of your paragraph. In the examples below, notice the embedded references and the punctuation.

> Northrop Frye agrees with this statement, declaring, "All writers are conventional." (17)

> Lear is eloquent in his description of his children's cruelty as "sharper than a serpent's tooth." (1.4.279)

Indicate that your quotation spans a line break using a forward slash mark:

> Lear warns Goneril that her sister will fight fiercely for him: "with her nails / She'll flay thy wolvish visage." (1.4.298–99)

5. Always introduce a quotation. For quotations incorporated into paragraphs, see the three examples above. When using block form, introduce the quotation with a sentence ending with a colon and follow it up with an explanation or summation that relates back to the thesis. For example:

> There is no escaping the irony in the Director's words to Bernard:
>
>> Alphas are so conditioned that they do not have to be infantile in their emotional behaviour. But that is all the more reason for their making a special effort to conform. It is their duty to be infantile, even against their inclination. (Huxley 88)
>
> The Director is preaching to the converted—Bernard's behavior is always immature, even when he is trying to be adult.

6. Always place a buffer sentence between quotations if you are using them one after the other.

7. Avoid any statement that makes reference to the essay as an essay or to the quotations as quotations. Don't talk about the thesis or arguments, either. The reader is smart enough to know that s/he is reading an essay and that it contains arguments supported by quotations. So DO NOT SAY things like the following:

> The following quotation will prove the point of this argument.
> As the quotation above shows, . . .
> Here is a quotation that will illustrate . . .

The Literary Essay Assignment 7
Revision, Editing, and Proofreading

✍ **YOU WILL NEED**

- All the materials from the previous assignments
- WLR 2–PROOFREAD WITH A PARTNER checklist (class set)
- WLR 3–LITERARY ESSAY ASSESSMENT RUBRIC (class set)

INTRODUCTION

1. Each student receives a copy of the PROOFREAD WITH A PARTNER checklist and the teacher and class go over it together, discussing each item to ensure that students understand the expectations.

2. Students also need to understand the following, which the teacher may wish to write on the board in condensed form as a reminder:

   - *Student authors are the owners of their own writing and take final responsibility for the completeness and correctness of the work that is handed in for marking.*
   - *Peer-editing partners are not to make corrections or changes to other authors' work. They may point out words to be checked for spelling or suggest improvements to wording, punctuation, and so on, but the author is the one who actually makes revisions to the text.*

PRACTICE

1. Students pair up with a working partner (different from all previous pairings) and designate themselves Author A and Author B. Together, both partners work on Author A's essay, reading it aloud and discussing the criteria on the PROOFREAD WITH A PARTNER checklist. Author A reads with a pencil in hand, making changes and improvements to his or her own work. As each item on the checklist has been discussed, Author A's editing partner checks it off in the left-hand column of Author A's sheet.

2. The process is then repeated for Author B's essay. The teacher circulates meanwhile, offering encouragement and assistance as needed.

FINAL PRODUCT

1. Each student receives a copy of the assessment rubric and the teacher goes over it with the class, discussing each item to ensure that students understand the criteria that will be used to evaluate their work.

   NOTE TO THE TEACHER: The rubric supplied with this module has been developed for and used successfully with grade 12 classes. It is included because it contains a complete listing of criteria, giving you a starting point from which you may create your own assessment tool. Feel free to shorten, reword, simplify, or reformat the rubric to make it suit the needs and abilities of your own classes, at all grade levels.

RUBRIC DEFINITIONS: APPLICATION

Functional—superficial level of analysis—answers are found in the text
Associative—middle level of analysis—answers are found by comparing the text to the real world
Thematic—the deepest level of analysis—answers are found within the reader's own imagination and judgment

2. That night, each student goes over his or her edited draft once more, making final changes and improvements and checking off items on the PROOFREAD WITH A PARTNER checklist (right-hand column) as they are completed. The student also refers to the assessment rubric to ensure that all the evaluation criteria have been met.

3. Before the due date specified for the essay, the student types or prints out a clean final draft of the essay, checking to make sure that the first page is formatted as outlined on the essay assignment sheet.

4. The student also gathers all the elements required for the submission package and assembles them as specified by the teacher. For example:

   Final draft essay on top, with student name, course code, and submission date on the first page, THEN
   Assessment rubric, THEN
   Edited rough draft of the essay with peer-editing checklist behind it, THEN
   Essay planning materials, including brainstorming, outline, chart, etc.

5. The submission package is then stapled together, ready to be handed in for evaluation on the due date.

REVISE, EDIT, AND PROOFREAD WITH A PARTNER
LITERARY ESSAY CHECKLIST

Author's Name: _____

Editing Partner's Name: _____

Checked by Partner	EDITING AND PROOFREADING CRITERIA	Improved by Author
	The essay has an interesting, descriptive title.	
	The opening paragraph of the essay is complete with a theme statement, elaboration, harnessing statement, and thesis statement.	
	The essay has a clear, focused, argumentative thesis that answers the question posed by the topic.	
	The thesis statement appears at the end of the introductory paragraph and again, rephrased, at the beginning of the concluding paragraph.	
	Each paragraph in the body of the essay contains a complete argument, strongly supported by a well-chosen quotation from the literary work. The closing sentence of each argument relates it back to the thesis of the essay.	
	The body paragraphs of the essay strongly support the thesis and are in the most effective order.	
	Each quotation in the essay is formatted in proper block style, with an embedded reference in parentheses at the end. Lines of poetry have been kept in their original format. Each quotation is sandwiched between an introduction (ending with a colon) and an explanation or summary.	
	The conclusion of the essay is complete, mirroring the structure of the opening paragraph and ending with a thought-provoking statement (not a question).	
	The language used in the essay is formal, not slangy. "I," "we," and "you" have been avoided. There are no contractions, abbreviations, or symbols in the text. The present tense is used throughout. The author is never referred to by first name only.	
	The grammar, spelling, and punctuation have been checked and corrected if necessary. There are no sentence fragments, run-on sentences, or ambiguous pronoun references in the text.	

Remember to attach this checklist (filled out) to the back of your edited draft when assembling your package for submission.

RUBRIC: LITERARY ESSAY

STUDENT NAME: _____

CRITERIA	REMEDIAL 0 to 2 out of 5	LEVEL 1 2.5 out of 5	LEVEL 2 3 to 3.5 out of 5	LEVEL 3 4 out of 5	LEVEL 4 4.5 to 5 out of 5
Knowledge The student's chart and planning materials are well organized and demonstrate a clear understanding of both the topic and the literary work.	Chart and/or materials are missing. Material is incomplete, poorly organized, trivial, and/ or irrelevant. Little or no understanding of topic and/ or literary work.	Chart and materials are completed and show an attempt at organization. Material is on topic but could be more helpful. Some understanding of topic and literary work.	Chart and materials show some skill at organization. Material is both relevant and helpful. Moderate understanding of topic and literary work.	Chart and materials are well organized. Selection of material demonstrates considerable understanding of both topic and literary work.	Chart and materials are skillfully organized. Selection of material demonstrates insightful understanding of both topic and literary work.
Thinking The student has arrived at a thesis that is on topic, clear, focused, and argumentative.	The thesis is missing, off-topic, or simplistic. Or, the student has mistaken an argument for a thesis.	The thesis is present and on topic but weak. Generalized and/or lacking conviction. Unfocused, not argumentative.	The thesis is present and on topic but could be more focused and argumentative.	The thesis is on topic, focused, and argumentative.	The thesis is strong and thought provoking.
The student presents sufficient significant evidence from text to support an appropriately sophisticated level of argumentation.	Evidence is lacking. Arguments digress to side issues or are incomplete, trivial, or simplistic. (greatly below grade level)	Evidence is present but weak—not specific or relevant enough to be convincing. (below grade level)	Evidence is present and on topic, but quotations could have been better chosen. (nearing grade level)	Arguments are well reasoned and supporting quotations are specific and relevant. (at grade level)	Arguments are creative and insightful. Quotations strongly support them. (above grade level)
Communication The student has structured each paragraph of the essay for best effect.	Missing elements weaken introduction and/ or conclusion. Body is cluttered, wordy, or disorganized.	Introduction and conclusion are complete but weak. One or more body paragraphs lack topic sentences, concluding sentence, and/or transition phrases.	Introduction and conclusion are complete. Body paragraphs are complete but need better transitions and stronger relevance to thesis.	Introduction and conclusion are well organized. Body paragraphs are complete, coherent, and connected.	Maximum effect. Writing is completely transparent.
The student has correctly and smoothly integrated quotations into the essay.	Limited effectiveness. Multiple formatting and punctuation errors. No embedded references.	Some effectiveness. Multiple formatting or punctuation errors. Embedded references are attempted.	Moderate effectiveness. Several formatting and/ or punctuation errors. Embedded references are present and mostly correct.	Considerable effectiveness. No formatting errors. Some punctuation errors. Embedded references are present and all correct.	Impressive writing! No formatting or punctuation errors. All embedded references are correct.
The student has correctly used conventions of standard English.	Numerous major and minor errors, often affecting meaning (15+ errors). Word choice often inappropriate.	Numerous major and minor errors, sometimes affecting meaning (10+ errors). Limited word choice, at times inappropriate.	Several major and minor errors but meaning not affected (8 to 10 errors). Word choice generally appropriate, few lapses.	Few major and minor errors (4 to 7 errors). Word choice is precise and appropriate.	Impressive writing! Virtually error-free (0 to 3 errors). Word choice is precise, appropriate, sophisticated, and effective.
Application The student has effectively connected the topic to a greater truth within the work.	Limited effectiveness. Connections are weak and on the functional level only.	Some effectiveness. The essay makes solid connections on the functional level.	Moderate effectiveness. The essay shows an attempt to connect on functional and associative levels.	Considerable effectiveness. The essay makes solid connections on functional and associative levels.	Maximum effectiveness. Strong connections on functional, associative, and thematic levels.

Studying Poetry

The STUDYING POETRY module is divided into four sections, from which you may mix and match activities to suit the requirements of the curriculum and your students' needs and interests.

The first section of the module provides students with a "toolkit" to appreciate and analyze poetry. Among the tools in the kit are a glossary of terminology, three levels of analysis, and a range of poetic devices that operate on each level. Students practice answering effectiveness questions on a variety of poems, then write a sight test. Especially recommended for grade 9 classes or students new to the study of poetry, this section can easily serve as a self-contained poetry unit at any grade level. Depending on the grade and ability levels of your class, each assignment may take from one to several periods to complete.

The second section focuses in turn on each of three different kinds of poetry: narrative, lyric, and dramatic. These assignments afford students ample opportunity to use the analytical tools in their kit but also encourage them to go beyond the poem on the page with creative media and writing challenges. The sample units provided may be used as is or adapted. All have been successfully taught at various grade levels.

The third section gives students practice at producing short and essay-length written dialectical, personal, and analytical responses to poetry. If your students have already worked through the LITERARY CRITICISM 101 module, this is an excellent opportunity for them to apply their critical viewpoint "lenses."

The fourth section is included specifically to help students hone their timed writing skills in preparation for writing final examinations and taking the Advanced Placement English exam. It isn't easy to write an entire essay from scratch in under forty-five minutes, but by sprinkling these exercises and activities throughout the course, you can help your students do their best when the pressure is on.

STUDYING POETRY ultimately focuses on close reading and analysis of short and longer poetry of various types; however, it may be implemented in tandem with related skill sets and assignments from other parts of the program. As with every module of *Literacy: Made for All*, each of the assignments can be taught at any grade level, from 9 through 12. Here are some further recommendations to help ensure that both you and your students derive the greatest possible benefit from STUDYING POETRY:

1. There are writing activities included throughout this module. Should you decide to use one of these for formative or summative assessment, give students the opportunity to practice peer assessment and self-assessment of their work. Let them pair up or form groups to help edit one another's first or second drafts. It may be beneficial as well to teach a preliminary lesson on ways to deliver constructive criticism.

   I have three effective rules for the English classroom, which you may find useful in yours:

   a) *Every person in this class is entitled to form her or his own opinions, and every expressed opinion has value. (But in order to earn marks, an opinion must be convincingly supported by examples or quotations.)*

   b) *Every expressed criticism of another student's work must be constructive. (A chart may be posted on the wall to suggest constructive openings for critical comments and to serve as a reminder that the purpose of criticism is to help the other author to improve.)*

c) Always try your best. (Areas where a student needs to improve will thus be easier to identify. Also, trying one's best to be constructive at all times will speed everyone's progress toward fluent, effective writing.)

2. Do not hesitate to repeat any of the activities in this program if, in your opinion, the students need to deepen their understanding or improve their analytical skills. Rather than feeling bored because of lesson repetition, students will become more familiar with the structure of the activity and therefore more confident about undertaking it. Increased confidence makes students more willing to take risks, and risk taking helps students to learn and grow. So, don't worry about repeating the segments in consecutive grades, or even about repeating a particular activity in two or more consecutive English periods. As your students "get into" this module, you may even find them asking to repeat an activity they have particularly enjoyed.

AIMS AND OBJECTIVES OF *STUDYING POETRY*

Aims:

Students shall have opportunities to:

1. compare themselves as poets with the writers whose work they are studying in class;

2. deepen their understanding of the ways in which poets use various writing techniques to make text effective;

3. understand the role that language, literature, and the media play in the exploration of intellectual issues and in the establishment of personal and societal values;

4. use their critical and analytical skills to respond to ideas communicated through a variety of styles and types of poetry; and

5. become thoughtful, literate readers of a range of poetic texts.

Objectives:

Through this module, students will be encouraged to:

1. become better communicators of their own thoughts and observations;

2. develop a greater understanding and acceptance of other points of view through group discussions;

3. develop a better understanding of themselves and others;

4. hone and channel their analytical abilities through close and thoughtful reading of a range of poetic texts; and

5. become effective editors of their own writing and that of others.

Studying Poetry Part 1
Build Your Toolkit

✍ **YOU WILL NEED**

- SPR 1–PROSE AND POETRY handout (class set)
- SPR 2–LEVELS OF ANALYSIS: POETRY (class set)
- SPR 3–A GLOSSARY OF POETICAL/LITERARY TERMS (class set)
- SPR 4–ANSWERING AN EFFECTIVENESS QUESTION (TECHNICAL) (class set)
- SPR 5–ANSWERING AN EFFECTIVENESS QUESTION (ASSOCIATIVE) (class set)
- SPR 6–ANSWERING AN EFFECTIVENESS QUESTION (THEMATIC) (class set)
- SPR 7–POETRY TERMINOLOGY QUIZ (optional)
- SPR 8–LEVELS OF ANALYSIS: EFFECTIVENESS (class set)
- SPR 9 to 11–POETRY IN *A Midsummer Night's Dream* (optional)
- SPR 12–TIPS FOR WRITING A TEST (optional)
- SPR 13–POETRY SIGHT TEST—ON THE SONNET (optional)
- SPR 14–POETRY SIGHT TEST—THE SCARECROW (optional)
- SPR 15–POETRY SIGHT TEST—I SEE BEFORE ME THE GLADIATOR LIE (optional)
- SPR 16–ANSWERING AN EFFECTIVENESS QUESTION EDITING CHECKLIST (class set)
- SPR 17–ANSWERING AN EFFECTIVENESS QUESTION ASSESSMENT SHEET (half a class set)
- A selected poem 15 to 20 lines long on a handout (class set, for Assignments 5 and 6)
                                        PLUS
- A photocopied study package containing 10 to 12 selected short poems (class set)
                                        OR
- A class set of a poetry anthology and a list of 10 to 12 preselected short poems for study during this part of the module

---

PURPOSE

In this series of activities, students will begin to familiarize themselves with the language of literary analysis. They will practice using correct terminology as they describe and discuss poetry at three levels of complexity: technical, associative, and thematic. In the process, they will hone their analytical and communication skills.

Assignment 1: Define Poetry

INTRODUCTION

1. The teacher explains to the class that just as a carpenter needs to learn how to use a variety of tools in order to build something, students need to practice with tools in order to fully understand and appreciate a work of literature. Poetry is an especially dense and powerful form of writing, and analyzing it will no doubt pose a challenge to their skills. However, having the right tools for the job will not only make the job a lot easier, it will also make it a lot more fun to do. The purpose of this unit is to give students the tools they need in order to enjoy working with poetry.

2. The teacher now hands out a copy of the PROSE AND POETRY sheet to each student. Teacher and class together read aloud and discuss the first pair of examples to determine which one is poetry and why. *(Example A is poetry, because it has a musical beat or rhythm, as well as some rhyming. It's also laid out in lines rather than stretching across the page as a sentence.)*

3. The teacher puts up two headings on the board or an overhead transparency: *Poetry* and *Prose*. As students suggest reasons for selecting example *A* and not example *B*, the teacher records them under the appropriate headings. *(Students may also point out that the first example shows what the second one is telling the reader—that the children are having fun. The beat is bouncy and energetic, and having just two words per line makes the poem read very fast.)*

4. The teacher points out that what the students have noticed is the form of the poem (how it looks on the page) and how it sounds. They have begun a technical analysis. The teacher now writes the word *Technical* on the board beside the students' reasons for choosing example *A*.

5. Students are directed to the second pair of examples and the teacher asks: Which one is poetry and why? *(Example B—it sounds like a snake moving through the grass. Again, the prose sentence tells what is happening but the poetry lets the reader hear it for himself or herself.)* The reason for picking example *B* is recorded on the board or overhead transparency, and the teacher points out that this is another instance of technical analysis.

6. Teacher and students now look at the third pair of examples. Which one is poetry? *(Example A—It compares the hostile and confusing world to a battlefield at night. It's a more powerful description than just saying, "We're surrounded by people who don't understand us.")* The teacher records students' answers under the appropriate headings, then points out that what the students have noticed is how comparisons give the poem a much stronger impact on the reader. They have begun an associative analysis. The teacher writes the word *Associative* on the board beside the students' reasons for choosing this example.

7. Teacher and students look at the final pair of examples. Which one is poetry? *(Example A—besides being laid out in lines and having a regular beat, it shows how the speaker is feeling by the words that he uses: idle, barren crag, still hearth, mete, and dole. The sentence in example B just sums it up.)* The teacher records students' answers under the appropriate headings, then points out that what students have noticed is the emotional baggage associated with the words chosen by the poet. They have begun a thematic analysis. The teacher writes the word *Thematic* on the board beside the students' reasons for choosing this example.

   NOTE TO TEACHER: This exercise is a good diagnostic tool, as you will find out what your students already know about poetry and poetic devices.

8. In whole class, teacher and students now recap what they've determined about poetry. The list may be recorded on the board by a student secretary and should include the following:

- Poetry shows rather than tells.
- Poets choose their words carefully to have a particular effect on the reader.
- Poetry uses comparisons to paint vivid pictures in the reader's mind.
- The look and sound of a poem is an important part of expressing its meaning.
- Not all poetry is serious, and not all poems use rhyme.

IMPORTANT: From this point on, the teacher should begin each English period by reading aloud to the class a different one of the selected poems from the anthology, then leading a brief discussion regarding its theme and content. This "poem of the day" will be the one students work on while practicing their skills in class, both with partners and independently.

POETRY AND PROSE

1. (a) Hippity-hoppity
   No time to stoppity,
   Children come tripping
   and skipping
   and jumping
   and running
   and laughing
   to Butterscotch Square.

   (b) Butterscotch Square attracts many children. They have fun there.

   Which one is poetry, and why?

2. (a) The snake moved through the grass.

   (b) The snake slithered sinuously between stalks of tall grass.

   Which one is poetry, and why?

3. (a) Ah, love, let us be true
   To one another! for the world, which seems
   To lie before us like a land of dreams, . . .
   Hath really neither joy, nor love, nor light, . . .
   And we are here as on a darkling plain
   Swept with confused alarms of struggle and flight,
   Where ignorant armies clash by night.
   (from "Dover Beach" by Matthew Arnold)

   (b) It's us against the world, sweetheart.

   Which one is poetry, and why?

4. (a) It little profits that an idle king,
   By this still hearth, among these barren crags,
   Matched with an aged wife, I mete and dole
   Unequal laws unto a savage race,
   That hoard, and sleep, and feed, and know not me.
   (from "Ulysses" by Alfred Lord Tennyson)

   (b) My life is so boring!

   Which one is poetry, and why?

Assignment 2: Analyze on the Technical Level

Before the assignment begins, the teacher goes over the list of technical devices on the LEVELS OF ANALYSIS handout and selects the ones most appropriate for each class to learn and practice analyzing. The devices chosen will depend on the grade and ability levels of the class.

NOTE TO TEACHERS: It is not necessary or desirable to deal with all the technical devices at once. For grade 9 classes, I generally focus on sound devices, as these are the easiest to identify and the most likely to engage younger students: alliteration, sibilance, onomatopoeia, and rhyme. Once that groundwork has been laid, other technical devices can be added to their "toolkit." Except for iambic pentameter, which is the natural rhythm of the English language and therefore the most commonly found meter in English poetry, I have found that it's best to reserve such things as meter and scansion for pre-AP and college-bound grade 12 classes. Once students are already "hooked" on poetry, they shouldn't mind tackling its more academic aspects.

Here is a suggested progression for technical devices that has worked well in my classes.

Grade 9 or beginners—alliteration, sibilance, onomatopoeia, rhyme
Grade 10—review of the above devices plus: assonance, repetition, line length, line and word placement
Grade 11—review of the above devices plus: free, blank, and formal verse forms; iambic pentameter
Grade 12—review of the above devices plus: meter, enjambment, caesura

I make a point of repeating certain poems and poets from one grade to the next. What really opens students' eyes to the expansion of their "toolkits" from year to year is going back to poems that have already been studied and discovering how much easier they are to understand and how much more depth of meaning they reveal the second and third times they are read.

INTRODUCTION TO TECHNICAL ANALYSIS

1. The teacher reads aloud to the class a short poem from the anthology, selected because it contains examples of the technical devices students are going to be working with during this assignment.

2. Following a brief discussion of the theme and content of the poem, the teacher hands out a copy of the LEVELS OF ANALYSIS: POETRY sheet to each student, directing the class to the section headed "Technical." The teacher identifies the devices that will be the focus of this assignment (ideally, no more than four) and instructs students to underline, star, or otherwise highlight them on their copies of the sheet.

3. Each student now receives a copy of the GLOSSARY OF POETICAL/LITERARY TERMS. Students are instructed to find each of the selected devices in the glossary and highlight them. Together, teacher and students review each of the highlighted definitions, ensuring that everyone understands what these devices are and what they do. *Students may be asked for extra examples of each selected device, to be added to its definition on the handout.*

4. The devices are numbered and students form groups with that same number of members *(that is, if three devices are being introduced, students should be divided into groups of three).* Within each group, students number off to determine which device will be each group member's "specialty."

5. Each student takes a sheet of blank paper and folds it lengthwise, forming two columns. Over the left-hand column, the student writes *Examples.* Over the right-hand column, the student writes *Effectiveness.*

6. Students are directed to the poem read aloud earlier (in Step 1). The teacher reads it aloud once more and asks students to identify an example from the poem of one of the technical devices highlighted on their sheets. The teacher then models on the board the format students are to use when recording examples in the left-hand column of their worksheet. For example:

"Several startled civilians gasped aloud" (l.7)

Students should be instructed that when quoting examples of sound devices, they will need to copy the entire line onto their sheet, underlining the words or letters that contain the device.

7. Each "specialist" proceeds to identify examples of his or her technical device in the poem, recording each example on the left side of the worksheet. When done, each student shares his/her findings with the rest of his/her group.

8. In whole class, the teacher asks each group to quote its favorite example from the poem, and these are recorded in a list on the board. The teacher then asks each group to explain what made this example stand out for them. *(Typically, it will be because the example helped them to do something—imagine being there with the speaker of the poem, share what the speaker was feeling at the time, and so on.)*

   The teacher points out that what the students have just described is the impact that the example had on them. In other words, they've begun to explain what makes the example *effective*.

9. Each student now receives a copy of the ANSWERING AN EFFECTIVENESS QUESTION (Technical) handout, and teacher and students together go over the entire sheet. The teacher points out that although the wording of an effectiveness question may not be exactly as shown on the handout, it's still asking for the same thing. In order to be considered complete (and get full marks on a test or exam), the answer to an effectiveness question must contain all of the important elements listed on the sheet, including how the example relates to the main idea or theme of the poem.

   The teacher should point out to students that the LEVELS OF ANALYSIS handout gives them a menu of ways in which a poetical device can contribute to the overall effectiveness of a poem ("Effective Poetry Has") and that the sample response on the ANSWERING AN EFFECTIVENESS QUESTION handout concludes with an item from this list.

10. The teacher then selects one of the quoted examples from the board and leads a whole-class discussion of what makes it effective. Students should be encouraged to choose words from the two lists provided on the handout when describing what the example does and what it helps the reader to do. Using point form, the teacher records the class response on the board, ensuring that all the important elements are present and that the response concludes by stating how the example contributes to the overall effectiveness of the poem (that is, by giving it immediacy, vividness, evocativeness, or provocativeness).

11. The students in each group now work together to discuss all of their found examples and fill in the right-hand side of their worksheets in point form, following the pattern modeled on the board. *(That is, each student will be talking about all of the selected technical devices but writing about only the one that is his or her "specialty.")*

12. (OPTIONAL) Each student "specialist" pairs up with one or two others specializing in the same technical device to compare and discuss their completed worksheets.

   At teacher's discretion, these worksheets may be handed in for a completion check mark.

PRODUCT

To demonstrate their understanding of the technical level of analysis, students may be asked to do one or more of the following:

• Compose a short poem or paragraph including examples of each of the technical devices studied so far. (The examples would need to be highlighted or underlined, then labeled.) These can be handed in for formative assessment.
• Over a period of one or two days, compile a list of technical devices they have seen or heard used in the media, in their other reading, or in real life. Students can assemble in groups to compare and discuss their lists.
• Create visual representations of the sound devices studied so far *(for example, a tree in the wind with S-shaped leaves)*. These can be posted around the room for others to admire.

LEVELS OF ANALYSIS: POETRY

LEVEL I: TECHNICAL (How does the poem look and sound?)

This type of analysis focuses on external aspects of a poem, rather than the content.

> Rhyme—internal, end-of-line
> Meter—patterns of stressed and unstressed beats in a line
> Free, blank, and formal verse—ways to organize lines of poetry
> Alliteration—repetition of consonant sounds
> Onomatopoeia—words sound like what they mean
> Repetition—of words, phrases, ideas, and lines
> Assonance—repetition of vowel sounds
> Sibilance—repetition of *s*, *sh*, *z*, and *zh* sounds
> Line length—short vs. long lines, for effect
> Line and word placement—to illustrate or emphasize an aspect of the poem
> Enjambment—one line flowing into another without stopping
> Caesura—a full stop in the middle of a line

LEVEL II: ASSOCIATIVE (How does the poem relate to the world of reality?)

This type of analysis focuses on comparison and contrast within the content of a poem.

> Simile—a figurative comparison using "like" or "as"
> Metaphor—a figurative comparison that does not use "like" or "as"
> Personification—giving human characteristics to abstract ideas or inanimate objects
> Objectification—giving people the characteristics of objects
> Imagery—sensory detail
> Contrast—placing opposites side by side to emphasize the difference between them
> Oxymoron—words with contrasting meanings linked in a phrase
> Metonymy—substitution of the quality for the thing or the container for the thing contained
> Synecdoche—substitution of the part for the whole or the whole for the part

LEVEL III: THEMATIC (How does the poem relate to my personal experience?)

This type of analysis focuses on what the reader brings to the reading of a poem.

> Recurring imagery—multiple sensory details that create or reinforce a single impression
> Symbolism—concrete things that represent abstract ideas
> Allusion—references to mythology, history, literature, or religion
> Irony—something that means or turns out to be the opposite of what is expected
> Connotation—the associations that some words carry with them

EFFECTIVE POETRY HAS:

> **IMMEDIACY—a sense of "you are there right now"**
> **VIVIDNESS—making the reader experience the poem with all of his or her senses**
> **EVOCATIVENESS—making the reader feel an emotion**
> **PROVOCATIVENESS—making the reader think**
> **ECONOMY OF LANGUAGE—saying a lot in very few words**

A GLOSSARY OF POETICAL/LITERARY TERMS

ALLITERATION
When two or more words that are close together begin with the same consonant sound. (Examples: *freedom forever, Daffy Duck*)

ALLUSION
A reference to something outside the work of literature (from history, mythology, religion or other literary works) for the purpose of deepening the reader's appreciation of the work. (Examples: a *Herculean* task, to meet one's *Waterloo*)

ASSONANCE
The use of same vowel sounds in words with different consonants to create an 'almost rhyme'. (Example: *plumber* and *mother*) Also, the repetition of vowel sounds within words. (Example: "Lots of green cheese, please!")

BLANK VERSE
Lines of iambic pentameter with no end-of-line rhyme. Usually found in dramatic poetry and in the plays of Shakespeare.

CAESURA
A full stop for effect in the middle of a line of poetry.

CONNOTATION
The associations that attach to a word, giving it additional emotional impact or levels of meaning in the context of a piece of writing. Unlike the dictionary definition (denotation), connotation may vary from reader to reader.

CONTENT
The subject matter of a piece of writing. The structured presentation of the subject matter is the FORM.

CONTRAST
Two opposite things or ideas placed side by side to emphasize the differences between them.

DICTION
An author's choice of words. In a poem every word is important, so poets choose their words carefully for effect.

ENJAMBMENT
When a phrase or an idea flows beyond the end of one line of poetry and into the next.

FOOT
A pattern of stressed and unstressed beats that is repeated a set number of times per line to create the METER of a poem. (Example: An *iambic* foot has two beats, the first unstressed and the second one stressed.)

FORMAL VERSE
Poetry that has a regular meter, rhyme scheme, line length, and/or pattern of stanzas. (Examples: haiku, sonnet)

FREE VERSE
Poetry without any regular meter, rhyme, line length, or pattern of stanzas.

IMAGERY
The sensory details in a piece of writing—descriptions of what can be seen, smelled, heard, touched, or tasted. Sensory details help to give a poem a sense of immediacy.

IRONY
When something means or turns out to be the opposite of what would normally be expected. (Example: *An Olympic skier wins a gold medal, then falls off the podium and breaks his leg.*) Verbal irony, or sarcasm, means the opposite of what the words seem to be saying. (Example: *Well, that was the bright move of the century!*)

LINE LENGTH
Lines of poetry may be shortened to provide emphasis for the words in them, to make the poem seem to move faster, or to create a look on the page that illustrates or reinforces the theme of the poem. (Example: A poem about trees is shaped like a tree on the page by the use of long and short lines.) Long lines, like long words, will tend to slow down the pace of a poem, so a poet may put a longer line where the reader is expected to stop and think.

LINE AND WORD PLACEMENT
Broken lines and words that sit apart from the rest of the poem are often used by poets to create emphasis or focus the reader's attention on a particular thought.

METAPHOR
A figurative comparison that does not use "like" or "as." (Example: *She is a glutton for punishment.*)

METER
A regular rhythm created by repeating a pattern of stressed and unstressed beats a set number of times per line of a poem. (Example: *Iambic pentameter* has ten beats per line—five repetitions of the iambic two-beat pattern.)

METONYMY
A substitution device which replaces a thing with one of its qualities (Example: *sailing on the deep*) or puts a container in place of the thing contained (Example: *I'm boiling the kettle for tea. Would you like a cup?*).

OBJECTIFICATION
Giving a person the characteristics of an object. (Example: a warrior described as though he were a sword—*burnished and lethal.*)

ONOMATOPOEIA
A word sounds like what it is describing. (Examples: *sizzle, crash*)

OXYMORON
Two words of opposite meaning combined in a phrase. (Examples: *jumbo shrimp, pretty ugly*)

PERSONIFICATION
Attributing human characteristics or qualities to abstract or inanimate objects. (Examples: *a haughty mountain, courageous love*)

POETRY
A type of literature in which the music and the meaning of words combine in order to reach the reader on an emotional level. Poetry says a great deal using few words and is consequently the most powerful way to communicate using written language.

PROSE
A style of literature that uses sentences and paragraphs rather than lines and stanzas to communicate. Prose can employ poetical techniques when it needs to be powerful but tends to be used for the expression of less emotionally laden ideas than poetry.

RECURRING IMAGERY
A pattern of sensory details that creates a single strong impression or an unstated message (a subtext). (Example: a series of courtroom references when someone feels as though he's being judged unfairly)

REPETITION
Repeating words and phrases can create or imitate a rhythm in a poem as well as serve to emphasize an image or an idea. (Example: *A thousand thousand years* emphasizes how long a time a million years really is.)

RHYME
The matching of words that have different beginning sounds but identical-sounding conclusions. (Examples: *erase* and *displace, contentment* and *resentment, fair* and *bear*)

SIBILANCE
A type of alliteration in which the repeated consonant sound is an *s, z, sh,* or *zh.*

SIMILE
A figurative comparison that uses "like" or "as." (Example: Jenny defended her project *as fiercely as a mother bear protecting a cub* OR *like a mother bear protecting a cub.*)

STANZA
A stanza is to poetry what a paragraph is to prose. It's a grouping of lines within the overall structure of a poem.

STRUCTURE
How a literary work in its entirety has been designed or organized.

STYLE
An author's individual way of expressing him/herself. An author's style includes his/her particular choice of words, use of figurative language, and anything else that makes it distinctive.

SYMBOLISM
The use of a concrete object to represent an abstract idea. (Examples: The color white symbolizes purity or innocence; a balancing scale symbolizes justice.)

SYNECDOCHE
A substitution device in which the whole represents the part (Example: *The town has decided to amend the law.*) or the part represents the whole (Example: *a fleet of a hundred sails*).

SYNTAX
All the ways that words are put together to create meaning. Syntax includes phrases, clauses, sentence fragments, and punctuation, as well as sentence lengths, patterns, and organization.

TEXTURE
In literature, this refers to the complexity and density of a work, as shown by the various levels on which it can be analyzed and appreciated.

THEME
The author's message contained in a poem or story; the topic of an essay or other work of nonfiction.

THESIS
The central idea or purpose of an essay. The thesis may be supported by a variety of techniques, including examples, argumentation, and weight of factual evidence.

TONE
This term refers to a writer's/speaker's attitude—consciously or unconsciously expressed—toward his/her subject and sometimes toward the reader and/or the speaker him/herself.

UNDERSTATEMENT
The opposite of exaggeration (hyperbole), a statement that downplays something, thereby suggesting much more. (Example: *That was no small feat.* This means it was a huge accomplishment.)

ANSWERING AN EFFECTIVENESS QUESTION
(TECHNICAL LEVEL OF ANALYSIS)

Question: How does the use of alliteration make the following poem more effective?

ROCKS OF AGES

One thousand thousand years from now,
On a sandy beach
Will proudly lie

                        a pebble
Hammered smooth by the sea.

A. F. Marks

Notice that the following response tells us:

- **the example of the device to be analyzed**
- **what the example does**
- **what it helps the reader to do**
- **how it increases the impact of the poem on the reader.**

The repetition of the **s** sound in "smooth by the sea" is an example of **alliteration**. By **recreating the sound** of rushing water, it **helps the reader to imagine** being at the seashore and hearing the waves break on the beach. It gives the poem **immediacy** and makes it more **vivid** in the reader's mind.

Here are some things that literary devices do:

compare	*contrast*	*recreate sounds*	*paint pictures*
connect	*emphasize*	*focus (on)*	*slow down*
speed up	*suggest*	*make memorable*	*reflect*
create subtext	*exaggerate*	*understate*	*refer to*
create rhythm	*add layers of meaning*		

Here are some things that literary devices help readers to do:

imagine	*visualize*	*understand*	*appreciate*
share (the speaker's feeling)	*focus (on)*	*consider*	
connect	*relate*	*hear*	*empathize*
feel/sense	*recognize*	*think about*	*associate*

Assignment 3: Analyze on the Associative Level

Before the assignment begins, the teacher goes over the list of associative devices on the LEVELS OF ANALYSIS handout and selects the ones most appropriate for each class to learn and practice analyzing. The devices chosen will depend on the grade and ability levels of the class.

NOTE TO TEACHERS: It is not necessary or desirable to deal with all the associative devices at once. For grade 9 classes or those new to the study of poetry, I generally focus on simile, metaphor, and personification, as these are the easiest devices to identify and therefore the ones most likely to engage younger students. Once that groundwork has been laid, other associative devices can be added to their "toolkit."

Here is a suggested progression for associative devices that has worked well in my classes.

Grade 9/beginners—simile, metaphor, personification
Grade 10—review of the above devices plus: imagery and contrast
Grade 11—review of the above devices plus: objectification and oxymoron
Grade 12—review of the above devices plus (for enriched or AP classes): metonymy and synecdoche

I make a point of repeating certain poems and poets from one grade to the next. What really opens students' eyes to the expansion of their "toolkits" from year to year is going back to poems that have already been studied and discovering how much easier they are to understand and how much more depth of meaning they reveal the second and third times they are read.

INTRODUCTION TO ASSOCIATIVE ANALYSIS

1. The teacher reads aloud to the class a short poem from the anthology, selected because it contains examples of the associative devices students are going to be working with during this assignment.

2. Following a brief discussion of the theme and content of the poem, the teacher tells students to take out their copy of the LEVELS OF ANALYSIS: POETRY sheet given out earlier. Students are directed to the section headed "Associative." The teacher identifies the devices that will be the focus of this assignment and instructs students to underline, star, or otherwise highlight them on their copies of the sheet.

3. Each student now takes out his or her copy of the GLOSSARY OF POETICAL/LITERARY TERMS. Students are instructed to find each of the selected associative devices in the glossary and highlight them, using a different color or method than before. Together, teacher and students review each of the highlighted definitions in turn, ensuring that everyone understands what these devices are and what they do. *Students may be asked for extra examples of each selected device, to be added to its definition on the handout.*

4. The devices are numbered and students form groups with that same number of members *(that is, three devices = groups of three)*. Within each group, students number off to determine which device will be each group member's "specialty."

5. Each student takes a sheet of blank paper and folds it lengthwise, forming two columns. Over the left-hand column, the student writes the heading *Examples*. Over the right-hand column, the student writes the heading *Effectiveness*.

6. Students are directed to the poem read aloud earlier (in Step 1). The teacher reads it aloud once more and asks students to identify an example from the poem of one of the associative devices highlighted on their sheets. The teacher then models on the board the format students are to use when recording examples in the left-hand column of their worksheet. For example:

> *she rears to unexpected height,*
> *a sudden wall none dare to breach* (ll. 6–7)

It should be pointed out to students that line 7 alone is not a complete metaphor because associative devices are comparisons, and both sides of the comparison *(here, the woman and the wall that she is being compared to)* need to be present in each example quoted.

7. Each "specialist" identifies examples of his or her associative device in the poem and records each example on the left side of the worksheet. When done, each student shares his/her findings with the rest of his/her group.

8. In whole class, the teacher asks each group to quote its favorite example from the poem, and these are recorded in a list on the board. The teacher then asks each group to explain what made this example stand out for them. *(Typically, it will be because the example helped them to do something—imagine the scene more clearly or vividly, recognize a connection between themselves and the natural world, and the like.)*

   The teacher points out that the students have just described the impact that the example had on them. In other words, they've begun to explain what makes the example *effective*.

9. Each student now receives a copy of the ANSWERING AN EFFECTIVENESS QUESTION (Associative) handout, and teacher and students together go over the entire sheet. The teacher reminds the class that although the wording of an effectiveness question may not be exactly as shown on the handout, it will still be asking for the same thing. In order to be considered complete (and get full marks on a test or exam), the answer to an effectiveness question must contain all of the important elements listed on the sheet, including how the example relates to the theme or main idea of the poem.

   Students should be reminded that the LEVELS OF ANALYSIS handout gives them a menu of ways that a poetical device can contribute to the overall effectiveness of a poem: "Effective Poetry Has." The sample response on the ANSWERING AN EFFECTIVENESS QUESTION handout concludes with an item from this list.

10. Students are directed to look at the sample response on the previous ANSWERING AN EFFECTIVENESS QUES-TION (Technical) worksheet and compare it with the one on the associative-level handout. What differences do they notice between the two responses? *(The first response is shorter, simpler, and more superficial than the second. The first presents a sensory image, while the second presents an idea, and so on.)* The teacher points out that both responses are about the same poem, demonstrating that an effective poem is one that can be analyzed on more than one level.

    NOTE TO TEACHERS: When explaining the levels of analysis to my students, I have had success with the following analogy: Analyzing a poem is like peeling an onion. The technical level gives you the outermost layer of meaning that identifies the poem as a poem. Peel that away and you have the associative level, a deeper layer of meaning where you can explore connections between the poem and the rest of the world. Peel that away and you have reached the thematic level. This is the core of the poem, its deepest level of meaning where the poem connects with the life of the reader—his or her knowledge, experience, thoughts, feelings, and memories. You have to work to get there and keep working to stay there, but the result is worth the effort.

11. The teacher then selects one of the quoted examples from the board and leads a whole-class discussion of what makes it effective on the associative level. Students should be encouraged to choose words from the two lists provided on the handout when describing what the example does and what it helps the reader to do. Using point form, the teacher records the class response on the board, ensuring that all the important elements are present and that the response concludes by stating how the example contributes to the overall effectiveness of the poem.

12. The students in each group now work together to discuss all of their examples and fill in the right-hand side of their worksheets in point form, following the pattern modeled on the board. *(That is, each student will be* talking *about all of the selected associative devices but* writing *about only the one that is his or her "specialty.")*

13. (OPTIONAL) Each student "specialist" partners with one or two others specializing in the same associative device to compare and discuss their completed worksheets.

    At the teacher's discretion, these worksheets may be handed in for a completion check mark.

PRODUCT

To demonstrate their understanding of the associative level of analysis, students may be asked to do one of the following:

- Compose a short poem or paragraph including examples of each of the associative devices studied so far. (The examples would need to be highlighted or underlined, labeled, and explained.) These can be handed in for formative assessment.
- Find an example of an associative device used by the media and write a paragraph-long analysis, being sure to include all the important elements specified on the ANSWERING AN EFFECTIVENESS QUESTION handout. Students can assemble in small groups and share their examples and analyses with one another.
- Draw a visual representation of one of the associative devices studied so far *(for instance, a personified car)*. These can be posted around the room for others to admire.

ANSWERING AN EFFECTIVENESS QUESTION
(ASSOCIATIVE LEVEL OF ANALYSIS)

Question: How does the use of personification make the following poem more effective?

ROCKS OF AGES

One thousand thousand years from now,
On a sandy beach
Will proudly lie

                    a pebble
Hammered smooth by the sea.

A. F. Marks

Notice that the following response tells us:

- **the example of the device to be analyzed**
- **what the example does**
- **what it helps the reader to do**
- **how it increases the impact of the poem on the reader.**

The **personification** of "will proudly lie a pebble" **gives the pebble the human ability** to remember that it was once a mighty rock and to feel proud of itself for standing up to the ocean waves for so long. Anyone who has had to stand his or her ground against a persistent and powerful opponent can identify and empathize with this pebble. By **helping the reader to connect** with nature on an emotional level, this example makes the poem more **evocative** and therefore more effective.

Here are some things that literary devices do:

compare	*contrast*	*recreate sounds*	*paint pictures*
connect	*emphasize*	*focus (on)*	*slow down*
speed up	*suggest*	*make memorable*	*reflect*
create subtext	*exaggerate*	*understate*	*refer to*
create rhythm	*add layers of meaning*		

Here are some things that literary devices help readers to do:

imagine	*visualize*	*understand*	*appreciate*
share (the speaker's feeling)	*focus (on)*	*consider*	
connect	*relate*	*hear*	*empathize*
feel/sense	*recognize*	*think about*	*associate*

Assignment 4: Analyze on the Thematic Level

Before the assignment begins, the teacher goes over the list of thematic devices on the LEVELS OF ANALYSIS handout and selects the one or ones most appropriate for each class to learn and practice analyzing. The devices chosen will depend on the grade and ability levels of the class.

NOTE TO TEACHERS: It is not necessary or desirable to deal with all the thematic devices at once. For those new to the study of poetry, I generally begin with word connotations, then proceed to irony. Once that groundwork has been laid, other thematic devices can be added to their "toolkit."

Here is a suggested progression for thematic devices that has worked well in my classes:

Grade 10/beginners—connotation and/or irony
Grade 11—review of the above device(s) plus: connotation or irony, recurring imagery
Grade 12—review of the above devices plus: symbolism and allusion

I make a point of repeating certain poems and poets from one grade to the next. What really opens students' eyes to the expansion of their "toolkits" from year to year is going back to poems that have already been studied and discovering how much easier they are to understand and how much more depth of meaning they reveal the second and third times they are read.

INTRODUCTION TO THEMATIC ANALYSIS

1. The teacher reads aloud to the class a short poem from the anthology, selected because it contains examples of the thematic device or devices students are going to be working with during this assignment.

2. Following a brief discussion of the theme and content of the poem, the teacher tells students to take out their copy of the LEVELS OF ANALYSIS: POETRY sheet given out earlier. Students are directed to the section headed "Thematic." The teacher identifies the devices that will be the focus of this assignment and instructs students to underline, star, or otherwise highlight them on their copies of the sheet.

3. Each student now takes out his or her copy of the GLOSSARY OF POETICAL/LITERARY TERMS. Students are instructed to find each selected thematic device in the glossary and highlight it, using a different color or method than before. Together, teacher and students review the highlighted definitions, ensuring that everyone understands what thematic devices are and what they do. *Students may be asked for extra examples of each selected device, to be added to its definition on the handout.*

4. Students pair up with working partners for the rest of the assignment. If the class will be studying two devices, then within each pair, students decide which of the selected devices will be each partner's "specialty."

5. Each student takes a sheet of blank paper and folds it lengthwise, forming two columns. Over the left-hand column, the student writes the heading *Examples*. Over the right-hand column, the student writes the heading *Effectiveness*.

6. Students are directed to the poem read aloud earlier (in Step 1). The teacher reads it aloud once more and asks students to identify an example from the poem of one of the thematic devices highlighted on their sheets. The teacher then models on the board the format students are to use when recording examples in the left-hand column of their worksheet. For example:

> *That 'twas his very care to preserve her life*
> *Impelled her to end it.* (ll. 11–12)

It should be pointed out to students that when a device involves comparison (with irony it is between what one would normally expect and its opposite), then both sides of the comparison *(here, the husband's determination and its effect on his wife)* need to be present in the example quoted.

7. Each "specialist" identifies examples of his or her thematic device in the poem and records each example on the left side of the worksheet. When done, each pair of students share their findings with each other.

8. In whole class, the teacher asks for several of the students' favorite examples from the poem, and these are recorded in a list on the board. The teacher then asks students to explain what made the example stand out for them. *(Typically, it will be because the example helped them to do something—relate to the person whose actions are being described, appreciate a point of view the reader hadn't considered before, and so on.)*

The teacher points out that what the students have just described is the impact that the example had on them. In other words, they've begun to explain what makes the example *effective*.

9. Each student now receives a copy of the ANSWERING AN EFFECTIVENESS QUESTION (Thematic) handout, and teacher and students together go over the entire sheet. The teacher reminds the class that although the wording of an effectiveness question may not be exactly as shown on the handout, it will still be asking for the same thing. In order to be considered complete (and get full marks on a test or exam), the answer to an effectiveness question must contain all of the important elements listed on the sheet, including how the example relates to the theme or main idea of the poem.

Students should be reminded that the LEVELS OF ANALYSIS handout gives them a menu of ways a poetical device can contribute to the overall effectiveness of a poem: "Effective Poetry Has." The sample responses on all three of the ANSWERING AN EFFECTIVENESS QUESTION handouts conclude with items from this list.

10. Students are directed to look at the sample responses on the previous ANSWERING AN EFFECTIVENESS QUESTION sheets (both the technical and associative levels) and compare them with the one on the thematic-level handout. What differences do they notice among the three responses? *(The responses keep getting longer and more complex. The first presents a sensory image, while the second and third present ideas, and so on.)* The teacher may wish to create a chart on the board or on an overhead transparency to serve as a visual aid during the discussion.

The teacher points out that all three responses were written about the same poem—each one reaching deeper to pull out meaning. In fact, a truly effective poem is one that can be analyzed on all three levels.

NOTE TO TEACHERS: When explaining the levels of analysis to my students, I have had success with the following analogy: Analyzing a poem is like peeling an onion. The technical level gives you the outermost layer of meaning, which identifies the poem as a poem. Peel that away and you have the associative level, a deeper layer of meaning where you can explore connections between the poem and the rest of the world. Peel that away and you have reached the thematic level. This is the core of the poem, its deepest level where meaning connects with the life of the reader, drawing from his or her knowledge, experience, thoughts, feelings, and memories. You have to work to get there and keep working to stay there, but the result is worth the effort.

11. The teacher then selects one of the quoted examples from the board and leads a whole-class discussion of what makes it effective on the thematic level. Students should be encouraged to choose words from the two lists provided on the handout when describing what the example does and what it helps the reader to do. Using point form, the teacher records the class response on the board, ensuring that it contains all the important elements noted on the handout, and concludes by stating how the device contributes to the overall effectiveness of the poem.

12. The students now work with their partners to discuss all of their examples and fill in the right-hand side of their worksheets in point form, following the pattern modeled on the board. *(That is, each student will be talking about both of the selected thematic devices but writing about only the one that is his or her "specialty.")*

13. (OPTIONAL) Each student "specialist" partners with one or two others specializing in the same thematic device to compare and discuss their completed worksheets.

At the teacher's discretion, these worksheets may be handed in for a completion check mark.

PRODUCT

To demonstrate their understanding of the thematic level of analysis, students may be asked to do one of the following:

- Compose a short poem or paragraph, including examples of the devices studied in this assignment. (The examples would need to be highlighted or underlined, labeled, and annotated.) These can be handed in for formative assessment.
- Select an example from one of the other poems studied so far and write a paragraph-long thematic analysis, being sure to include all the important elements listed on the ANSWERING AN EFFECTIVENESS QUESTION handout. Students can form small groups and read their analyses aloud to one another.
- Create a visual representation of one of the thematic devices studied so far *(for example, two panels representing an ironical situation, the first showing what would normally be expected and the second depicting its opposite)*. These can be posted around the room for others to admire.

OPTIONAL PRODUCT: AN OBJECTIVE QUIZ

As a consolidation exercise between assignments 4 and 5, you may want to consider administering an objective quiz like the one provided with this module (SPR 7). I have used this one formatively with grade 10 and 11 classes and diagnostically with grade 12 classes. The format works well, and it can be taken and marked quickly. With some content modification, it could be administered to students at any grade level.

ANSWERING AN EFFECTIVENESS QUESTION
(THEMATIC LEVEL OF ANALYSIS)

Question: How does the use of allusion make the following poem more effective?

ROCKS OF AGES

One thousand thousand years from now,
On a sandy beach
Will proudly lie

                  a pebble

Hammered smooth by the sea.

A. F. Marks

Notice that the following response:

- **identifies the example and the device to be analyzed**
- **elaborates and explains the relationship contained in the device**
- **tells what it helps or makes the reader do**
- **states how it makes the poem more effective**

The title of this poem is an **allusion** to a religious hymn about the power of faith to endure. Like faith in times of trouble, the rock on the beach is standing its ground, enduring the constant pounding of the waves. After a million years, the rock will be reduced to a pile of sand, but its heart, the pebble, will survive. By **providing a religious connection** for the poem, the title **turns the reader's focus** away from the awe-inspiring power of the ocean to the stubborn strength of the rock, thus making the poem more **thought provoking** and increasing its overall impact on the reader.

Here are some things that literary devices do:

compare	*contrast*	*recreate sounds*	*paint pictures*
connect	*emphasize*	*focus (on)*	*slow down*
speed up	*suggest*	*make memorable*	*reflect*
create subtext	*exaggerate*	*understate*	*refer to*
create rhythm	*add layers of meaning*		

Here are some things that literary devices help readers to do:

imagine	*visualize*	*understand*	*appreciate*
share (the speaker's feeling)	*focus (on)*	*consider*	
connect	*relate*	*hear*	*empathize*
feel/sense	*recognize*	*think about*	*associate*

POETRY TERMINOLOGY QUIZ

Your Name: _____

PART 1: MATCHING

Match each literary device at the left with the correct definition or description at right by printing the letter of the description in the blank beside each term:

_____	Allusion	A. Sensory detail
_____	Enjambment	B. Concrete things that represent abstract ideas
_____	Oxymoron	C. One line flowing into another without stopping
_____	Symbolism	D. A reference to mythology or history
_____	Connotation	E. Words with contrasting meanings linked in a phrase
_____	Simile	F. Associations that some words carry with them
_____	Imagery	G. A figurative comparison using "like" or "as"

PART 2: MULTIPLE CHOICE

Circle the letter beside the most correct answer to each question below:

1. Prose is divided into paragraphs; formal poetry is divided into _____.
   (a) beats
   (b) stanzas
   (c) lines
   (d) syllables

2. "Crash! Boom! Sizzle!" is an example of _____.
   (a) meter
   (b) alliteration
   (c) onomatopoeia
   (d) metaphor

3. Which word or phrase below is NOT part of syntax?
   (a) diction
   (b) sentence lengths
   (c) punctuation
   (d) phrases

4. A poem or story has a theme; an essay has a _____.
   (a) tone
   (b) texture
   (c) structure
   (d) thesis

5. Which answer below is NOT about differences?
   (a) contrast
   (b) oxymoron
   (c) irony
   (d) rhyme

6. What is the difference between "evocativeness" and "provocativeness"?
   (a) one moves forward; the other moves backward
   (b) one is about feeling; the other is about thinking
   (c) one is about the author; the other is about the reader
   (d) one is about speaking; the other is about acting

7. Which answer below does NOT refer to blank verse?
   (a) used for dramatic poetry
   (b) does not rhyme
   (c) limited to fourteen lines
   (d) iambic pentameter

8. Which answer below is an example of assonance?
   (a) heaps of cheese, please
   (b) see you later, alligator
   (c) my marvelous mom
   (d) snakes sliding slowly southward

TOTAL SCORE: /15

Assignment 5: Practice Close Reading of Poetry

Before beginning the assignment: The teacher picks a short poem (10 to 20 lines long) from the anthology or from another source, ensuring that the poem contains examples of the studied devices at all three levels of analysis. The teacher then transfers it to the middle of a letter-sized sheet of paper, leaving wide margins for note-making, and uses this to create both a class set of student handouts and an overhead transparency for modeling purposes.

1. Together, teacher and students review all the poetical devices that have been studied so far. These may be listed on the board to serve as reference during the assignment.

2. The teacher explains to the class that in a poem, no words are wasted and every word is important. Words and phrases in a poem tend to multitask. A single word can even be working on all three levels of analysis at the same time. For that reason, a poem needs to be closely and carefully read, going line by line and even word by word to identify everything meaningful about it. Close reading is what the students will be practicing during this assignment.

3. The teacher hands out a copy of the selected short poem to each student and puts the transparency up on the overhead screen. The poem is read aloud and there is a brief discussion regarding its theme and content. Using an overhead marker, the teacher records the agreed-upon theme in one of the upper corners of the transparency, instructing students to do the same on their copies of the poem.

4. The teacher and class together then proceed to read the poem one or two lines at a time, pausing to identify and discuss examples of all the devices they have been working with during this part of the module. The teacher can use three different colors of overhead marker (one per level of analysis) to underline each identified example before drawing a color-coded arrow to the space in the margin where the device is named. Students can do the same on their copies of the poem, using three different colors of highlighter to distinguish the three levels of analysis.

   As they go through this exercise, students should be able to see and realize how each word and phrase of the poem contributes to its depth of meaning and its impact on the reader.

   Students should be instructed to save their completed handouts for Assignment 6.

5. Each student now selects one of the listed poems from the anthology and works independently to conduct a close reading, determining the theme and identifying examples of all the devices worked with during this part of the module.

   To accomplish this, students can copy the poem into the middle of a sheet of blank paper and repeat the exercise just practiced using different colored highlighters. Alternatively, they can create a chart or placemat using blank paper, then copy and label quotations under the appropriate heading of the chart or in the appropriately labeled space of the placemat.

   Unless you are actually focusing on how to make and use a particular type of graphic organizer, I would recommend giving students a menu of options and letting them choose and use the method they are most comfortable with to complete this activity.

6. When done, students can pair up with partners who have read the same poem and compare worksheets. Partners may help each other by making suggestions for improvement of their work.

   Students should be instructed to save their worksheets to use for Assignment 6.

Assignment 6: Practice Analyzing Poetry

1. The teacher reviews with the class: What are the characteristics of an effective poem? *(immediacy, vividness, evocativeness, and provocativeness, as listed on the LEVELS OF ANALYSIS: POETRY handout)* These four words are now listed on the board and discussed in whole class to ensure that students understand what they mean.

2. Each student then receives a copy of the LEVELS OF ANALYSIS: EFFECTIVENESS handout and the teacher goes over it with the class. For each item listed under "Thus helping the reader to," the teacher and students identify the characteristics of an effective poem to which the item contributes. Students should record this information on their handouts for reference during the rest of the assignment.

   NOTE TO TEACHER: It should be pointed out to the students that the items at each level of analysis are stated in general terms (for instance, recreates a sound) because they are talking about poetry in general. When analyzing a specific poem, students will need to explain exactly what that sound is (for example, recreates the sound of galloping hoof beats) and what it helps the reader to do (such as, imagine standing at the side of the road as the horseman rides past).

3. Students are now directed to take out the example poem that the whole class worked on in Assignment 5. The teacher puts his or her copy up on the overhead screen and reviews with the class what the main idea or theme of the poem is. Together, the teacher and class now go through all the devices that they identified and select the ones that most strongly relate to the theme of the poem. These should be starred or circled.

4. Each student now takes a sheet of paper and folds it in half lengthwise to form two columns, one headed *Example* and the other *Effectiveness*. The starred examples from the handout are copied into the left-hand column of the page, using the format modeled earlier by the teacher.

5. The teacher writes an effectiveness question on the board and explains that the students will be applying this question to each of the starred examples on their worksheets: *How does this example enhance the effectiveness of the poem?*

   Students are referred to their ANSWERING AN EFFECTIVENESS QUESTION handouts for the list of important elements to include in each of their responses.

6. Together, the teacher and students discuss the first starred example on the overhead transparency as the teacher records their point-form analysis on the board. After a check to ensure that all the important elements have been included, students copy this first response onto their worksheets.

7. Students then work in pairs or small groups to complete their worksheets, being sure to include all the important elements in each response and to conclude by stating how each example contributes to the overall effectiveness of the poem.

8. Pairs can combine to form groups of four or six for sharing their work, and each group can then choose a spokesperson to present its favorite example and analysis to the whole class.

9. Each student now takes out his or her independent work from Assignment 5 and proceeds to follow the process just practiced: select and star or circle the examples most strongly related to the theme of the poem, copy them onto a separate sheet of paper, and write out a point-form analysis of each one in response to the effectiveness question on the board.

10. Each student writes up his or her favorite response in sentence and paragraph form and hands it in to the teacher as the student's "ticket out the door."

This work may be formatively assessed by the teacher. I generally award a total of five points as follows: one for correctly identifying the device contained in the example, one for correctly formatting the quoted example, one for fully explaining what the example (not the device) does, one for satisfactorily explaining what it helps the reader to do, and one for satisfactorily describing how the example contributes to the overall effectiveness of the poem.

LEVELS OF ANALYSIS: EFFECTIVENESS

LEVEL I: FORM AND TECHNICAL DEVICES (How does the poem look and sound?)

Sound devices are effective because they:
> recreate a sound
> link two or more words in a poem, thus linking their meanings and
> > associations as well
> mark or create the rhythm (beat) of a poem
> make a phrase or a line more memorable

Thus helping the reader to:
> imagine that he or she is right there, hearing what is being described
> understand and appreciate a deeper level of meaning to the words
> hear and appreciate the music of the poem
> feel or sense the mood of the poem more intensely

The form of a poem is effective because it:
> creates emphasis using short and long lines and word placement
> may create a shape on the page that reflects or enhances the theme
> suggests a level (or lack) of organization that matches the theme

Thus helping the reader to:
> focus more clearly on what the poet is trying to say
> appreciate the artistry of the poem

LEVEL II: ASSOCIATIVE DEVICES (How does the poem relate to the world?)

Associative devices are effective because they:
> paint vivid pictures using very few words
> create unexpected comparisons, leading to thought-provoking associations
> attribute human qualities to things in the world around us

Thus helping the reader to:
> visualize more easily what is being described
> understand and appreciate a deeper level of meaning to the words
> relate better to the feelings being expressed in the poem
> recognize and think about the relationships that exist all around us

LEVEL III: THEMATIC DEVICES (How does the poem relate to my own life?)

Thematic devices are effective because they:
> create thought-provoking associations
> allow the reader to tap into his or her own knowledge and experiences to flesh
> > out the meaning of a poem
> use existing associations to emphasize the emotion expressed in the poem
> create a subtext (a secret meaning) which gives the poem added depth

Thus helping the reader to:
> personalize the message in the poem
> discern and appreciate a deeper level of meaning in the poem
> share the feelings being expressed in the poem
> recognize and think about the relationships between the poet's experiences and his or her own

Extension Activity

Analyzing the Poetry of a Shakespearean Play

If your class is studying a Shakespearean play, you might want to insert a mini-unit on poetical analysis. For grade 9 or 10 classes, I would suggest using handouts like the ones provided with this module (SPR 9 through SPR11), based on A Midsummer Night's Dream. *Teacher and students can work on these together in whole class, or they can be done for homework after an in-class review of the poetic devices involved and then taken up in class the next day. With a grade 11 or 12 class, I have had success with oral presentations, as outlined below.*

Before the activity begins: The teacher selects from the play being studied ten to twelve passages of 15 to 20 lines each (or longer, if they are soliloquies) and lists them on the board or on an overhead transparency. The teacher also drafts a peer-assessment handout, identifying each of the passages and leaving space for five assessment criteria to be added *(see Step 6 below).*

NOTE TO TEACHER: Grade 11 students can partner up before selecting or being assigned a passage to analyze. Grade 12 students, however, should be able to work on Step 3 of this activity independently.

1. The teacher explains the assignment to the class: Each student or pair of students will have time in class to conduct a close reading and analysis of one of the selected passages. Following that, the students who worked on each passage will form a focus group to prepare a ten-minute presentation of their passage to the class. One group member will give a dramatic reading of the passage, and the others will follow up with their analysis of the poetical devices that make the passage effective.

2. The teacher reminds students that poetry is a very dense literary medium. They will need to read the text closely and carefully, going line by line and even word by word to pull out all the meaning they can.

   It may be beneficial at this time to review with students the three levels of analysis and what makes them effective, and the overall characteristics of an effective poem—immediacy, vividness, evocativeness, and provocativeness.

3. Individually or in pairs, students select or are assigned passages to work on from the list on the board or on the overhead screen. Students then proceed with the first part of the assignment. *(Depending on the class, you may decide to allow either one or two full class periods for students to conduct their close reading and analysis. Any work still not completed may then be done for homework.)*

4. Next period, the teacher leads a whole-class discussion of what should be included in the oral presentation, recording students' suggestions on the board. The list should include the following:

   • a brief explanation by the student performing the dramatic reading, to "set the stage" and provide a context for the passage being presented
   • the reading, rehearsed and delivered as though by an actor on an actual stage
   • an introduction to the analysis, outlining the main idea or ideas being expressed by the passage

190

- a required number of examples from each level of analysis
- each example separately analyzed but related to the overall effectiveness of the passage
- the entire presentation should be rehearsed and timed—and should not exceed 10 minutes in length

Students are instructed to copy this list into their notes for reference.

5. Students then form their focus groups and work together to prepare their oral presentations. *(Allow no more than two class periods for this part of the assignment.)*

6. The teacher explains that these presentations are going to be peer-assessed and asks the class for a list of characteristics to be evaluated. A student secretary can record these on the board. The teacher and students then identify the five most important items from the list to go on the audience "ballots." The teacher makes a note of these and finishes preparing a peer-assessment handout (photocopied double-sided if necessary) that each audience member can quickly fill out during the presentations.

   NOTE TO TEACHER: It is important to ensure that each group member's part of the presentation be represented on the "ballot" and that the criteria include both presentation skills and the analysis itself. For example:

The dramatic reading was clearly and confidently acted.	*Yes*	*Part of it*	*None of it*
Each example analyzed was firmly tied to the main idea.	*All*	*Some*	*None*
The analysis contained all the important elements.	*All*	*Some*	*One/None*
The presenters were easy to understand.	*Yes*	*Somewhat*	*Not really*
The presentation flowed smoothly from start to finish.	*Yes*	*Sort of*	*Choppy*

7. *Presentation days:* The order of presentations can be determined by drawing numbers from an envelope or by following the chronological sequence of the play. Each group presents its work and is assessed by peers and by the teacher (diagnostic or formative assessment).

   ALTERNATIVE PRESENTATION FORMAT: The presentation could also take the form of a "fishbowl" discussion in which the members of the presenting group sit around a desk or table in the middle of the room, surrounded by an audience of their fellow students, and proceed to analyze the excerpt aloud, talking among themselves for a set period of time. The discussion is then thrown open to comments and questions from the audience and continues for another set number of minutes. The advantage of a format like this is that you can assess not only the group presenting but also selected audience members (for a participation mark).

POETRY IN *A MIDSUMMER NIGHT'S DREAM*

Level 1: Sound Devices
(alliteration, assonance, repetition, rhyme, onomatopoeia)

For each underlined word or phrase in the excerpts below, identify the device being used and explain what makes it effective:

Fairy:
    Over hill, over dale,
    Thorough bush, thorough brier,
    Over park, over pale,
    Thorough flood, thorough fire
    I do wander everywhere,
    <u>Swifter than the moon's sphere;</u>
    And I serve the fairy <u>queen,</u>
    To dew her orbs upon the <u>green.</u>
    The cowslips tall her pensioners be:
    In their gold coats spots you see;
    Those be rubies, <u>fairy favours,</u>
    <u>In those freckles</u> live their savours. . . .

                        (2.1.2–13)

Puck:
    . . . And now they never <u>meet</u> in grove or <u>green,</u>
    By fountain <u>clear,</u> or spangled starlight <u>sheen,</u>
    But they do square, that all their elves for fear
    Creep into acorn cups and hide them there.

                        (2.1.28–31)

Puck:
    I'll follow you, I'll lead you about a round,
    <u>Through bog, through bush, through brake, through brier;</u>
    Sometime a horse I'll be, sometime a hound,
    A hog, a headless bear, sometime a fire;
    And <u>neigh, and bark, and grunt, and roar,</u> and burn,
    Like horse, hound, hog, bear, fire at every turn.

                        (3.1.98–104)

REMEMBER: *Sound devices are effective because they*:
    recreate a sound
    link two or more words in a poem, thus linking their meanings and associations as well
    mark or create the rhythm (beat) of a poem
    make a phrase or line more memorable

thus helping the reader to:
    imagine that he is right there, hearing what is being described
    understand and appreciate a deeper level of meaning to the words
    hear and appreciate the music of the poem
    feel or sense the mood of the poem more intensely

POETRY IN *A MIDSUMMER NIGHT'S DREAM*

Level 2: Associative Devices
(simile, metaphor, personification, imagery)

For each underlined word or phrase in the excerpts below, identify the device being used and explain what makes it effective:

Lysander: Or, if there were a sympathy in choice,
     War, death or sickness did lay siege to it,
     Making it momentary as a sound,
     Swift as a shadow, short as any dream;
     Brief as the lightning in the collied night,
     That, in a spleen, unfolds both heaven and earth,
     And ere a man hath power to say "Behold!"
     The jaws of darkness do devour it up:
     So quick bright things come to confusion.

                          (1.1.141–149)

Titania: Set your heart at rest:
     The fairyland buys not the child of me.
     His mother was a votaress of my order:
     And, in the spiced Indian air, by night,
     Full often hath she gossip'd by my side,
     And sat with me on Neptune's yellow sands,
     Marking the embarked traders on the flood,
     When we have laugh'd to see the sails conceive
     And grow big-bellied with the wanton wind;
     Which she, with pretty and with swimming gait
     Following—her womb then rich with my young squire—
     Would imitate, and sail upon the land,
     To fetch me trifles, and return again,
     As from a voyage, rich with merchandise.

                          (2.1.122–34)

REMEMBER: *Associative devices are effective because they*:
    create unexpected comparisons, leading to thought-provoking associations
    attribute human qualities to things in the world around us
    paint vivid pictures with very few words

thus helping the reader to:
    visualize more easily what is being described
    understand and appreciate a deeper level of meaning to the words
    relate to the feelings being expressed in the poem
    recognize and think about the relationships all around us

POETRY IN *A MIDSUMMER NIGHT'S DREAM*

Level 3: Thematic Devices
(*allusion, irony, symbolism, imagery, connotation, hyperbole, understatement*)

For each underlined word or phrase in the excerpts below, identify the device being used and explain what makes it effective:

Theseus: Lovers and madmen have such seething brains,
Such shaping fantasies, that apprehend
More than cool reason ever comprehends.
The lunatic, the lover, and the poet
Are of imagination all compact:
One sees more devils than vast hell can hold,
That is, the madman; the lover, all as frantic,
Sees Helen's beauty in a brow of Egypt:
The poet's eye, in a fine frenzy rolling,
Doth glance from heaven to earth, from earth to heaven,
And as imagination bodies forth
The forms of things unknown, the poet's pen
Turns them to shapes and gives to airy nothing
A local habitation and a name.

                                           (5.1.4–17)

Puck: My fairy lord, this must be done with haste,
For night's swift dragons cut the clouds full fast,
And yonder shines Aurora's harbinger,
At whose approach, ghosts, wandering here and there,
Troop home to churchyards: damned spirits all,
That in crossways and floods have burial,
Already to their wormy beds are gone;
For fear lest day should look their shames upon,
They wilfully themselves exile from light
And must for aye consort with black-brow'd night.

                                           (3.2.378–87)

REMEMBER: *Thematic devices are effective because they*:
      create thought-provoking associations
      allow the reader to tap into his or her own knowledge and experiences to flesh out
      the meaning of a poem
      use existing associations to emphasize the emotion expressed in the poem
      create a subtext for the poem (a secret meaning) which gives it added depth

thus helping the reader to:
      personalize the message in the poem
      understand and appreciate a deeper level of meaning in the poem
      share the feelings being expressed in the poem
      recognize and think about the relationships between the poet's experiences and his/her own.

Summative Product: Write a Sight Test (Optional)

The day before test day: The teacher explains to the class that they will be concluding the poetry unit with a sight test. A sight test is not about their eyes—it's a test of their ability to answer questions about a poem that they will be reading for the first time on the day of the test.

The teacher reveals some sample questions on the board and explains that today they will be working on their time management while practicing how to answer the kind of questions that will be on the sight test.

Over the years I have found that the vast majority of marks/points that are lost by students on tests and exams are the direct result of two things: not following instructions and not answering the question that has been asked. Here are some test-taking tips you may wish to share with your class to help students do their best. They are provided as a reproducible handout as well.

Tips for Writing a Test

1. Relax. Breathe. You won't be asked to do anything on this test that you haven't been practicing in class. Keep telling yourself: *I am prepared. I can do this.*

2. Before you do any writing (in this case, before you read the poem), read all of the questions. Underline the words in the questions that tell you what you are being asked to do. Notice where you're being asked to make a choice, and circle the word "or." (On a poetry test, notice which poetic devices you're being asked to find. This will program your brain to recognize what's important about the poem as you are reading it.)

3. Read with a pencil in your hand and make notes on the test paper. It's yours, so go ahead and mark it up. As soon as you think of something to include in an answer, jot it down so you won't forget it.

4. Answer the easy questions first. This ensures that you will get all the credit you deserve for what you know and what you can do. If you tackle the hard questions first, you might get bogged down and run out of time before you can complete the test.

5. To avoid getting bogged down, use the marking scheme to determine how much time you should spend on each question. If the test is out of thirty and the period is over in forty-five minutes, then you should be spending about one-and-a-half minutes per mark/point. So, if a question is out of five, it's reasonable to spend about seven minutes on it. If the next question is out of ten, it should take about fifteen minutes to answer. Jot a time limit in the margin beside each question. Then watch the clock (or your watch) and time yourself.

6. Follow instructions carefully and answer the question that is asked. If you're told to pick five out of eight items to discuss, don't discuss all eight. If you're told to answer in full sentences, don't use point form. If you're told to use ink, don't use a pencil. If you're asked to identify the theme of the poem, then state in a sentence what the main idea is. If you're asked to find and quote an example of a particular poetic device, then write, "An example of _____ is . . ." and copy the example from the poem. Don't analyze an example unless the question requires you to do so. Doing extra work on a test won't earn you extra marks/points no matter how brilliant your answer is, but it will take extra time—time that you could be putting to better use answering the questions that have been asked.

7. If you have time left once you've answered all the questions, go back and reread what you've written. Make sure you haven't left out any words or information. Remember that your answers have to be specific to the poem. When answering an effectiveness question, you must tell the reader what the example does *(e.g., The toaster is given the human ability to feel anger at the way it is treated.)*, not what the device does *(e.g., The toaster is an inanimate object given human characteristics.)*

8. Don't stress or second-guess yourself after the test is over. Nobody—including yourself—can ask any more of you than your best effort.

NOTE TO THE TEACHER: Following this part of the module, you will find three sight tests that I have given at different grade levels. The poems are in the public domain. Please feel free to use these tests, either as templates or as is:

ON THE SONNET: Suitable for a grade 12, enriched grade 11, or pre-AP class.

Keats has written a "protest sonnet" about the restrictions placed on the form of a sonnet. He uses an irregular rhyme scheme to rebel against the standard sonnet rhyming patterns. He throws out the traditional eight-six division of lines, enjambing lines 8 and 9 without even a pause. He personifies the sonnet and puts her in chains, as though she were the mythological figure Andromeda. He compares writers and scholars counting syllables to the legendary miser Midas, counting his coins. He advocates collecting dead leaves from the victory wreaths of winners, those that have burst their chains and stood out from the pack, and using garlands made of those leaves to restrain the Muse of poetry herself. (You can practically hear Keats ranting: Shackle the sonnet? Why stop there? Why not shackle the Muse?)

THE SCARECROW: Suitable for a grade 9 or 10 class.

This lovely lyric poem is written from the point of view of a scarecrow who sees himself as a knight on guard duty, keeping the wheat field safe from enemies. At his post year-round, he is proud to serve and feels that he is doing a good job. The descriptions are vivid, full of technical and associative devices. Spring is personified as a child who brings forth a host of other children—it is a time of birth and rebirth—including the seedlings in the field, and their appearance attracts crows, the foes of the scarecrow's "strange master, Man." (For grade 9 students, I remove "connotation" from question 3.)

I SEE BEFORE ME THE GLADIATOR LIE: Suitable for all grade levels, depending on the amount of background information provided and the kinds of questions asked. The test provided here was given to a class of nonacademic grade 11 students. (They quite enjoyed the poem.)

Byron travels to Rome and is filled with both pity and anger when he sees the statue of a dying slave. Forced to fight for the amusement of his masters, the gladiator has just lost his battle in the arena but has never truly been defeated. The poet imagines for us the final thoughts and emotions of the gladiator, using simile, metaphor, vivid imagery, and connotative language to inspire pity and anger in the reader at the senseless waste of a human life.

TIPS FOR WRITING A TEST

1. Relax. Breathe. You won't be asked to do anything on this test that you haven't been practicing in class. Keep telling yourself: *I am prepared. I can do this.*

2. Before you do any writing, read all of the questions. Underline the words in the questions that tell you what you are being asked to do. Notice where you're being asked to make a choice, and circle the word "or." (On a poetry test, notice which poetic devices you're being asked to find. This will program your brain to recognize what's important about the poem as you are reading it.)

3. Read with a pencil in your hand and make notes on the test paper. It's yours, so go ahead and mark it up. As soon as you think of something to include in an answer, jot it down so you won't forget it.

4. Answer the easy questions first. This ensures that you will get all the credit you deserve for what you know and what you can do. If you tackle the hard questions first, you might get bogged down and run out of time before you can complete the test.

5. To avoid getting bogged down, use the marking scheme to determine how much time you should spend on each question. If the test is out of thirty and the period is over in forty-five minutes, then you should be spending about one-and-a-half minutes per mark/point. So, if a question is out of five, it's reasonable to spend about seven minutes on it. If the next question is out of ten, it should take about fifteen minutes to answer. Jot a time limit in the margin beside each question. Then watch the clock (or your watch) and time yourself.

6. Follow instructions carefully and answer the question that is asked. If you're told to pick five out of eight items to discuss, don't discuss all eight. If you're told to answer in full sentences, don't use point form. If you're told to use ink, don't use a pencil. If you're asked to identify the theme of the poem, then state in a sentence what the main idea is. If you're asked to find and quote an example of a particular poetic device, then write, "An example of _____ is" and copy the example from the poem. Don't analyze an example unless the question asks you to do so. Doing extra work on a test won't earn you extra marks/points, no matter how brilliant your answer is, but it will take extra time—time that you could be putting to better use answering the questions that have been asked.

7. If you have time left once you've answered all the questions, go back and reread what you've written. Make sure you haven't left out any words or information. Remember that your answers have to be specific to the poem. When answering an effectiveness question, you must tell the reader what the example does (*e.g., The toaster is given the human ability to feel anger at the way it is treated.*), not what the device does (*e.g., The toaster is an inanimate object given human characteristics.*)

8. Don't stress or second-guess yourself after the test is over. Nobody—including yourself—can ask any more of you than your best effort.

ON THE SONNET

If by dull rhymes our English must be chain'd,
    And, like Andromeda, the Sonnet sweet
Fetter'd, in spite of pained loveliness;
Let us find out, if we must be constrain'd,
    Sandals more interwoven and complete
To fit the naked foot of poesy;
Let us inspect the lyre, and weigh the stress
Of every chord, and see what may be gain'd
    By ear industrious, and attention meet;
Misers of sound and syllable, no less
Than Midas of his coinage, let us be
    Jealous of dead leaves in the bay-wreath crown;
So, if we may not let the Muse be free,
    She will be bound with garlands of her own.

John Keats, 1819

l.3, *Fetter'd*—shackled
l.4, *find out*—discover, find
l.6, *poesy*—poetry
l.9, *meet*—appropriate, proper
l.12, *bay-wreath*—laurel wreath, a symbol of victory

This is an excellent example of Form, Music, and Meaning all reinforcing one another.

Write your answers in complete sentences and in good paragraph form on a separate sheet of paper.

1. In a sentence, state the main idea or theme of the poem. (-/1)

2. How does Keats use each of the following devices or techniques to reinforce his theme? (Give an example of each from the poem and discuss its effectiveness.)
   (a) rhyme scheme (-/4)
   (b) personification (-/4)
   (c) metaphor (-/4)
   (d) allusion (-/4)
   (e) assonance (-/4)
   (f) connotation (-/4)

3. BONUS: (-/3) Explain the significance of the last line, "She will be bound with garlands of her own."

TOTAL SCORE: _____ **/25**

THE SCARECROW

All winter through I bow my head
    Beneath the driving rain;
The North Wind powders me with snow
    And blows me black again;
At midnight in a maze of stars
    I flame with glittering rime,
And stand, above the stubble, stiff
    As mail at morning-prime.
But when that child, called Spring, and all
    His host of children, come,
Scattering their buds and dew upon
    These acres of my home,
Some rapture in my rags awakes;
    I lift void eyes and scan
The skies for crows, those ravening foes
    Of my strange master, Man.
I watch him striding lank behind
    His clashing team, and know
Soon will the wheat swish body high
    Where once lay sterile snow;
Soon shall I gaze across a sea
    Of sun-begotten grain,
Which my unflinching watch hath sealed
    For harvest once again.

Walter de la Mare

l.6, *rime*—frost
l.8, *mail at morning-prime*—armor at dawn
l.13, *rapture*—joy
l.14, *void*—empty
l.15, *ravening*—hungry
l.23, *watch hath sealed*—vigilance has guaranteed

Write your answers in complete sentences and in good paragraph form on a separate sheet of paper.

1. How does the scarecrow feel about himself and his job? (-/2)

2. Why is the image of the scarecrow standing like a suit of armor ("stiff as mail at morning-prime") especially effective? (-/3)

3. Give one example each from the poem of FOUR of the following devices or techniques and discuss how each one enhances the effectiveness of the poem:

    (a) alliteration (-/4)   (d) onomatopoeia (-/4)
    (b) personification (-/4)   (e) connotation (-/4)
    (c) metaphor (-/4)   (f) simile (-/4)

I SEE BEFORE ME THE GLADIATOR LIE

I see before me the Gladiator lie:
He leans upon his hand—his manly brow
Consents to death, but conquers agony,
And his droop'd head sinks gradually low—
And through his side the last drops, ebbing slow
From the red gash, fall heavy, one by one,
Like the first of a thunder-shower; and now
The arena swims around him: he is gone,
Ere ceased the inhuman shout which hail'd the wretch who won.

He heard it, but he heeded not—his eyes
Were with his heart, and that was far away;
He reck'd not of the life he lost nor prize,
But where his rude hut by the Danube lay,
There were his young barbarians all at play,
There was their Dacian mother—he, their sire,
Butcher'd to make a Roman holiday—
All this rush'd with his blood—Shall he expire,
And unavenged?—Arise! ye Goths, and glut your ire.

George Gordon, Lord Byron

l.12, *He reck'd not of*—He wasn't thinking about
l.17, *expire*—die
l.18, *glut your ire*—satisfy your rage

This poem was inspired by a statue titled The Dying Slave, found in the Capitoline Museum in Rome. Imagine what it was like to live as a captured "barbarian" forced to fight as a gladiator in ancient Roman times.

Dacia, where Roumania is now, was once a Roman province. Goths was the name given to the race of "barbarians" who lived there and had been conquered by the Romans. Eventually, the Goths, along with other barbarian tribes, were able to rise up and invade Rome.

1. What two emotions did the poet feel when he saw the statue in Rome? (-/2)

2. What picture does he paint with words in order to make the reader feel the same emotions? (Give at least four details.) (-/4)

3. What two words does the poet use to show the reader that this captive was never truly conquered? (–/2)

4. A simile is a figurative comparison using the words "like" or "as." Find and quote a simile from this poem (-/2). Explain what is being compared (-2) and describe how the comparison helps the reader to "get into" the poem (-/2).

5. A metaphor is a figurative comparison that does not use the words "like" or "as." Find and quote a metaphor from this poem (-/2). Explain what is being compared (-/2) and how the comparison makes the poem more powerful (-/2).

SUMMATIVE PRODUCT: ANSWER AN EFFECTIVENESS QUESTION

Throughout this section of the module, students have been practicing the analysis of poetry by answering effectiveness questions in point form. Writing a paragraph-long answer to an effectiveness question is one of the foundation skills of writing analytical responses and literary essays. It would therefore be appropriate and beneficial for students to mark the conclusion of this unit by selecting one of the studied poems and completing for summative assessment a written response to the question:

How does the poet's use of (a specified poetic device) make the poem more effective?

INTRODUCTION TO THE ASSIGNMENT

1. The teacher reviews with the class what they have done up to this point in the unit and explains that the final assignment will be a paragraph-long written response to one of the poems already studied, in answer to an effectiveness question.

2. Teacher and students together discuss what constitutes a paragraph: *the topic (opening) sentence*, *the body*, and *the concluding sentence*. The teacher lists these on the board.

3. The teacher then leads a whole-class discussion on the important elements to include in an answer to an effectiveness question, and these are listed on the board as well. Together, teacher and students determine where in the paragraph each of the important elements ought to go. Lines are drawn between the two lists to illustrate the outcome of the discussion.

4. The teacher writes the effectiveness question on the board, then instructs students to go back through their notes and reread all the poems studied so far. Working independently, each student is to select the poem that will be the focus for his or her response to that question.

5. *Homework:* Each student selects one of the poems studied so far and performs a close reading and analysis to determine which of the poetic devices appears with the greatest frequency and/or has the greatest impact on the reader, thus making the greatest contribution to the effectiveness of the poem.

   NOTE TO THE TEACHER: Depending on the grade level of the class, this summative assignment may be done as either an in-class or an out-of-class activity. There are pros and cons for each approach. My general preference for summative written work is to have students produce their first draft in class under test conditions. I collect the first drafts and photocopy them, then keep the originals for my files and return the photocopy to the students for completion of the assignment. I have found that there are fewer problems with academic dishonesty that way.

THE FIRST DRAFT

1. Each student comes to class having selected a poem and determined its predominant poetic device.

2. Each student then proceeds to identify the strongest example of that device to analyze in his or her written response. *(Depending on grade and ability levels, students may be given the option of including more than one example. In that case, the response will include a separate paragraph for each example.)*

3. Working independently, each student writes the effectiveness question at the top of a sheet of lined paper, inserting the predominant poetic device in the blank. The student then writes a first-draft response that cites and analyzes the selected example(s).

The teacher collects the students' first-draft work to look over diagnostically. *The teacher may decide to offer encouragement by adding a marginal comment or suggestion as well.*

COMPLETING THE ASSIGNMENT

1. Each student receives back his or her first-draft work and a copy of the peer editing checklist. The teacher and class go over the checklist together, discussing each item to ensure that students understand what they will be expected to produce.

   Students also need to understand the following, which the teacher may wish to write on the board in condensed form as a reminder:

   - *Student authors are the owners of their writing and take final responsibility for the completeness and correctness of the work that is handed in for marking.*
   - *Peer-editing partners are not to make corrections or changes to other authors' work—they may point out words to be checked for spelling or suggest improvements to wording, punctuation, and so on, but the author is the one who actually makes revisions to the text.*

2. Students pair up with a different partner from all previous pairings and designate themselves Author A and Author B.

3. Together, both partners work on Author A's response, reading it aloud and discussing the criteria on the editing checklist. Author A reads with a pencil in hand, making changes and improvements to his or her own work. As each item on the checklist has been discussed, Author A's editing partner checks it off in the left-hand column of Author A's sheet.

4. The process is then repeated for Author B's response. The teacher circulates meanwhile, offering encouragement and assistance as needed.

FINAL PRODUCT

1. Each student receives a copy of the assessment sheet and the teacher goes over it with the class, discussing each item to ensure that students understand the criteria that will be used to evaluate their work.

   NOTE TO THE TEACHER: The peer editing and assessment checklists supplied here (SPR 16 and SPR 17) have been used successfully in my classes and may be used as is. Alternatively, you may consider them a starting point from which to create your own marking tool. Feel free to shorten, reword, simplify, or reformat either or both of the checklists to suit the needs of your own classes, at all grade levels.

2. *Homework:* That night, each student goes over his or her edited draft once more, making final changes and improvements and checking off items on the editing checklist (right-hand column) as they are completed. The student also refers to the assessment sheet to ensure that all the evaluation criteria have been met.

3. Before the specified submission date, the student types or prints out a clean final draft of the response. The student also gathers all the elements required for the submission package and assembles them as instructed by the teacher. For example:

   Final draft on top, with student name, course code, and submission date in the upper left corner, THEN
   Assessment sheet, THEN
   Edited rough draft with peer-editing checklist behind it, THEN
   Planning materials, including notes, outline, and so on.

   The submission package is then stapled together, ready to be handed in for summative assessment.

ANSWERING AN EFFECTIVENESS QUESTION
PEER-EDITING CHECKLIST

Written by: _____ Edited by _____

Checked by Partner	EDITING CRITERIA	Improved by Author
	1. The paragraph is complete. It has a topic sentence, body, and concluding sentence.	
	2. The paragraph is on topic. It answers the question that has been asked.	
	3. The paragraph is specific. It identifies the poem and states its theme or main idea. It names the poetic device being used and provides a quotation from the poem (with line number) as an example.	
	4. The example is fully developed: the paragraph tells what the example does, what it helps the reader to do, how it reinforces the theme, and how it contributes to the overall effectiveness of the poem (immediacy, vividness, evocativeness, provocativeness).	
	5. The writing is grammatically as correct as possible: • Spellings are accurate (including use of capital letters). • Punctuation is complete and correct (including quotation marks around the example from the poem). • Every sentence is complete. There are no fragments or run-ons.	
	6. Linking words and phrases have been used to make the writing flow from one sentence to the next.	

PEER EDITOR SAYS:

One thing I really like about this paragraph is _____

_____

One thing that I think would improve this paragraph is _____

_____

AUTHOR SAYS:

The reason I chose this poem to write about is _____

_____

The thing I found hardest about this assignment was _____

_____

ASSESSMENT CHECKLIST: ANSWER TO AN EFFECTIVENESS QUESTION

Student's Name: _____ TOTAL SCORE: ___ /15

Knowledge/Understanding_____/5

The student's choice of example shows
   solid comprehension of both the poem and
   the question.

                           5   4   3   2   1

Thinking_____/5

The way the example is developed
   demonstrates an appropriately
   sophisticated level of thinking.

                           5   4   3   2   1

Communication_____/5

The paragraph is well organized and
   demonstrates correct use of the conventions
   of standard English.

                           5   4   3   2   1

Comments:

ASSESSMENT CHECKLIST: ANSWER TO AN EFFECTIVENESS QUESTION

Student's Name: _____ TOTAL SCORE: ___ /15

Knowledge/Understanding_____/5

The student's choice of example shows
   solid comprehension of both the poem and
   the question.

                           5   4   3   2   1

Thinking_____/5

The way the example is developed
   demonstrates an appropriately
   sophisticated level of thinking.

                           5   4   3   2   1

Communication_____/5

The paragraph is well organized and
   demonstrates correct use of the conventions
   of standard English.

                           5   4   3   2   1

Comments:

Studying Poetry Part 2
Analyzing Narrative Poetry
"David" by Earle Birney

✍ **YOU WILL NEED**

- Copies of the narrative poem(s) to be studied (one of each per student)
  OR
- A class set of an anthology containing one or more narrative poems to be studied
  PLUS
- SFR 4–THREE TYPES OF CONFLICT chart (class set)
- SFR 6–STORY OUTLINE chart (class set)
- SPR 2–LEVELS OF ANALYSIS: POETRY (class set, if not already handed out)
- SPR 8–LEVELS OF ANALYSIS: EFFECTIVENESS (class set, if not already handed out)
- SPR 18–THE HERO (class set, optional)
- SPR 19–DAVID worksheet (class set, optional)

PURPOSE

In a close examination of a narrative poem, students will practice using correct terminology as they discuss aspects of the poem and consider and respond to questions on all three levels of analysis. In the process, they will come to appreciate how powerful a story is when told through the medium of poetry.

ASSIGNMENT 1: THE STORY IN THE POEM

1. The teacher puts a list on the board: *The Odyssey, The Iliad, The Aeneid, Beowulf, Gilgamesh, The Eddas*. The teacher and students discuss each item on the list, establishing that each one is actually a heroic adventure tale, written long ago. (*The Odyssey* is about Odysseus's struggles to return home after the Trojan War. *The Iliad* is about the war itself and the heroes who died fighting it. *The Aeneid* tells of a Trojan prince named Aeneas who fled Troy after the war, traveled around having adventures, and went on to found a new city. *Beowulf* is about a monster-slayer who was eventually killed by a dragon. *Gilgamesh* describes an ancient king who formed a relationship with a "wild man" and had adventures with him. *The Eddas* tell stories about the exploits of the earliest Icelandic heroes.)

2. The teacher explains to the class: Although storytelling is as old as humankind itself, the first people ever to write stories down were traveling poets called "bards." They went from town to town, spreading news and singing about the exploits of gods and heroes. In fact, the only way you could become a hero back then was to have your deeds immortalized in poetry by an admiring bard. (And yes, sometimes the bard exaggerated a little for the sake of a good story.)

Narrative poetry is therefore a very old and well-established form of literature. Like prose fiction, it can be very long (an epic poem, like *Beowulf*), but it can also be fairly short (a ballad, like "The Highwayman" by Alfred Noyes). What all narrative poems have in common is that each one tells a story that is made vivid and powerful—and, ultimately, memorable—by the use of poetry as a storytelling medium.

In this unit, students are going to be reading poetry that is a blend of story and song. In order to appreciate it fully, they will need to approach it from two directions at once: as a poem and as a work of fiction containing all the elements of a story: plot, characters, setting, conflict, and theme.

3. Each student receives a copy of either the first poem to be studied or the anthology containing the poem. The students follow along as the teacher reads the poem aloud (or plays it, if using a song lyric).

   NOTE TO TEACHER: All ballads are narrative poems, but not all narrative poems are ballads. When selecting a narrative poem for study, you may find that students engage more readily with something from a modern poet like Robert Frost ("Home Burial," "The Death of the Hired Hand") or Robert Service ("The Cremation of Sam McGee") or with a song lyric ("In the Ghetto" sung by Elvis Presley) than with a traditional British ballad like "The Highwayman" or "Lochinvar." A mainstay of my grade 10 and 11 English courses has always been "The Dying Eagle" by E. J. Pratt. During the World Series, my nonacademic classes really engaged with "Casey at the Bat" by Ernest Thayer. And, of course, there's "David" by Earle Birney, which I've taught at every grade level.

4. The teacher draws a copy of the STORY OUTLINE chart on the board. In whole-class discussion, the events of the story told in the poem just read (or listened to) are discussed and the teacher records them in order on the chart, highlighting the inciting incident and climactic moment of the story.

5. Each student receives a STORY OUTLINE chart and proceeds to copy the information from the board onto his or her handout.

6. The teacher now hands out a copy of the THREE TYPES OF CONFLICT chart to each student and writes the headings of the chart across the board. Together, teacher and students identify each of the principal characters in the poem, and these are listed on the board under the *Protagonist* heading, along with two or three details provided in the poem about each character. On their personal dramatic conflict charts, students record the information from the board, giving each main character his or her own line of the chart.

7. Students form groups of four and work together to complete the lines of their conflict charts. As they reread and discuss the poem, each group is to identify and make a note on their charts of the lines of the poem that provide information about the characters' goals, motivations, and obstacles to be overcome.

8. In whole-class discussion, the groups can share their findings and flesh out their personal dramatic conflict charts.

   The teacher asks: *Did the fact that this was a poem make it easier or more difficult to locate the elements of Dramatic Conflict? Why do you think this was so?*

9. Teacher and class together discuss the remaining narrative elements of the poem: the setting *(What are the time and place—the when and where—of this poem?)* and the theme *(What message do you think the poet wants us to carry away from reading this poem?)*. Students record the resulting information on the back of their STORY OUTLINE handout.

10. The teacher now asks a thought question that will engage the class in a discussion of all the elements of the story.

    NOTE TO TEACHER: I have found that the most effective questions at this stage of the unit are those that ask why, how, *what is the result or effect,* and *what is the extent. For "The Dying Eagle" I generally ask why the eagle is dying. For "David" I often ask how much of what happens in the story is caused by the characters and how much by the setting.*

ASSIGNMENT 2: IDENTIFY A FOCUS

1. The teacher explains to the class that in a story, more emphasis is often placed on one or two elements than on the others. Stories in which action and conflict lead to further action and conflict are said to be *plot-driven*. Stories in which the characters' personalities and choices play the greatest role in determining plot events are described as *character-driven*. Stories can also be built around interesting or evocative settings, making them *mood-driven* (the classic horror stories are the best example of this). And in a *theme-driven* story what matters most is delivering a message from the author to the reader.

   The teacher lists these four types of stories on the board and asks the class: *Which kind of story is being told in this narrative poem?*

2. The teacher stars or circles the one or two narrative elements that form the focus of the poem. The teacher then directs students to take out their copy of the LEVELS OF ANALYSIS: POETRY handout and look at the list on the bottom of the page ("Effective Poetry Has").

   The teacher lists on the board the four characteristics of an effective poem: *immediacy*, *vividness*, *evocativeness*, and *provocativeness*.

3. Students pair up with "elbow partners" to discuss which of these four characteristics would match up with each of the four story types listed on the board. *(Allow up to five minutes.)* In whole class, the student pairs share what they discussed as the teacher draws lines on the board linking the following:

   > Immediacy to plot-driven and mood-driven
   > Vividness to plot-driven, character-driven, and mood-driven
   > Evocativeness to character-driven and mood-driven
   > Provocativeness to theme-driven

4. Referring to the story type or types contained in the poem under study, the teacher highlights on the board the poetic characteristics that would make this story especially powerful and memorable.

5. The teacher then sums up the focus of the poem study: *Students will be examining how the techniques employed by the poet simultaneously enhance the effectiveness of the poetry and strengthen or underline the narrative elements of the story.*

ASSIGNMENT 3: PERFORM A CLOSE READING

NOTE TO TEACHER: If the narrative poem under study is quite long, you might want to consider dividing the poem into sections and assigning each one to a different group of students for close reading and analysis. In fact, if the class is studying an epic poem that has been made into a film, it might be more practical to show them the movie before beginning the unit, then select significant excerpts from the text for reading, discussion, and analysis. (My grade 11 pre-AP class included a number of Muslim students, so I showed them *The 13th Warrior* before we tackled parts of *Beowulf*. Subsequent discussions comparing the two versions of the story were quite animated and engaging.)

1. The teacher reminds the students that close reading involves going line by line and word by word to identify and label as many poetic devices as they can find, on all three levels of analysis. Students should be directed to their copies of the LEVELS OF ANALYSIS: POETRY handout for a listing of the various devices.

2. If the poem under study is on a photocopied handout, students may be instructed to highlight each example and draw an arrow to a note in the margin. If the poem is in an anthology, then students will need to copy the examples they find onto a separate sheet of paper, indicating for each which device has been used. (Words and phrases that are "multi-tasking" should be copied multiple times, once for each device they represent.)

3. Students pair up or form groups of three and conduct a close reading of the poem (or of the part each group has been assigned). Each student should ensure that s/he makes a personal copy of the group's work.

4. If the poem was divided up for close reading, the students now "jigsaw" into new groups, ensuring that the entire poem is represented in each group. Group members share their findings and identify repetitions and commonalities among the sections of the poem.

   If all students have read the entire poem, then the class forms groups of four to compare notes and discuss the devices each member found. Students can take the opportunity to flesh out their notes with examples that they may have missed.

5. Groups can share their favorite examples in a teacher-led whole-class discussion.

ASSIGNMENT 4: ANALYZE THE POEM

1. The teacher writes on the board the focus question that will inform the class's analysis of the narrative poem under study: How do the poetic devices used by the poet make the (plot, characters, setting/mood, theme) of the story more powerful and memorable by giving the poem (immediacy, vividness, evocativeness, provocativeness)? (*Pick the choices that apply.*)

   Students get back into their groups from Assignment 3, Step 4, and take out their notes on the narrative poem under study.

2. The teacher explains that while any poem is a treasure trove of poetic devices, the purpose of analysis is to determine the answer to a question. Crime scene investigators analyze evidence to discover who committed the crime and how—but not all the evidence leads to an answer. Meteorologists analyze data to find out what the weather is likely to be tomorrow—but they have a lot more information than they need for a local forecast. If the students are going to analyze this poem to answer the question on the board, then they first need to identify and isolate their most relevant findings.

3. The teacher instructs the class to begin by going through all the examples of devices they've identified and selecting the ones that most strongly fit the criteria in the question. Each group should be able to find at least five to eight strong examples in a short poem (like "The Dying Eagle") and proportionately more in a longer poem.

4. Students work in their groups to identify the examples they will be using for their analysis of the poem, testing each one by comparing it with the question on the board. Each group member then stars or circles the selected examples in his or her notes.

5. The groups dissolve. Each student folds a clean sheet of lined paper lengthwise to form two columns, headed *Example* and *Analysis*, and copies the selected examples from his or her notes into the first column. Referring to his or her copy of the LEVELS OF ANALYSIS: EFFECTIVENESS handout, the student writes a point-form note in the second column for each of the examples, explaining what the example does, what it helps the reader to do, how it contributes to the overall effectiveness of the poem, and how it enhances or reinforces the dominant narrative elements of the story.

6. Students can pair up or get into groups of three to compare notes and offer one another suggestions for improvement.

ASSIGNMENT 5: SUMMATIVE PRODUCTS

NOTE TO TEACHER: Most of the assignments listed below can be found in other parts of this program:

Write an effectiveness paragraph—*see* "Build Your Toolkit" (Studying Poetry Part 1)
Write a literary response—*see* "Write a Literary Response to a Poem" (Studying Poetry Part 5)
Write a letter to the poet—*see* "Write a Formal Letter" (*Wordsmithing*)
Write a short story—*see* Getting Started (*Story Crafting*)
Write a literary essay—*see* Writing the Literary Essay (*Enjoying Literature*)
Write a comparative report—*see* "Write a Report" (*Wordsmithing*)

When giving students a summative assignment based on the above unit, you may wish to remind them that while they are encouraged to have fun with it, the purpose of the activity is to let them demonstrate both their analytical skills and their understanding of the poems or poems just studied. Each submitted assignment should therefore include reference to both the narrative and the poetical elements of the selected works.

IN GRADE 9: Students may choose from a menu including three or more of the following:

• Complete and hand in a paragraph about the effectiveness of one of the devices used in a narrative poem.
• Complete and hand in a written response (dialectical or personal) to a narrative poem.
• Create a visual representation of a scene or chapter from a narrative poem, illustrating the associative devices used by the poet. (If a group of students does this assignment, each group member can illustrate a different scene and the pictures can be posted on the wall in sequential order to form a mural.)
• Imagine that a narrative poem is being made into a film and create a poster or radio promo for it.
• Compose a diary entry by one of the characters in a narrative poem.
• Write a letter to the author of a narrative poem, commenting on his or her use of narrative elements and poetical devices.

IN GRADE 10: Students may choose from a menu including three or more of the following:

• Complete and hand in a written response (personal or analytical) to a narrative poem.
• Write up a news report based on a narrative poem.
• Compose a diary entry by one of the characters in a narrative poem (same day or one year later).
• Dramatize a scene from a narrative poem (or dramatize the entire poem if it is short enough).
• Rewrite a narrative poem to include themselves as characters in the story.

IN GRADE 11: Students may choose from a menu including three or more of the following:

• Complete and hand in a written response (personal or analytical) to a narrative poem.
• Write up a report comparing a narrative poem to a film or a short story (may be based on the same story as the poem or contain similar elements).
• Rewrite a narrative poem as a short story.
• Reimagine a narrative poem in video or graphic novel format.

IN GRADE 12: Students may choose from a menu including three or more of the following:

• Complete and hand in a written analytical response to a narrative poem.
• Complete and hand in a literary essay based on a narrative poem.
• Conduct and write up a comparative analysis between two poems, one of them narrative.
• Prepare and participate in a fishbowl discussion about a narrative poem in response to the focus question posed in Assignment 4.
• Compose their own narrative poem in the same style and using the same poetical devices as a poem under study.

TEACHING "DAVID" BY EARLE BIRNEY

NOTE TO TEACHER: I have enjoyed teaching this poem to classes at all grade levels, by tweaking the assignments outlined above as follows:

GRADE 9

Before beginning the poem: Introduce students to the concept of heroes and heroism. In whole-class discussion, identify the defining characteristics of a hero and list them on the board. Then hand out THE HERO worksheet. Question 1 has just been answered on the board, and students can copy the information onto their handouts.

Organize students into groups of three or four and assign each group question 2, 3, or 4 from the sheet to answer. Allow about five to seven minutes for group discussion.

In subsequent whole-class discussion, go over all the questions on the sheet. Make notes on the board and encourage students to write the answers on their handouts.

OPTIONAL CREATIVE ACTIVITY:

Complete each of the following sentences with as many words as you can think of that would apply:

A hero is (brave, loyal . . .).
A hero is someone who (rescues people, protects the weak . . .).
A hero needs (a sword, a shield . . .).
Heroes do things (swiftly, confidently . . .).

Now pick one of the following:

1. Write an illustrated how-to booklet: "So You Want to Be a Hero?"
2. Imagine that you're in trouble and need a hero to get you out of it. Create a "Help Wanted" ad. Then write a letter applying for the job.
3. You've decided to make a career out of being a hero. Create a poster advertising your services.

Begin the poem: Explain that the focus of this poetry study will be heroism, and the question they will be trying to answer is this: Of the two characters, David and Bobby, which one is the greater hero, and why?

As the unit proceeds, relate everything back to heroism: What are the poetical devices that emphasize the heroic nature of David and what he does? The heroic nature of what Bobby does? What are the story elements that help or hinder heroism? How are David's and Bobby's differing levels of heroism reflected in various aspects of the setting?

The summative assignment is a written or creative response to the focus question: Which of the boys is the greater hero?

• Write an opinion paragraph explaining why you think either David or Bobby is the greater hero.
• Complete and hand in a written response (dialectical or personal) to the poem, focusing on heroism.
• Create a visual representation of a scene or chapter from the poem, illustrating the associative devices used by the poet to reflect or emphasize the heroic nature of one of the boys.
• Imagine that the poem is being made into a film and create a poster or radio promo for it.
• Compose two diary entries, one by David and one by Bobby, that demonstrate which one is more heroic.
• Write a letter to Earle Birney, commenting on his use of narrative elements and poetical devices to make one of the boys appear more heroic.

GRADE 10

At this grade level, we focus on the fact that there are two contrasting stories in this poem—David's and Bobby's.

Before beginning the poem: Review with the class the structure of a short story and the storytelling devices that make fiction enjoyable to read (*foreshadowing, irony, suspense, contrast, symbolism*). Discuss definitions and record them on the board or on an overhead transparency.

Hand out the double-sided worksheet (SPR 19) and go over it with the students. Organize the class into working groups of four. Explain that this poem is too long to be taken in all at once, so the students will be examining one section per day, first discussing it in their groups, then sharing their findings in whole class.

Begin the poem. Tell the students in general terms what happens in this story: *Two boys spend their summer mountain climbing together, tackling tougher and tougher challenges. On the toughest peak of all there is an accident, and only one of the boys climbs back down.*

Read aloud the first "chapter" of the story, clarifying or defining any difficult vocabulary. *(Having only three dictionaries for my class, I appointed three students to be our "word wizards" for the duration of the poem study. The strategy worked so well that I adopted it for every unit of the course.)* Give the student groups about twenty minutes to work on filling in the handout, then lead a whole class discussion in which they can share their findings. (Each student should ensure that s/he has a personal written record of his or her group's work.)

As the unit proceeds, follow this pattern to the end of the poem (read aloud and clarify, group analysis, whole-class discussion), covering one numbered section per day. Change up the groups each day to help ensure that students are making personal notes. Once a question from the handout has been satisfactorily answered, record the response on the board or on an overhead transparency so that students can add any missing information to their own personal worksheets.

When the poem has been read all the way through, ask the students: If you were in Bobby's place and had to make the same decision as he does, what would you do? *(Allow plenty of time for the discussion of Bobby's ethical dilemma.)*

Have students remain in their most recent groups. Hand out a copy of the DRAMATIC CONFLICT sheet to each student and divide the class into two sections, Group A to chart David's goal, motivation, and antagonists and Group B to chart Bobby's goal, motivation, and antagonists. After the groups have had time to discuss the poem and fill in their assigned line of the chart, lead a whole-class discussion to determine: Whose story is this, anyway? Is it David's? Or is it really Bobby's?

Groups are dissolved. Have the students number off from one to nine, then come together in focus groups, one per numbered section of the poem. Each group is to perform a close reading and analysis of its assigned section in response to the following question: *How do the poetical devices presented in each section contribute to making the entire poem a more powerful story?*

The summative assignment is a written or creative response to one of the major questions discussed during the unit: Whose story is it? How do the poetical devices in the poem contribute to making the story more powerful?

- Complete and hand in a written response (personal or analytical) to the poem.
- Write up a news report based on the poem.
- Compose two contrasting diary entries by one of the characters in the poem.
- Dramatize a scene from the poem (or dramatize the entire poem if it is short enough).
- Rewrite a section of the poem to include yourself as a character in the story.

GRADE 11

In my pre-AP class, "David" followed our study of Beowulf, *so the similarities between the two narrative poems (both their writing style and the epic hero qualities displayed) were immediately evident.*

Before beginning the poem: Show students a movie version of the Beowulf story. Discuss in whole class what an epic hero is and does, and record the list of characteristics on the board. Students should be able to volunteer additional examples of epic heroes from films or TV shows they've seen—compare these with the list on the board. Ask the students: Is it possible for anyone in this room to become an epic hero? If so, how? (That is, what distinguishes an epic hero from an ordinary hero?)

Begin the poem. Tell the students in general terms what happens in this story: *Two boys spend their summer mountain climbing together, tackling tougher and tougher challenges. On the toughest peak of all there is a mishap, and only one of the boys climbs back down.*

Read the poem aloud in class, stopping between sections to discuss and clarify the events of the story so far. Draw comparisons as you go between David and Beowulf (and between Bobby and Wiglaf) and chart them on the board. Review the structure of a short story and identify the inciting incident and climactic moment of "David." Compare these to the same points in the Beowulf story.

Introduce the focus question to guide students' close reading and analysis: *How do the poetical devices used in this poem underline the epic nature of the story being told?*

Students can work in pairs or groups of three to conduct a close reading and analysis of the poem, with each person making his or her own personal notes. In whole-class discussion, students can share their findings. Particularly strong examples of repeatedly used devices can be identified and missing information added to students' notes for use in one of the summative products.

The summative product is a written or creative response to the focus question:

• Complete and hand in a written analytical response or a literary essay based on the poem.
• Write a report comparing the poem to a film or a short story (may be based on the same story as the poem or contain similar elements).
• Rewrite the poem as a short story.
• Reimagine the poem in video or graphic novel format, emphasizing its epic characteristics.

GRADE 12

My grade 12 university-bound English course was nicknamed "Tragedy 101" because it focused on the three kinds of tragic heroes: classical Greek, Shakespearean, and modern. "David" fit in perfectly with the major works I'd selected for study: *King Oedipus* (Sophocles), *King Lear* (Shakespeare), and *The Wars* (Timothy Findley).

Before beginning the poem: Students should already have studied at least one major work in the course. Discuss with students the nature of tragedy and the three kinds of tragic heroes:

Classical Greek: a high-born individual whose pride pits him against the gods (leading to his death or utter ruin)
Shakespearean: a figure of high social standing whose "fatal flaw" leads him to make disastrous choices, which are not recognized as such until it is too late to rectify them (resulting in his death, madness, or utter ruin)
Modern: an average person who opposes one of the "systems" of society in a hopeless cause, refusing to back down, and pays dearly for it (death or utter ruin)

Point out that literature builds on what has gone before: a classical tragedy only has one kind of tragic hero, but a Shakespearean tragedy can have two kinds—classical as well as Shakespearean—and a modern work can have all three kinds, sometimes all at once (as does *The Wars*, a novel with multiple tragic figures).

Begin the poem: Read the poem aloud in class, stopping between sections to discuss and clarify the events of the story so far. Draw comparisons as you go between "David" and a previously studied major work and chart them on the board. Review the structure of a story and identify the inciting incident and climactic moment of "David." Compare these to the same points in the previously studied work. Discuss which kind of tragic hero pattern David fits most closely. Could Bobby also be considered a tragic hero? Which kind?

Introduce the focus question to guide students' close reading and analysis: *How do the poetical devices used in this poem underline the tragic nature of the story being told?*

Students can work independently, in pairs, or in groups of three to conduct a close reading and analysis of the poem, with each person making his or her own personal notes. In whole-class discussion, students can share their findings. By referring to both the focus question and the handout (SPR 20), students can identify particularly strong examples of poetical devices and add any missing infomation to their notes for use in one of the summative products.

The summative product is a written, oral, or creative response to the focus question:

- Write a detailed analytical response to the poem.
- Write a literary essay based on the poem (you may compare it to a previously studied work).
- Prepare and participate in a fishbowl discussion about the poem.
- Compose your own tragic narrative poem in the same style and using the same poetical devices as "David."

THE HERO

1. What makes a person or an action heroic?

2. Is every protagonist in a story a hero? Why or why not?

3. What are the advantages and disadvantages of being considered a hero?

4. Is it a good thing or a bad thing for a person to have a hero? Why?

5. Explain the differences between:

   a hero and a martyr

   a hero and a celebrity

   a hero and a role model

6. What is meant by each of the following phrases?

   An unsung hero

   A hometown hero

   A war hero

   A cheap hero

   Hero worship

7. What is a hero sandwich? Why do you think it was given that name?

"DAVID" by Earle Birney

1. What is the inciting incident in this story? How do you know?

_____

_____

_____

2. What is the climactic moment of the story for David? For Bobby? How do you know?

_____

_____

_____

Find and quote examples from the poem that contribute to the reader's enjoyment of "David" as a story:

NARRATIVE DEVICE	QUOTATION/EXAMPLE	EXPLANATION
Foreshadowing		
Irony		
Suspense		
Contrast		
Symbolism		

(continued on back)

3. What is Bob's attitude toward David at the beginning of the poem? At what point does his attitude shift? Find and quote examples from the poem to support your answers to both questions.

_____

_____

_____

_____

_____

Fill in the chart with at least ONE example of each poetic device.

POETIC DEVICE	QUOTE EXAMPLE	EFFECTIVE BECAUSE
Alliteration		
Sibilance		
Onomatopoeia		
Simile		
Metaphor		
Personification		
Imagery		

GROUP POETRY ASSIGNMENTS
"DAVID"

In your group, take turns rereading your assigned section of the poem aloud. Discuss what is happening in the story, then work together to answer the questions below. Each member of the group should be sure to make personal notes on the discussion:

PART I. INTRODUCTION

The first part introduces the characters, establishes the setting and the point of view, and sets up the Dramatic Conflict.

(A) What do we learn about David and Bobby in this part of the poem?
(B) What three reasons are given for going mountain climbing?
(C) Find examples in this part of the poem of each of the following:

      alliteration   metaphor

Each mountain gets its own part of the poem, like a chapter in the story, and Bobby learns something from each peak the boys attempt.

PART II. MOUNT GLEAM

(A) What does David teach Bobby in this section of the poem?
(B) Find examples in this part of the poem of each of the following:

      personification   alliteration   simile

      metaphor   onomatopoeia   sibilance

PART III. RAMPART

(A) What metaphor does the name of this mountain suggest?
(B) What does David teach Bobby on this mountain?
(C) What other interesting thing does Bobby learn, and what might it foreshadow?
(D) Find examples in this part of the poem of each of the following:

      alliteration   metaphor   sibilance

PART IV. INGLISMALDIE

(A) How can we tell that there used to be a sea where the mountains are now?
(B) Find examples in this part of the poem of each of the following:

      assonance   metaphor

PART V. SUNDANCE

(A) How do we know that Bobby is becoming a much stronger mountain climber?
(B) What does David's reaction to the injured robin reveal about his attitude to life?
(C) Find examples in this part of the poem of each of the following:

       contrast   personification   connotation
       foreshadowing

PART VI. THE FORTRESS

(A) How do we know that this mountain was much more difficult to climb?
(B) What lesson does Bobby learn from this experience?
(C) Find examples in this part of the poem of each of the following:

       simile   alliteration   personification

PART VII. THE FINGER

(A) We are approaching the Climax to the story, and it takes place on this mountain. How does each of the following hint at a future tragedy?

- There is a great deal of personification in this part of the poem.
- The Finger is hooked, not a straight climb like the others.
- The boys' first attempt at the base of the Finger is unsuccessful.

(B) What is a cairn, and why would the boys form one?
(C) Find examples in this part of the poem of each of the following:

       metaphor   imagery   personification
       sibilance

PART VIII. THE FINGER

(A) Why does David insist on blaming himself for the accident on the mountain?
(B) What does he want Bobby to do, and why?
(C) This is a friend's last request. If you were in Bobby's place, what would be your decision?
(D) Find examples in this part of the poem of each of the following:

       simile   imagery   personification
       alliteration

PART IX. THE DESCENT FROM THE FINGER

(A) What is "It" (line 4, first stanza)?
(B) Bobby has to retrace his steps down the mountain. Compare the way the landscape is described in this part of the poem with the description in part VII.
(C) Explain the meaning of the last line of the poem.
(D) Find examples in this part of the poem of each of the following:

       imagery   alliteration   personification
       metaphor   connotation

Studying Poetry Part 3
Analyzing Lyric Poetry
The Sonnet

✍️ **YOU WILL NEED**

- A list of 6 to 10 sonnets to be studied, provided to the students as one of:
    A photocopied package containing 1 sonnet per side of a page (class set)

    OR

    A class set of an anthology that contains the sonnets

    PLUS
- An example sonnet (not in the package) on an overhead transparency
- An overhead projector and colored markers
- SPR 2–LEVELS OF ANALYSIS: POETRY and SPR 8–LEVELS OF ANALYSIS: EFFECTIVENESS (class sets, if not already handed out)
- SPR 4 to SPR 6–ANSWERING AN EFFECTIVENESS QUESTION (class sets, if not already handed out)

PURPOSE

In a close examination of a lyric poem, students will practice using correct terminology as they discuss aspects of the poem and consider and respond to questions on all three levels of analysis. In the process, they will come to appreciate the artistry and economy of poetry.

ASSIGNMENT 1: INTRODUCTION TO THE SONNET

1. The teacher explains to the class that there are different kinds or classifications of poetry: narrative poetry tells a story, dramatic poetry is a monologue expressing the thoughts and feelings of a character called "the speaker," and lyric poetry conveys the thoughts and feelings of the poet.

   Lyric poetry can be free or formal verse. In this unit, the teacher and students are going to explore a formal type of lyric poetry called the sonnet.

2. The teacher writes the word *sonnet* on the board, then puts the example sonnet up on the overhead screen.

   NOTE TO TEACHER: I generally begin a sonnet unit with "Portrait of a Machine" by Louis Untermeyer. The octave and sestet are physically separated on the page and the shift in tone between them is easy to discern. With grade 9 or 10 students, I have also had success with "The Railway Station" by Archibald Lampman and "Ozymandias" by Percy Bysshe Shelley.

3. The teacher reads the poem aloud to the class, then asks: What do you notice about this poem?

As the students offer their observations about the poem on the screen, the teacher begins recording a list of characteristics on the board. The teacher adds whatever is missing, then goes over each item to ensure that everyone understands:

- two parts, the first eight lines long and the second six lines long, for a total of fourteen lines
- rhyme scheme—abbaabba cdcdcd OR abbaabba cdecde
- regular meter—iambic pentameter (ten beats per line, repeating an unstressed-stressed pattern five times)

4. The teacher then asks the class: What is the poet saying in the first eight lines of the poem? *(In "Portrait of a Machine," it's how beautiful the machine is and how well it is working.)* And what is the poet saying in the last six lines of the poem? *(In "Portrait of a Machine," it's what the machine might be thinking and feeling about its master, Man. It hates us and enjoys the fact that we have become so dependent on machines and technology.)*

The teacher points out that in a sonnet of this type, there is a shift or contrast of some kind between the first eight lines, called the "octave" and the last six lines, called the "sestet." (These terms are written under the word *sonnet* on the board.) In "Portrait of a Machine," for example, the poet shifts from admiring the outward appearance of the machine to speculating darkly about its inner thoughts.

The teacher adds this final characteristic to the list on the board:

- a shift or contrast between the octave and the sestet (Petrarchan sonnet)

5. Students are instructed to copy the list from the board into their notes.

NOTE TO TEACHER: Depending on the grade and ability levels of your students and on the sonnets chosen for study, you may want to consider spending some time going over the differences between Petrarchan (Italian) and Elizabethan (Shakespearean) sonnets, and pointing out the various rhyme schemes students might encounter as they proceed through the unit:

   Petrarchan sonnet—octave (abbaabba or abbacddc) + sestet (efefef or efgefg)

There is a shift or contrast between the octave and sestet of a Petrarchan sonnet.

   Shakespearean sonnet—three quatrains (abbacddceffe or ababcdcdefef) + a couplet (gg)

The rhyming couplet at the end of a Shakespearean sonnet firmly concludes the poem, often by summing it up or by drawing a logical inference from the content of the preceding three quatrains.

ASSIGNMENT 2: CLOSE READING AND ANALYSIS OF A SONNET

1. Referring students to the example sonnet on the overhead screen, the teacher asks: What message, concern, or emotion is the poet expressing in this poem? *(i.e., What is the theme or main idea of the sonnet?)* The teacher then asks: How does the shift between the octave and the sestet underline or reinforce that theme or main idea?

The teacher records the students' best answers, either on the board or on the overhead transparency.

NOTE TO TEACHER: If you have included any descriptive sonnets in the study package, this would be a good time to mention to the class that sonnets are often written to celebrate the beauty of the natural world. These poems may have no message or concern to convey. They may simply be a sharing of the poet's perceptions and resulting appreciation of the world around him or her.

2. Teacher and students together perform a close reading of the example poem, going line by line and word by word to identify and label all the poetic devices they can find. Using three different colored markers (one per level of analysis), the teacher underlines each example with the appropriate color, then draws an arrow to the margin and identifies the device being used.

   In the case of an extended metaphor or multi-detail personification, more than one arrow may be drawn to the same label.

3. Students assemble in groups of three or four. Each group selects or is assigned a different sonnet from the teacher's list on which to focus.

   NOTE TO TEACHER: Not every poem on the list needs to be assigned for group work. It's recommended that you reserve a couple for students' summative work later in the unit.

4. The students in each group now read aloud their assigned poem, draw a line between lines 8 and 9 (or between lines 12 and 13 of a Shakespearean sonnet), and discuss the various shifts and contrasts that members can see between the octave and the sestet (or the role performed by the rhyming couplet of the Shakespearean sonnet). Each group member makes a personal note of the group's findings, either on his or her own copy of the poem or on a separate sheet of paper.

5. Each group member works independently to perform a close reading of the group's assigned poem. When done, the group reassembles so that members can share their findings and help one another to complete the work.

6. The teacher refers students once again to the example poem on the overhead screen and reviews with the class the main idea or theme of the poem, the shift that takes place between lines 8 and 9, and the ways in which the shift underlines or reinforces that main idea or theme.

7. Teacher and class now go through all the examples of devices identified earlier and select those that relate directly to the theme or main idea and contribute most strongly to the poem's effectiveness. These examples (there should be at least three) are highlighted, circled, or starred on the overhead transparency.

8. The teacher copies the examples onto the board, modeling the format to be used by students when quoting and citing lines of poetry. Leaving the overhead transparency on the screen for reference, the teacher then asks the students: *How does the poet's use of poetic devices make the sonnet more effective?*

9. Students take out their ANSWERING AN EFFECTIVENESS QUESTION handouts, and teacher and class together review the important elements to include when answering the question in Step 8. *(The following should be included: What does the example do, what does it help the reader to do, how does it relate to the theme/main idea of the poem, and how does it contribute to the overall effectiveness of the poem by giving it immediacy, vividness, evocativeness, and/or provocativeness?)*

10. Together, teacher and class discuss and analyze each of the examples on the board as the teacher or a student secretary records point-form notes containing the important elements for each one.

11. Students work together in their groups to select and analyze examples from each group's assigned sonnet, following the process just modeled by the teacher. Each group member copies the selected examples onto his or her own separate sheet of paper and makes personal notes based on the group's discussion. Each member's notes should then be checked by at least one other person in the group to ensure that all the important elements have been included.

12. *Next day:* Students jigsaw to form new groups containing one representative from each of four different previous groups. Group members take turns orally presenting their sonnet analyses to the rest of the group. The sonnets are first read aloud and then analyzed, using the personal notes each student made during the earlier group discussion. *(Each presentation should take approximately ten minutes, for a total of about forty to forty-five minutes.)*

ASSIGNMENT 3: SUMMATIVE PRODUCTS

NOTE TO TEACHER: When giving students a summative assignment based on the above unit, you may wish to remind them that while they are encouraged to have fun with it, the purpose of the activity is to let them demonstrate both their analytical skills and their understanding of the poem or poems just studied.

Some of the assignments listed below can be found elsewhere in this program:

Write a literary response—*see* "Write a Literary Response to a Poem" (Studying Poetry Part 5)
Write a letter to the poet—*see* "Write a Formal Letter" (*Wordsmithing*)
Write a literary essay—*see* Writing the Literary Essay (*Enjoying Literature*)

IN GRADE 9: Students may choose from a menu including three or more of the following:

• Complete and hand in a point-form sonnet analysis (using a different poem than in Assignment 2).
• Complete and hand in a written response (dialectical or personal) to a sonnet from the teacher's list.
• Create a visual representation of a sonnet from the teacher's list, showing both sides of the shift between lines 8 and 9. (When done, these can be posted on the wall for others to admire.)
• Write a letter to one of the poets from the teacher's list of sonnets, commenting on his or her use of the sonnet form and poetical devices.

IN GRADE 10: Students may choose from a menu including three or more of the following:

• Complete and hand in a written response (personal or analytical) to a sonnet from the teacher's list.
• Prepare and orally present a sonnet analysis (using a different poem than in Assignment 2).
• Write an original sonnet inspired by something in a different medium (for example, a TV ad).
• Complete and hand in a point-form sonnet analysis (using a different poem than in Assignment 2).

IN GRADE 11: Students may choose from a menu including three or more of the following:

• Complete and hand in a written response (personal or analytical) to a sonnet from the teacher's list (using a different poem than in Assignment 2).
• Prepare and orally present an analysis comparing a sonnet from the teacher's list to something in another medium (for example, a famous painting or song).
• Write an original sonnet inspired by the natural world.
• Translate a sonnet from the teacher's list into a different medium, being sure to represent both sides of the shift between lines 8 and 9 and to include at least two of the poet's selected literary devices.

IN GRADE 12: Students may choose from a menu including three or more of the following:

• Complete and hand in a written analytical response to a sonnet from the teacher's list (using a different poem than in Assignment 2).
• Complete and hand in a literary essay based on a sonnet from the teacher's list.
• Prepare and orally present an analysis comparing two sonnets from the teacher's list.
• Write an original sonnet on the same theme as a sonnet from the teacher's list.

STUDYING LYRIC POETRY: CREATIVE AND WRITING CHALLENGES

CHALLENGE 1. WRITE AN ORIGINAL LYRIC POEM BASED ON A NEWS ARTICLE

Instructions for Students:

1. Read the newspaper article supplied by the teacher. Select an emotion that would have been present in the situation described.

2. Now close your eyes and visualize the situation with your chosen emotion inside it. What shape would the emotion take? What color would it be? How would it move? What would it do? If it could speak, what would it say? What would it look like, smell like, feel like, taste like, and sound like? Brainstorm words and phrases to describe this emotion and how it would behave in that situation.

3. Now choose one or two phrases or short sentences from the article to incorporate into your poem. Write them out.

4. Write a rough draft of your poem. It should be about ten lines long. Edit your draft to be sure you have included at least one poetic device from each of the three levels of analysis. Look at each word of each line. Does it sound like the emotion you are trying to portray? Are all your action words strong and interesting? Does your poem paint a vivid word picture?

5. Share your poem with a classmate. Get feedback and suggestions for improvement. Then polish up a good draft and hand it in for teacher assessment.

    NOTE TO TEACHER: *I wrote this poem in response to an article about a courtroom trial and used it as an exemplar when challenging my students.*

> Sticky and red as the blood he shed,
> Anger spatters the courtroom walls.
> > *Three dead, one injured. . . .*
> It bursts from the gallery,
> Drips from the ceiling,
> Onto the judge's desk.
> > *He shows no remorse.*
> Outrage flares, furnace-hot;
> The gavel smashes down.
>
> Justice is a dare, accepted.

A. F. Marks

CHALLENGE 2. TRANSLATE A QUOTATION ABOUT POETRY INTO A MEDIA PRODUCT

NOTE TO TEACHER: *Before issuing this challenge, you will need about ten interesting quotations about the nature of poetry. They aren't difficult to find—just go online to www.quotegarden.com/poetry/ and pick a bouquet. List the quotations on a handout under the instructions to students, below.*

Choose one of the quotations about poetry below and use it as the basis for a creative response. Your response may take the form of a story, a poem, a video, a photo album or montage, a drawing, or whatever else occurs to you.

Whichever form you choose, it must be accompanied by a 250-word commentary, explaining how this form and this product express your feelings about poetry and relate to the quotation you selected.

Two days will be selected as "gallery days," when you will place your response on display for peer and teacher assessment.

CHALLENGE 3. USE POETIC DEVICES TO WRITE DESCRIPTIVELY (100 TO 250 WORDS)

1. Write a lyric poem or a descriptive paragraph about the relationship between a person and an object. *(For example, you could write about a man and his motorcycle, a boy and a pizza, a woman and a credit card, a chef and his or her favorite frying pan, and so forth.)* Give the piece a one-word title naming the emotion felt by the person.

2. Using simile, metaphor, and imagery, describe a place from two different points of view. *(For instance, describe a hospital corridor from the point of view of a patient and then the same corridor from the point of view of a family member visiting the patient.)*

3. Personify something in your house. Give it a purpose in life that nobody would ever suspect. Now write a monologue from the point of view of the chosen item, describing in colorful and connotative language how it feels about YOU!

4. Imagine a race. Perhaps it's a race to answer the phone before your younger brother or sister does. Perhaps it's a race to take the pot off the stove burner before the soup boils over or to get downstairs and put the fabric softener into the washing machine before the rinse cycle ends. Describe this race, using sound devices such as alliteration, sibilance, and onomatopoeia.

5. Write a poem or paragraph about a change *(such as from ugly to beautiful, useful to useless, hot to cold, and so on)*. Describe this transformation using poetic devices so that the reader can vividly imagine being there and witnessing the change as it takes place.

6. Write a poem in honor of your favorite meal. Call it "Ode to _____" and use plenty of sensory details. Make it sound so delicious that the reader gains weight while reading your poem.

   NOTE TO TEACHER: For each of these written assignments, students will need to be given time in class for sharing and peer-assisted revision before they finish editing and polishing their final draft for submission.

Studying Poetry Part 4
Analyzing Dramatic Poetry
"Ulysses" by Alfred Lord Tennyson

✍ YOU WILL NEED

- Copies of the dramatic poem or soliloquy to be studied (1 of each per student)
  OR
- A class set of an anthology that contains the dramatic poem or soliloquy
  PLUS
- SPR 2–LEVELS OF ANALYSIS: POETRY (class set, if not already handed out)
- SPR 8–LEVELS OF ANALYSIS: EFFECTIVENESS (class set, if not already handed out)
- SPR 4 to SPR 6–ANSWERING AN EFFECTIVENESS QUESTION (class sets, if not already handed out)
- SPR 21–ULYSSES, by Alfred Lord Tennyson (class set, optional)
  AND
- A copy of the dramatic poem or soliloquy to be studied, on an overhead transparency
- Overhead projector and colored overhead markers

PURPOSE

In a close examination of a dramatic poem, students will practice using correct terminology as they discuss aspects of the poem and consider and respond to questions on all three levels of analysis. In the process, they will come to appreciate how powerful poetry is as a medium for the communication of thoughts and emotions.

ASSIGNMENT 1: INTRODUCTION TO DRAMATIC POETRY

1. The teacher explains to the class that there are different kinds or classifications of poetry: narrative poetry tells a story, lyric poetry conveys the thoughts and feelings of the poet, and dramatic poetry is a monologue expressing the thoughts and feelings of a character called "the speaker." In this unit, the teacher and students are going to explore dramatic poetry.

NOTE TO TEACHER: If your class has already studied a Shakespearean play, then you might want to reach back and make the connection between dramatic poetry and drama. If your class is presently studying a Shakespearean play, then this unit can be modified and inserted the first time you want them to perform a close analysis of a long speech or a soliloquy.

2. The teacher projects the dramatic monologue to be studied on the overhead screen and points out to the class that the word *dramatic* means the poem was written to be acted out, as though upon a stage. The teacher then reads the poem aloud to the class, with as much feeling and as many dramatic flourishes as possible.

3. The teacher then asks the students what they notice about the form of the poem. *(Students might note that the lines don't rhyme but they're all the same length, ten beats per line, alternating stressed and unstressed syllables.)* The teacher writes the phrase "blank verse" on the board and explains that this is the standard format for dramatic poetry, including Shakespeare's plays, and the common meter for blank verse is iambic pentameter.

   The teacher selects a line from the poem on the overhead screen and uses a marker to put a short horizontal line above each unstressed syllable and a forward slash mark above each stressed syllable. A longer vertical line is put after each slash mark to show that there are five repetitions of the iambic pattern (thus putting the "pent" in pentameter). The teacher points out that what s/he has just done is called "scanning."

   At the teacher's discretion, the students may practice scanning several more lines of the poem to confirm that the meter remains unchanged throughout.

4. The teacher lists on the board the characteristics of a dramatic poem and instructs students to copy this information into their notebooks. The list should include, in some form, the following:

   • poet is acting the role of a character, expressing the character's thoughts and feelings
   • speaker may address the reader (or audience) directly, may be speaking to another character, or may simply be thinking aloud
   • written in blank verse (no rhyme scheme, iambic pentameter)
   • no prescribed length
   • is both a poem and a dramatic speech, revealing information about the speaker while pulling a reaction from the listener

5. Referring students to the dramatic monologue on the overhead screen, the teacher asks: When you're watching a film or a play, how do you know that an actor is being effective? *(Students may note that s/he makes you believe s/he really is the character, you begin to have positive or negative feelings about the character, everything the character says and does reveals something about him or her, and the like.)*

   The teacher explains to the students that just as real people are always revealing things about themselves by what they say and do, a well-scripted and well-acted character will reveal things about himself or herself through both speech and behavior.

6. The teacher then asks: How do you know that a poem has been effective? (Students can be referred to the list on the LEVELS OF ANALYSIS: POETRY sheet: an effective poem uses literary devices to create immediacy, vividness, evocativeness, and provocativeness.)

   The teacher explains that in order to analyze and appreciate a dramatic monologue, the students are going to have to approach it from two directions at once, treating it as both poetry and drama.

7. The teacher writes the heading *Drama* on the board and asks the class: Who is the speaker of this poem? *(That is, who is the poet pretending to be? Whose thoughts and feelings are being expressed in the monologue?)* What do the speaker's words reveal about both the character and his or her situation?

   As students provide responses to these questions, the teacher begins a point-form note under the heading on the board, supplying additional background information if necessary about the character. *(This would be a good opportunity to model for students the correct format for quoting and citing lines of poetry in support of a drawn inference.)*

8. The teacher then writes the heading *Poetry* on the board and asks: What message, concern, or emotion is the speaker expressing in this poem? *(That is, what is the theme or main idea of the poem?)* As students respond to this question, the teacher begins a point-form note under the heading on the board.

9. The teacher then sums up the focus of the poem study:

Students will be examining how the techniques employed by the poet simultaneously enhance the effectiveness of the poetry and strengthen or underline the dramatic elements of the monologue.

ASSIGNMENT 2: PERFORM A CLOSE READING

1. The teacher reminds the students that close reading involves going line by line and word by word to identify and label as many poetic devices as possible, on all three levels of analysis. Students should be directed to their copies of the LEVELS OF ANALYSIS: POETRY handout for a list of the various devices.

2. If the poem under study is on a photocopied handout, students may be instructed to highlight each example and draw an arrow to a note in the margin. If the poem is in an anthology, then students will need to copy the examples they find onto a separate sheet of paper, indicating for each which device has been used. (Words and phrases that are "multi-tasking" should be copied out multiple times, once for each device they represent.)

3. Students pair up or form groups of three and proceed to conduct a close reading of the poem (or soliloquy). Each student should be sure to make a personal copy of the group's work.

4. Groups can share their most powerful examples in a teacher-led whole-class discussion.

ASSIGNMENT 3: ANALYZE THE POEM

1. The teacher writes on the board the focus question that will inform the class's analysis of the dramatic poem under study:

How do the poetical devices used by the author make this dramatic monologue more effective as both a character's spoken lines and a work of poetry by giving it immediacy, vividness, evocativeness, and/or provocativeness? *(Pick the choices that apply.)*

Students reassemble in different groups of four and take out their notes on the poem under study.

2. The teacher explains that while any poem is a treasure trove of poetic devices, the purpose of analysis is to determine the answer to a question. Crime scene investigators analyze evidence to discover who committed the crime and how—but not all the evidence leads to an answer. Meteorologists analyze data to find out what the weather is likely to be tomorrow—but they have a lot more information than they need for a local forecast. If the students are going to analyze this poem to answer the question on the board, then they first need to identify and isolate their most relevant findings.

3. The teacher instructs the class to begin by going through all the examples of devices they've identified and selecting the ones that reveal the most about the character and at the same time contribute most strongly to the effectiveness of the poem. Each group should be able to find at least five to eight strong examples in a short poem and proportionately more in a longer poem.

4. Students work in their groups to identify the examples they will be using for their analysis of the poem, testing each one by comparing it with the question on the board. Each group member then stars or circles the selected examples in his or her notes.

5. The groups dissolve. Each student folds a clean sheet of lined paper lengthwise to form two columns, headed *Example* and *Analysis*, and copies the selected examples from his or her notes into the first column. Referring to his or her copy of the LEVELS OF ANALYSIS: EFFECTIVENESS handout, the student writes a point-form note in the second column for each of the examples, explaining what the example does, what it helps the reader to do, how it contributes to the overall effectiveness of the poem, and how it enhances or reinforces the dramatic aspects of the monologue.

6. Students can pair up or get into groups of three to compare notes and offer one another suggestions for improvement.

ASSIGNMENT 4: SUMMATIVE PRODUCTS

NOTE TO TEACHER: Most of the assignments listed below can be found in other parts of this program:

Write an effectiveness paragraph—*see* "Build Your Toolkit" (Studying Poetry Part 1)
Write a literary response—*see* "Write a Literary Response to a Poem" (Studying Poetry Part 5)
Write a letter to the poet—*see* "Write a Formal Letter" (*Wordsmithing*)
Write a short story—*see* Getting Started (*Story Crafting*)
Write a literary essay—*see* Writing the Literary Essay (*Enjoying Literature*)
Write a report—*see* "Write a Report" (*Wordsmithing*)

When giving students a summative assignment based on the above unit, you may wish to remind them that while they are encouraged to have fun with it, the purpose of the activity is to let them demonstrate both their analytical skills and their understanding of the poem or poems just studied. Each submitted assignment should therefore include reference to both the dramatic and the poetical elements of the selected work(s).

IN GRADE 9: Students may choose from a menu including three or more of the following:

• Complete and hand in a paragraph about the effectiveness of one of the devices used in the poem.
• Complete and hand in a written response (dialectical or personal) to the poem.
• Create a visual representation of the poem, illustrating the devices used by the poet.
• Imagine that a film is being based on this poem and create a poster or radio promo for it.
• Compose a diary entry by the speaker of the poem.
• Write a letter to the author of the poem, commenting on the dramatic effectiveness of his or her use of poetical devices.

IN GRADE 10: Students may choose from a menu including three or more of the following:

• Complete and hand in a written response (personal or analytical) to the poem.
• Imagine that the speaker has visited a psychotherapist or has been arrested and write up the resulting report.
• Memorize and perform the poem for the rest of the class in a way that demonstrates its poetical aspects.
• Respond to the poem in writing as though it were a blog post. (Your response should be at least 200 words long.)

IN GRADE 11: Students may choose from a menu including three or more of the following:

• Complete and hand in a written response (personal or analytical) to the poem.
• Write a scene around this poem, using blank verse and giving lines to at least one other character.
• Write a short story using the speaker as the main character.
• Reimagine the poem in video or graphic novel format.

IN GRADE 12: Students may choose from a menu including three or more of the following:

• Complete and hand in a written analytical response to the poem.
• Complete and hand in a literary essay based on the poem.
• Conduct and write up a comparative analysis between this poem and another one with the same theme.

- Prepare and participate in a fishbowl discussion about the poem in response to the focus question posed in Assignment 3.
- Compose a dramatic monologue using the same poetical devices as the poem under study.

TEACHING "ULYSSES" BY ALFRED LORD TENNYSON

NOTE TO TEACHER: I have enjoyed teaching this poem to classes at all grade levels by tweaking the assignments outlined above as follows:

GRADE 9

The focus: The drama of the past, Ulysses as a legendary hero.

Before beginning the poem: Tell students the story of the Trojan War and the *Odyssey*. Show a film or a couple of film excerpts to illustrate the part played by Odysseus in winning that war and the obstacles he had to overcome in order to get home to Ithaca afterward. (He was away for a total of twenty years.) Point out that Odysseus was no ordinary Greek general. Besides being brave, he was a shrewd negotiator and a great talker, able to persuade people to do and believe whatever he wanted them to. Odysseus was a favorite of Athena, the goddess of wisdom and strategy in battle.

In whole-class discussion, identify the defining characteristics of a hero *(for instance, strength, courage, intelligence, selflessness, devotion to the cause of justice, self-sacrifice, and so on)* and list them on the board. Elicit and record a further list of people whom the students would consider to be heroes, along with how and where these individuals have shown their heroic qualities. Then ask students: What happens to a hero when everything is calm and peaceful and the hero is no longer needed?

Begin the poem: Explain that Ulysses, the speaker of this dramatic monologue, finds himself in exactly this situation. He's won a war, fought his way home, reclaimed by force his wife and his kingdom—and for the past three years he has ruled peacefully, growing progressively more restless and dissatisfied with his life. Tell students that the focus of this poetry study and the question they will be trying to answer is this: *Is heroism a blessing or a curse?*

As the unit proceeds, relate everything back to the focus question: What are the poetical devices that emphasize the heroic nature of Ulysses's past and the unhappiness of his present situation? How realistic are his expectations for the future? Will it ever be possible for Ulysses to recapture the thrilling feeling of being a hero? In the end, was it worth risking his life?

The summative assignment is a written or creative response to the focus question:

- Write an opinion paragraph explaining why you think Ulysses will or will not succeed at the end.
- Complete and hand in a written response to the poem (dialectical or personal) focusing on how Ulysses remembers his heroic past deeds.
- Create a visual representation of a scene from the poem, illustrating the poetical devices used by the poet to reflect or emphasize the heroic nature of Ulysses's past life.
- Compose two diary entries for Ulysses, one written just after he's won back his kingdom and the other one written after a year or two of ruling it.
- Imagine that you were a soldier who served under Ulysses during the Trojan War. You've been home for ten years and have just received an invitation to join him on an adventure. What will your response be? (Be sure to give reasons for your answer.)

GRADE 10

The focus: The drama within the family, Ulysses as a father.

Before beginning the poem: Tell students the story of the Trojan War and the *Odyssey*. Show a film or a couple of film excerpts to illustrate the part played by Odysseus in winning that war and the obstacles he had to overcome in order to get home to Ithaca afterward. (He was away for a total of twenty years.) Point out that Odysseus was no ordinary Greek general. Besides being brave and a fierce fighter, he was a shrewd negotiator and a great talker, able to persuade people to do and believe whatever he wanted them to. Odysseus was a favorite of Athena, the goddess of wisdom and strategy in battle. He was widely considered to be a great hero.

Ask the class: What sort of father do you think a hero like Ulysses would have been? If he were your father, how well do you think you would have gotten along?

Now tell the students what happens to Ulysses's wife and son while he is away for twenty years:

> *Telemachus grows up in a single-parent home, raised by his mother and her handmaidens. Penelope remains loyal to her husband and never loses faith that he will return. Eventually, a mob of neighboring rulers invade and occupy Ulysses's palace, insisting that he must be dead and pressuring her to choose one of them as her new husband (and scheming to kill Telemachus once he is old enough to take the throne himself). Athena removes Telemachus from danger by helping him go in search of his long-lost father. Meanwhile, the pressure on Penelope to remarry keeps increasing. For years, she manages to keep the mob at bay. Then, just as it appears she is cornered, Ulysses comes back, in disguise. With the help of Telemachus and the loyal palace staff, he massacres the intruders and reclaims his rightful place as king of Ithaca. But he's been away for a long time. Ulysses's son was an infant when he left for Troy. Now Telemachus is a grown man. Penelope has been ruling the kingdom and has been forced to acquire kingly skills. This is not the same family as the one he left behind twenty years earlier.*

Begin the poem: Read the poem (with dramatic flourishes) all the way through, then direct students' attention to the section in which Ulysses talks about Telemachus. Ask the students: How do we know that Ulysses is disappointed by the way his son has turned out? What evidence does Ulysses see of the "womanly" influences in Telemachus's upbringing? How do you think Telemachus would have turned out if Ulysses had been around while the boy was growing up?

Tell students that the focus of this poetry study and the question they will be trying to answer is this: *What qualities does Ulysses reveal in this monologue that would make him a good or a bad father? How do the poetical devices chosen by the author reinforce or emphasize these qualities?*

As the unit proceeds: Relate everything back to the focus question, above.

The summative assignment is a written or creative response to the focus question:

- Complete and hand in a written response to the poem (personal or analytical).
- Write two blog entries posted by Telemachus, the first on the day after his father returns and the second one a year or two later.
- Imagine that Ulysses, Penelope, and Telemachus have gone for family counseling. Write up the resulting report.
- Ulysses "damns his son with faint praise." Rewrite this section of the poem so that it expresses what Ulysses is really feeling.
- Write a letter from Telemachus to his father, composed the night before Ulysses departs on his new adventure.

GRADE 11

The focus: The drama of contrast, Ulysses as a king versus Ulysses as an adventurer.

Before beginning the poem: Tell students the story of the Trojan War and the *Odyssey*. Show a film or a couple of film excerpts to illustrate the part played by Odysseus in winning that war and the obstacles he had to overcome in order to get home to Ithaca afterward. (He was away for a total of twenty years.) Point out that Odysseus was no ordinary Greek general. Besides being brave and a fierce fighter, he was a shrewd negotiator and a great talker, able to persuade people to do and believe whatever he wanted them to. Odysseus was a favorite of Athena, the goddess of wisdom and strategy in battle. After the war he was widely considered to be a great hero. Before the war, however, he had a young wife and an infant son; he ruled a peaceful kingdom; and he considered himself to be a lucky man. He didn't want to go to war, but he had sworn an oath and had to keep his promise.

Ask the class: Ulysses went from being a peacetime king to being a great war hero, then back to being a peacetime king, two very difficult transitions. Which one do you think would have been the harder, and why?

Begin the poem: Explain to the students that this poem begins three years after Ulysses's return to Ithaca. For three years he has been ruling a peaceful kingdom—and becoming progressively more restless and dissatisfied with his life.

Read the poem aloud, stopping between sections to discuss and clarify the attitudes and emotions being expressed. Draw comparisons between Ulysses and Telemachus and chart them on the board.

Introduce the focus question to guide students' close reading and analysis: *How do the poetical devices used in this poem underline the contrasts between Ulysses the peacetime king and Ulysses the war hero and adventurer, and between Ulysses the former hero and Telemachus the never-been hero?*

Students can work in pairs or groups of three to conduct a close reading and analysis of the poem, with each person making his or her own personal notes. In whole-class discussion, students can share their findings. Particularly strong examples can be identified and missing information added to students' notes for use in one of the summative products.

The summative product is a written or creative response to the focus question:

- Complete and hand in a written analytical response or a literary essay based on the poem.
- Create a visual representation of the contrasts contained in the poem.
- Write a dramatic poem in response to this one, but with Telemachus as the main character.
- Compose a scene of dialogue in which prewar Ulysses is speaking with postwar Ulysses.

GRADE 12

The focus: The drama within the character, Ulysses as a man.

Before beginning the poem: Tell students the story of the Trojan War and the *Odyssey*. Show a film or a couple of film excerpts to illustrate the part played by Odysseus in winning that war and the obstacles he had to overcome in order to get home to Ithaca afterward. (He was away for a total of twenty years.) Point out that Odysseus was no ordinary Greek general. Besides being brave and a fierce fighter, he was a shrewd negotiator and a great talker, able to persuade people to do and believe whatever he wanted them to. Odysseus was a favorite of Athena, the goddess of wisdom and strategy in battle. After the war he was widely considered to be a great hero. Before the war, however, he had a young wife and an infant son; he ruled a peaceful kingdom; and he considered himself to be a lucky man. He didn't want to go to war, but he had sworn an oath and had to keep his promise. Twenty years later, he returns to a wife and son who are strangers to him and a way of life that gives him no pleasure.

Begin the poem: Read the poem aloud in class, stopping between sections to discuss and clarify the thoughts and emotions being expressed. Draw comparisons as you go between Ulysses the war hero and adventurer and Ulysses the miserable peacetime king and chart them on the board. Elicit from students and record on the board all the different ways Ulysses might possibly be feeling toward his son. Ask the class: Is Ulysses running toward a new adventure or just away from the dreariness of his life on Ithaca? How do you know?

Introduce the focus question to guide students' close reading and analysis: *How do the poetical devices used in this poem underline the changes that have taken place in Ulysses as a result of the Trojan War? How complete are they? Is there still a king underneath that war hero?*

Students can work independently, in pairs, or in groups of three to conduct a close reading and analysis of the poem, with each person making his or her own personal notes. In whole-class discussion, students can share their findings. Particularly strong examples of poetical devices can be identified and any missing information can be added to students' notes for use in one of the summative products.

The summative product is a written, oral, or creative response to the focus question:

- Complete and hand in a written analytical response to the poem.
- Complete and hand in a literary essay based on the poem.
- Conduct and write up a comparative analysis between this poem and another one with the same theme (past glory interfering with present happiness).
- Prepare and participate in a fishbowl discussion about the poem, in response to the focus question.
- Imagine a character who is unhappy with his or her life and wishing to escape from it, then compose an original dramatic monologue with this character as the speaker. Be sure to use a variety of poetical devices to underline the character's thoughts and emotions.

ULYSSES

It little profits that an idle king,
By this still hearth, among these barren crags,
Match'd with an aged wife, I mete and dole
Unequal laws unto a savage race,
That hoard, and sleep, and feed, and know not me.
I cannot rest from travel; I will drink
Life to the lees: all times I have enjoy'd
Greatly, have suffer'd greatly, both with those
That loved me, and alone; on shore, and when
Thro' scudding drifts the rainy Hyades
Vext the dim sea: I am become a name;
For always roaming with a hungry heart
Much have I seen and known; cities of men
And manners, climates, councils, governments,
Myself not least, but honour'd of them all;
And drunk delight of battle with my peers,
Far on the ringing plains of windy Troy.
I am a part of all that I have met;
Yet all experience is an arch wherethro'
Gleams that untravell'd world, whose margin fades
For ever and for ever when I move.
How dull it is to pause, to make an end,
To rust unburnish'd, not to shine in use!
As tho' to breathe were life. Life piled on life
Were all too little, and of one to me
Little remains: but every hour is saved
From that eternal silence, something more,
A bringer of new things; and vile it were
For some three suns to store and hoard myself,
And this gray spirit yearning in desire
To follow knowledge like a sinking star,
Beyond the utmost bound of human thought.

      This is my son, mine own Telemachus,
To whom I leave the sceptre and the isle—
Well-loved of me, discerning to fulfil
This labour, by slow prudence to make mild
A rugged people, and thro' soft degrees
Subdue them to the useful and the good.
Most blameless is he, centred in the sphere
Of common duties, decent not to fail
In offices of tenderness, and pay
Meet adoration to my household gods,

When I am gone. He works his work, I mine.
        There lies the port; the vessel puffs her sail;
There gloom the dark broad seas. My mariners,
Souls that have toil'd, and wrought, and thought with me—
That ever with a frolic welcome took
The thunder and the sunshine, and opposed
Free hearts, free foreheads—you and I are old;
Old age hath yet his honour and his toil;
Death closes all: but something ere the end,
Some work of noble note, may yet be done,
Not unbecoming men that strove with Gods.
The lights begin to twinkle from the rocks:
The long day wanes: the slow moon climbs: the deep
Moans round with many voices. Come, my friends,
'Tis not too late to seek a newer world.
Push off, and sitting well in order smite
The sounding furrows; for my purpose holds
To sail beyond the sunset, and the baths
Of all the western stars, until I die.
It may be that the gulfs will wash us down:
It may be we shall touch the Happy Isles,
And see the great Achilles, whom we knew.
Tho' much is taken, much abides; and tho'
We are not now that strength which in old days
Moved earth and heaven, that which we are, we are;
One equal temper of heroic hearts,
Made weak by time and fate, but strong in will
To strive, to seek, to find, and not to yield.

Alfred Lord Tennyson

Studying Poetry Part 5
Writing a Literary Response

✍ **YOU WILL NEED**

- A short poem that the class has not already read (photocopied or in the anthology; class set)
- A blank overhead transparency
- Overhead projector and markers
- SPR 22–WRITING A RESPONSE sheet (class set)
- SPR 23–WRITING AN ANALYTICAL RESPONSE sheet (class set)
- SPR 24–PROOFREAD WITH A PARTNER: DIALECTICAL RESPONSE CHECKLIST
- SPR 25–PROOFREAD WITH A PARTNER: PERSONAL RESPONSE CHECKLIST
- SPR 26–PROOFREAD WITH A PARTNER: ANALYTICAL RESPONSE CHECKLIST
- SPR 27–ASSESSMENT CHECKLIST: DIALECTICAL RESPONSE
- SPR 28–ASSESSMENT CHECKLIST: PERSONAL RESPONSE
- SPR 29–ASSESSMENT CHECKLIST: ANALYTICAL RESPONSE
                                            PLUS
- A class set of an anthology and a list of poems already studied from the anthology

---

PURPOSE

As students practice writing three different kinds of responses to poetry—dialectical, personal, and analytical—they will be honing both their writing and their critical thinking skills.

INTRODUCTION

The teacher explains to the class that there are many different ways that a reader can respond to a poem, including putting it down and forgetting about it. In this section of the module, however, students are going to be learning and practicing how to create a response that can be shared with others.

NOTE TO THE TEACHER: There are three types of response in this assignment. In order of increasing difficulty, they are a dialectical response, a personal response, and an analytical response. Select the one(s) that would best suit the needs, abilities, and interests of your students.

ASSIGNMENT 1: WRITE A DIALECTICAL RESPONSE TO A POEM

MODELING

1. The teacher explains to the class that the simplest form of response is the dialectical or "double entry" journal in which the reader records his or her strong immediate impressions of the poem while reading it.

2. The blank transparency is put on the overhead projector. With a marker, the teacher draws a vertical line down the middle of the transparency, creating two columns of equal width. The teacher then prints a header at the top of each column: *Quotation* and *Response*.

3. Each student receives a copy of the example poem (or is directed to it in the anthology) and follows along as the teacher begins reading it aloud.

   The teacher stops after reading an interesting line or phrase and explains why it seemed to jump off the page at him or her: *the vivid description painted a picture in his or her mind, or the metaphor was especially powerful, or this situation reminded the teacher of one from his or her own past, and so on.*

4. The teacher then copies the line or phrase into the left-hand column of the transparency, modeling the correct format for extracting and citing quotations from a text, and proceeds to record his or her response to the quoted text in the right-hand column, elaborating with some detail the explanation given to the class a moment earlier.

GUIDED PRACTICE

1. The teacher now instructs the students to each take a clean sheet of lined paper, fold it vertically in half, and print the headings *Quotation* and *Response* over the resulting two columns.

2. Working independently, each student finishes reading the poem, recording his or her immediate responses to it in the form of a dialectical journal, as modeled by the teacher.

   Students should be instructed to select and respond to at least three separate quotations, filling one side of the page. The teacher circulates meanwhile, offering encouragement and assistance as needed. *(Allow up to twenty minutes for this exercise.)*

3. Students form groups of four or five to share and compare their responses and offer one another constructive suggestions for improvement. *(Allow up to ten minutes.)*

PRACTICE

1. Each student now chooses either a poem already studied or a new one from the anthology.

2. The student divides another clean sheet of lined paper in half lengthwise and proceeds to create a dialectical journal, filling at least one side of the page with correctly formatted quotations and detailed personal responses. *(Allow up to thirty minutes.)*

PRODUCT

1. Each student receives a copy of the peer-editing sheet (SPR 24). The teacher goes over each item with the class to ensure that students understand what they will be expected to produce.

2. *Homework:* That night, each student reads over the peer-editing sheet and his or her dialectical journal, expanding the responses with additional detail if necessary before recopying the journal onto a fresh sheet of paper. The student also checks to ensure that each quotation in the completed draft is correctly copied, formatted, and cited.

3. The finished product may be turned in for formative or summative assessment.

(See "Completing the Final Draft, All Responses," below.)

ASSIGNMENT 2: WRITE A PERSONAL RESPONSE TO A POEM

MODELING AND GUIDED PRACTICE

1. The teacher points out to the class that a written personal response is much more than just saying whether or not one likes the poem. The reader also has to be able to explain WHY s/he feels that way, WHAT about the poem is effective or ineffective, and HOW the story connects to the reader's own life. At the same time, students need to be aware that a personal response is not the answer to an effectiveness question.

2. The blank transparency is put on the overhead projector. With a marker, the teacher draws a box or circle in the middle, divides the rest of the transparency into three sections, and labels them: *Form and Sound, Comparison,* and *Ideas.* The teacher explains that while reading the poem, s/he is going to use this "placemat" to classify and record interesting quotations and his or her immediate strong responses to them.

3. Each student receives a copy of the example poem (or is directed to it in the anthology) and follows along as the teacher begins reading it aloud.

4. The teacher stops after reading an interesting line or phrase and explains how s/he is feeling right now and why: *pleasantly surprised by an interesting or unusual comparison, sympathetic to the speaker who is describing his estranged son, and so forth.*

5. The teacher then identifies what about the line or phrase has made him or her feel that way and copies it into the appropriate section of the placemat on the transparency, modeling the correct format for extracting and citing quotations from text. The teacher proceeds to record his or her response to the quotation in point form just below it, elaborating with some detail the explanation given to the class a moment earlier: *The father has no other family left, and the words he uses to describe his son make it clear how cruelly this child treats him and how lonely and afraid it makes him feel. Nobody wants to die alone.*

6. Students are instructed to take out a clean sheet of paper and create their own three-section placemat, leaving a fourth space in the middle. Working in groups of four, students are to continue reading the poem, monitoring and discussing their reactions to it and recording both the relevant quotations and the students' responses to them in the appropriate spaces on their placemats. The teacher circulates, offering encouragement and assistance where needed. *(Allow up to fifteen minutes for this exercise.)*

7. Each student now receives a copy of the WRITING A RESPONSE sheet, and the teacher and class go over it together, identifying and discussing the questions that relate to the quotation/reaction recorded on the exemplar placemat. The teacher expands the recorded material, adding further detail and explanation to answer the questions as the whole class discussion progresses.

8. The teacher explains that what they have just done is the PLANNING stage. The next step will be to create the OUTLINE for their response.

The teacher begins the process by picking from the handout the prompt question that generated the greatest amount of animated discussion. The question is copied into the circle or square in the middle of the placemat, and the teacher explains that the finished response is going to be the answer to that question.

PRACTICE

1. Students are instructed to choose for their response one of the poems already studied.

2. Working independently, each student takes a clean sheet of paper, creates a new placemat, and follows the steps modeled and practiced earlier to plan his or her personal response.

3. Each student then considers the list of prompt questions, makes further detailed notes, and finally selects the prompt question that relates most strongly and directly to his or her reaction to the text. This question that the student's response is going to answer is then copied into the space in the middle of his or her placemat.

4. If time permits, students can pair up and compare notes. Partners can offer each other constructive suggestions for improvement.

5. *Homework:* That night, each student goes over his or her notes and uses a colored marker to highlight the material—points, explanations, and quotations—that relates most strongly to the selected prompt question. This is the content that will be included in the finished response. The student copies the prompt question and the highlighted portions of his or her notes onto a fresh sheet of paper.

PRODUCT

1. Working independently in class, each student divides up his or her notes and quotations from the night before into paragraphs and proceeds to write a first-draft personal response in sentence and paragraph form.

2. Students now pair up with different partners and read each other's responses. Reading partners may offer suggestions for improved wording and organization of ideas but should not actually make changes to the other author's work.

3. *Homework:* That night, each student reads over his or her draft response and makes any necessary changes or improvements before recopying the response onto a fresh sheet of paper. The finished product may be turned in for formative or summative assessment.

(See "Completing the Final Draft, All Responses," below.)

WRITING A RESPONSE

WHAT IS A RESPONSE?

A response is a thoughtful and organized reaction to a piece of literature. In high school, students are asked to write two different kinds of essay-style responses.

A PERSONAL RESPONSE

A personal response is just what its name suggests—your personal reaction to the poem that you have just read. But it has to be a *thoughtful* reaction. "Wow, this is a great poem!" is just the beginning of your response. You now have to do the following:

THINK ABOUT THE WORK

- Why is this a great (or not-so-great) poem? What parts of it were really effective, which were ineffective, and why?
- Does it remind you of other poems you've read? How?
- What message do you think the poet wants the reader to get from reading this poem?

RELATE THE WORK TO YOURSELF

- Which parts of the poem did you like, and why?
- Which parts didn't you like? Why?
- How did reading this poem make you feel? Why?
- Does this poem remind you of anything that has happened to someone you know? Or of something that happened to you when you were younger?
- If you could rewrite any part of this poem, what part would it be? How would you make it different? Why?
- If you could speak with the poet, what would you like to say to him or her? Why?

PICK A QUOTATION FROM THE WORK AND RELATE IT TO YOURSELF

- Why did you choose this quotation? How does it relate to your feelings or your life?
- What do you think is the purpose of this quotation? Why do you think the poet chose to include it in the finished poem?

The teacher will tell you when assigning the response how long he or she wants it to be and whether you are to base it on a quotation or on the entire poem.

A FORMAL RESPONSE

A formal response is also called an "analytical response." Unlike the personal response, it isn't about your personal feelings or memories triggered by the poem or piece of literature. It's about the things that make the writing *work*. A formal response lets you show the teacher your critical thinking skills.

(continued on other side)

THE WRITING PROCESS

Whether personal or formal, any piece of writing that is to be turned in for marking must be put through the writing process:

PLANNING (sometimes called prewriting) is the stage of gathering information and organizing it. You might use a chart, a web, a concept map, or a Venn diagram to put your impressions or supported opinions in order. Then you must **OUTLINE THE RESPONSE**, either using a template supplied by your teacher or laying out the information in some arrangement or sequence that makes it meaningful for the reader.

Write out your **FIRST DRAFT**. It doesn't have to be perfect. Just get the information down on the page in sentence and paragraph form, being sure you haven't left anything out.

Now **REVISE THE FIRST DRAFT**. Make sure it has a beginning, a middle, and an end and that everything in it is on topic and in the most effective order. Does anything else need to be added? Should something be left out? Would it read better if you rearranged parts of it? Check the assessment rubric to ensure that you've included everything the teacher will be looking for when he or she marks your response. That's what revising is about—format and completion. When you're done, recopy the entire response as your SECOND DRAFT.

EDIT AND POLISH THE SECOND DRAFT. Now you are looking for:
- sentences that are incomplete or don't make sense
- words that have been left out or need to be left out
- words that have been incorrectly spelled (don't rely on your computer's spellchecker—it can't tell the difference between "again" and "a gain," but you can!)
- verb tenses that don't make sense
- symbols (&) or abbreviations (etc.) that need to be written out in full
- commas, apostrophes, and capital letters that are missing or out of place

When you're sure the response is as grammatically correct as you can make it, copy it out one last time as your **FINAL DRAFT**. Be sure to attach your assessment rubric, edited first draft, or whatever else your teacher has requested as part of the submission package.

ASSIGNMENT 3: WRITE AN ANALYTICAL RESPONSE TO A POEM

MODELING

1. The teacher hands out copies of WRITING AN ANALYTICAL RESPONSE to the class and goes over it with the students, discussing it item by item to ensure that the process is understood.

   The teacher should point out to the students that an analytical response is a piece of formal writing, unlike either the dialectical journal or the personal response, and that it is important that the rules on the handout be followed.

2. The blank transparency is put on the overhead projector. The teacher explains that while reading the poem, s/he is going to use a marker to make notes and record his or her immediate strong impressions as well as interesting quotations.

3. Each student receives a copy of the example poem (or is directed to it in the anthology) and follows along as the teacher reads aloud, modeling Steps 1 and 2 from the handout and writing out notes on the overhead transparency.

   By reading over the notes, the teacher and class together should be able to determine what the focus of the analysis will be.

PRACTICE

1. Working independently, each student chooses a poem to which to respond and completes Steps 1 and 2 from the handout, as modeled by the teacher. The teacher circulates, offering encouragement and assistance as needed.

2. Students are then instructed to go on, following Steps 3, 4, and 5 on the handout.

3. Students who complete the planning phase in class can pair up to share and discuss their written outlines (Step 5). Partners can make constructive suggestions for improving the wording of the focus statement and the order of presentation of the supporting points and quotations.

PRODUCT

1. Working independently, each student proceeds to write a first draft of his or her response, following the instructions in Step 6 on the handout.

2. *Homework:* At home, each student completes the first draft of his or her response. The student then reads over the draft to check that there are no missing or extra words and to ensure that the instructions on the handout have been followed.

3. The finished product may be turned in for formative or summative assessment.

   (See "Completing the Final Draft, All Responses," below.)

WRITING AN ANALYTICAL RESPONSE

An analytical response is not an essay, and it isn't a personal response—it's somewhere in between.

- It has no thesis statement and no formal introduction. However, there has to be a thread running through it, holding it all together.
- It is written in the third person (avoiding all use of "I," "you," "we," or any form thereof).
- It assumes a critical focus and maintains it throughout.
- It is written entirely in the present tense, in proper sentence and paragraph format. It avoids slang, contractions, abbreviations, and symbols, just like a formal essay.
- Unlike a formal literary essay, it may take a humorous tone.

Here are the steps to follow when preparing an analytical response to a poem. Be sure not to skip any!

1. Perform a close reading of the text and make plenty of notes in the margins and on separate pieces of paper. Poets make conscious decisions about what to include in their work and choose every word carefully. Notice everything that is there. Go line by line and word by word and pick everything apart, pulling as much meaning out of the text as you can. Identify and label all the literary devices you find.

2. Now that you fully understand the text, decide what your critical approach is going to be. Which of the following will you be focusing on in your analysis?

   - a literary device that runs like a thread through the poem, pulling it all together (for example, an extended metaphor or a contrast)?
   - the poet's "personal agenda" served by writing the poem?
   - a theme that is reflected in multiple parts of the poem?
   - echoes of a much older story (for instance, biblical references, mythology, or a fairy tale)?
   - gender-based discrepancies reflected in the poem (such as stereotypes or one gender dominating or excluding the other)?
   - a power imbalance or power struggle (perhaps between rich and poor or educated and uneducated)?
   - a relationship or association that is reflected in multiple parts of the poem?

3. Return to your notes and the original text, and identify two or three points or quotations that relate strongly to the focus you've chosen for your response. Copy them out in a list. They will form the backbone of your analysis.

(continued on other side)

4. Now turn your attention to each of the points or quotations in turn and begin analyzing in depth by thinking about and answering the following questions, making detailed notes as you go:

- Why do you think the poet chose to include this in the work?
- Why would s/he consider it important?
- What does this say about (the focus of your response)?
- How does this enhance or reflect or reinforce (the focus of your response)?
- How does it relate to the other points or quotations you've chosen?
- What is the effect on the reader? (In general, not just the effect on you—this is not a personal response.)

5. If you have thought deeply about the piece and made detailed notes, you should now have something insightful and meaningful to say about it. Express this as a written statement in your notes. Then, based on your answers to the analytical questions in Step 4, decide on the best order in which to present your two or three points and which strong examples (quotations) from your notes will support each one. Write this information out to serve as the outline for your response.

6. Begin writing your first draft, using the DFAR pattern.

- D—In the first paragraph, Define and Discuss the focus of the analysis and come to a Decision about it. This is not a thesis statement, but it provides a unifying purpose for your response.
- F, A, R—In each of the following paragraphs, Find an example, Analyze it, and Relate it back to the decision at the end of the first paragraph.
- Give each of your important points or quotations its own paragraph.
- Make sure you're not just answering effectiveness questions (although that is a good place to start). Go deeper and explain how the example connects with the critical focus of your response. Discuss what makes each example effectively support your decision statement. Show the reader that you've given this poem a close examination and a lot of thought.
- You don't need to have a concluding paragraph as long as your response ends on a completed thought.

7. Now put your completed first draft through the rest of the writing process: revise, edit, proofread, and polish, and create a final draft for submission.

COMPLETING THE FINAL DRAFT, ALL RESPONSES

INTRODUCTION

1. Each student receives a copy of the applicable PROOFREAD WITH A PARTNER checklist and the teacher and class go over it together, discussing each item to ensure that students understand the expectations.

   Students need to understand the following, which the teacher may wish to write on the board in condensed form as a reminder:

   - *Student authors are the owners of their writing and take final responsibility for the completeness and correctness of the work that is handed in for marking.*
   - *Peer-editing partners are not to make corrections or changes to other authors' work—they may point out words to be checked for spelling or suggest improvements to wording, punctuation, and so on, but the author is the one who actually makes revisions to the text.*

PRACTICE

1. Students pair up and designate themselves Author A and Author B.

2. Together, each pair work on Author A's response, reading it aloud and discussing the criteria on the PROOFREAD WITH A PARTNER checklist. Author A reads with a pencil in hand, making changes and improvements to his or her own work. As each item on the checklist has been discussed, Author A's editing partner checks it off in the left-hand column of Author A's sheet.

3. The process is then repeated for Author B's response. The teacher circulates meanwhile, offering encouragement and assistance as needed.

FINAL PRODUCT

1. Each student receives a copy of the assessment sheet and the teacher goes over it with the class, discussing each item to ensure that students understand the criteria that will be used to evaluate their work.

   NOTE TO THE TEACHER: The peer-editing and assessment checklists supplied here have been used successfully in my classes. You may use them as is or adapt them to suit the needs of your own classes, at all grade levels.

2. *Homework:* That night, each student goes over his or her edited draft once more, making final changes and improvements and checking off items on the PROOFREAD WITH A PARTNER checklist (right-hand column) as they are completed. The student also refers to the assessment checklist to ensure that all the evaluation criteria have been met.

3. Before the due date specified for the response, the student types or prints out a clean final draft of the response. The student also gathers all the elements required for the submission package and assembles them as specified by the teacher. For example:

   Final draft response on top, with student name, course code, and submission date on the first page, THEN
   Blank Assessment checklist, THEN
   Edited rough draft with peer-editing checklist behind it, THEN
   Planning materials, including notes, outline, and so forth.

   The submission package is then stapled together, ready to be handed in for evaluation on the due date.

REVISE, EDIT, AND PROOFREAD WITH A PARTNER
DIALECTICAL RESPONSE CHECKLIST

AUTHOR'S NAME: _____

EDITING PARTNER'S NAME: _____

Checked by Partner	EDITING AND PROOFREADING CRITERIA	Improved by Author
	The response has a descriptive title.	
	The response is organized on the page in two columns of equal width, headed "Quotation" and "Response."	
	The student has selected at least three different quotations to copy into the left-hand column.	
	Each quotation has been accurately copied from the text. There are no words left out and no spelling errors.	
	Each quotation has been correctly formatted and cited.	
	The student has responded to each of the selected quotations individually.	
	Each response is personal and thoughtful, fully describing the effect the quotation had on the responding reader.	
	Each response is detailed and specific rather than general.	
	Each response is written out in complete and correctly punctuated sentences.	
	The grammar and spelling have been checked and corrected if necessary.	

TO BE COMPLETED BY THE EDITING PARTNER:

One thing I especially enjoyed about reading this response was

_____

_____

_____

One thing that I think would improve this response is

_____

_____

_____

Remember to attach this checklist (filled out) to the back of your edited draft when assembling your package for submission.

REVISE, EDIT, AND PROOFREAD WITH A PARTNER
PERSONAL RESPONSE CHECKLIST

AUTHOR'S NAME: _____

EDITING PARTNER'S NAME: _____

Checked by Partner	EDITING AND PROOFREADING CRITERIA	Improved by Author
	The response has been given an interesting, descriptive title. ("Personal Response" is not going to do it.)	
	The response has been written out in complete sentence and paragraph form. (No jotted notes or point-form lists.)	
	The response follows the instructions given by the teacher: It is the correct length and is based on either the entire poem or the specified number of quotations.	
	The response begins with the answer to a specific prompt question from the list on the handout.	
	The response is a thoughtful personal reaction to a poem. It provides a detailed explanation for each statement the reader makes about the text: the "why," the "what," and the "how."	
	The response is well organized. Paragraphs have been put in the most effective order.	
	The response has coherence. Sentences and paragraphs are linked together so the writing flows from the opening to the closing sentence.	
	Each quotation used in the response has been correctly copied, formatted, and cited, as demonstrated by the teacher in class.	
	The language used in the response is not slangy. All words are written out in full. When referring to the poem, the responder has used the present tense. The poet is never referred to by first name only.	
	The grammar, spelling, and punctuation have been checked and corrected if necessary. There are no sentence fragments, run-on sentences, or confusing pronoun references in the text.	

Remember to attach this checklist (filled out) to the back of your edited draft when assembling your package for submission.

REVISE, EDIT, AND PROOFREAD WITH A PARTNER
ANALYTICAL RESPONSE CHECKLIST

AUTHOR'S NAME: _____

EDITING PARTNER'S NAME: _____

Checked by Partner	EDITING AND PROOFREADING CRITERIA	Improved by Author
	The response has been given an interesting, descriptive title.	
	The first paragraph *defines* and *discusses* a thread that runs through the poem and that will become the focus of the analysis.	
	The response is based on a *decision* the responder has made about the thread that runs through the poem.	
	The statement expressing this *decision* appears at the end of the introductory paragraph.	
	Each quotation chosen to illustrate the *decision* is analyzed in detail and is contained in its own paragraph.	
	The selected quotations strongly support the *decision* expressed in the first paragraph.	
	Each quotation in the response is correctly copied, formatted, and cited, as demonstrated by the teacher in class. Each quotation is smoothly integrated into the text of the response.	
	Each analytical paragraph concludes by relating the analysis to the *decision* at the end of the introductory paragraph. The response concludes with a completed thought.	
	The language used in the response is formal, not slangy. "I," "we," and "you" have been avoided. There are no contractions, abbreviations, or symbols in the text. The present tense is used throughout. The poet is never referred to by first name only.	
	The grammar, spelling, and punctuation have been checked and corrected if necessary. There are no sentence fragments, run-on sentences, or ambiguous pronoun references in the text.	

Remember to attach this checklist (filled out) to the back of your edited draft when assembling your package for submission.

ASSESSMENT CHECKLIST: DIALECTICAL RESPONSE

Student's Name: _____

ASSESSMENT CRITERIA:
Knowledge/Understanding /10

- Student's responses demonstrate a thoughtful, age-appropriate understanding of the chosen quotations.
- Student's work shows clear understanding of the form and purpose of a dialectical response—that is, the page is correctly organized and the selected quotations are responded to rather than summarized or explained.

Thinking /10

- Student's choice of quotations reflects a logical awareness of the greater meaning of the poem.
- Student's responses demonstrate an appropriately sophisticated level of thinking.

Comments:

ASSESSMENT CHECKLIST: DIALECTICAL RESPONSE

Student's Name: _____

ASSESSMENT CRITERIA:
Knowledge/Understanding /10

- Student's responses demonstrate a thoughtful, age-appropriate understanding of the chosen quotations.
- Student's work shows clear understanding of the form and purpose of a dialectical response—that is, the page is correctly organized and the selected quotations are responded to rather than summarized or explained.

Thinking /10

- Student's choice of quotations reflects a logical awareness of the greater meaning of the poem.
- Student's responses demonstrate an appropriately sophisticated level of thinking.

Comments:

ASSESSMENT CHECKLIST: PERSONAL RESPONSE

Student's Name: _____

ASSESSMENT CRITERIA:
Knowledge/Understanding   **/10**

- Student demonstrates *insightful understanding* of the poem being responded to and is able to make *interesting and thoughtful comments* about it.
- Student shows clear understanding of the *form of a personal response*—that is, the work under discussion is responded to rather than summarized or explained; student has written a response, not an essay.

Thinking   **/10**

- The writing is *well organized*. Ideas have been placed in the most effective order and linked together to create coherence.
- Student's comments demonstrate an *appropriately sophisticated level of thinking*. Example quotations are thoughtfully considered and firmly related to the responder's life and emotions.

Comments:

ASSESSMENT CHECKLIST: PERSONAL RESPONSE

Student's Name: _____

ASSESSMENT CRITERIA:
Knowledge/Understanding   **/10**

- Student demonstrates *insightful understanding* of the poem being responded to and is able to make *interesting and thoughtful comments* about it.
- Student shows clear understanding of the *form of a personal response*—that is, the work under discussion is responded to rather than summarized or explained; student has written a response, not an essay.

Thinking   **/10**

- The writing is *well organized*. Ideas have been placed in the most effective order and linked together to create coherence.
- Student's comments demonstrate an *appropriately sophisticated level of thinking*. Example quotations are thoughtfully considered and firmly related to the responder's life and emotions.

Comments:

ASSESSMENT CHECKLIST: ANALYTICAL RESPONSE

Student's Name: _____

ASSESSMENT CRITERIA:
Knowledge/Understanding /10

- Student demonstrates *insightful understanding* of the poem chosen for analysis and is able to make *interesting and specific comments* about it.
- Student demonstrates clear understanding of the chosen *critical focus*.
- Student shows clear understanding of *the form of an analytical response*—that is, the work under discussion is analyzed rather than summarized or explained; student has written a response, not an essay.

Thinking /10

- The writing is well organized. Response is *clearly focused* on the identified thread running through the poem and all quoted examples are strongly related to it.
- Student's analysis demonstrates an *appropriately sophisticated level of thinking*. Examples are thoughtfully examined, then solidly tied together.

Comments:

ASSESSMENT CHECKLIST: ANALYTICAL RESPONSE

Student's Name: _____

ASSESSMENT CRITERIA:
Knowledge/Understanding /10

- Student demonstrates *insightful understanding* of the poem chosen for analysis and is able to make *interesting and specific comments* about it.
- Student demonstrates clear understanding of the chosen *critical focus*.
- Student shows clear understanding of *the form of an analytical response*—that is, the work under discussion is analyzed rather than summarized or explained; student has written a response, not an essay.

Thinking /10

- The writing is well organized. Response is *clearly focused* on the identified thread running through the poem and all quoted examples are strongly related to it.
- Student's analysis demonstrates an *appropriately sophisticated level of thinking*. Examples are thoughtfully examined, then solidly tied together.

Comments:

Studying Poetry Part 6
Timed Writing Practice

✍ **YOU WILL NEED**

- Copies of the sight poems to be worked with (1 of each per student)
- SPR 2–LEVELS OF ANALYSIS: POETRY (class set, if not already handed out)
- SPR 30–INTRODUCTION TO SYNTAX (class set, optional)
- LCR 9–CLAUSES DETERMINE SENTENCE PATTERNS (class set, optional)
- SPR 31–PHRASES ENHANCE SENTENCE MEANING (class set, optional)
- SPR 32–SYNTACTICAL EFFECTS IN POETRY (class set)
- SPR 33–DICTION: THE ART OF CAREFULLY CHOOSING WORDS (class set)
- SPR 34–ANALYZING TONE IN LITERATURE (class set)
- SPR 35–HOW TO READ A LITERARY QUESTION (class set)
- A list of 5 or 6 practice-writing prompts on the board or on an overhead transparency
- SPR 36 to 39–TIMED WRITING FORMATIVE ASSESSMENT sheets (enough each for one-quarter of the class)
- SPR 40–TIPS FOR SUCCESS IN TIMED WRITING EXERCISES (class set)

PURPOSE

Students will learn and practice techniques that will help them do their best when answering essay-response questions on English examinations.

ASSIGNMENT 1: LAY THE FOUNDATIONS

NOTE TO TEACHER: The foundations of language literacy are diction and syntax. Diction describes an author's choice of words, and syntax describes how words are combined and organized in order to communicate meaning and create emphasis. An understanding of how language works is essential if a student is to develop and demonstrate the ability to analyze literature. Depending on the grade and skill levels of your class, a diagnostic quiz and some quick review at the start of the course may be all that's needed. Alternatively, you may decide to schedule a mini-unit on diction and syntax near the beginning of the semester or sprinkle mini-lessons on these two topics throughout the course. How the foundation is laid is up to you. What's important is that students have these analysis tools in their kits before you ask them to focus on writing timed responses to poetry.

Handouts have been provided, on each of which you may base one or several lessons. Feel free to use them as is or modify them to suit the needs and ability levels of your classes. Should you wish to teach a mini-unit, here is one that has worked for me:

INTRODUCTION: SYNTAX

1. The teacher defines the term *syntax* for the students and records the definition on the board:

    Syntax refers to the way that words are put together to create meaning and emphasis.

2. The teacher now writes or reveals on the board a pair of examples:

    The dog chased the cat.
    The cat chased the dog.

    The teacher points out that in English, word order is very important to the meaning of a sentence. The teacher then asks: Which is the most important word in these two examples? *("Chased" is the most important because it links the dog and the cat and tells you what is happening.)*

3. Each student receives a copy of the INTRODUCTION TO SYNTAX handout, and the teacher and students go over it together, stopping to review and clarify wherever necessary to ensure that everyone understands. The teacher and class then do the first question of the exercise together in whole class. The teacher records the correct answer on the board to serve as a model. Students then complete the rest of the exercise, independently or in pairs.

4. Students form groups of three or four to check over one another's work. The teacher circulates, providing assistance where necessary.

5. In whole class, the teacher and students take up only those questions that students have found especially challenging (if any) before moving on.

6. The teacher defines the word *clause* for the students (a group of words that has a subject and a complete verb) and points out that every sentence has at least one clause in it and often more than one. The teacher then writes or reveals on the board the following examples:

    The dog chases the cat around the yard.
    The dog chases the cat around the yard but he never catches her.
    He never catches her because she is so fast.
    The dog chases the cat around the yard, but he never catches her because she is so fast.

    Together, teacher and class look at each sentence in turn, locating and underlining each verb, and from the verb identifying each clause. The teacher may want to parse the examples more fully (identifying the independent and subordinate clauses and perhaps naming the sentence patterns as well) before distributing and going over the handouts.

7. Each student receives a copy of the CLAUSES DETERMINE SENTENCE PATTERNS handout, and the teacher and students go over it together, stopping to clarify and discuss wherever necessary to ensure that everyone is keeping up.

    The teacher and class then do the exercise together in whole class. The teacher projects the questions onto the overhead screen and records the correct answers on the transparency using colored markers (one color for independent clauses, a second one for subordinate clauses). Students can flesh out or correct their work from the model on the screen.

8. The teacher now explains to the class the difference between a clause and a phrase (a phrase is a group of words that together have meaning but do not have a subject or complete verb).

   The teacher reveals or writes on the board the following examples:

   under the desk   emergency response team   has been trying to call

   The teacher explains that each of these groups of words has more meaning than the individual words that make it up, and each is a different kind of phrase (prepositional, noun, and verb). The appropriate heading is put above each example. Students can then suggest additional examples of each type, which may be recorded on the board as well.

9. Each student receives a copy of the PHRASES ENHANCE SENTENCE MEANING handout, and the teacher and students go over it together, stopping to clarify and discuss wherever necessary to ensure that everyone is keeping up.

   NOTE TO TEACHER: For grade 9 and 10 classes, I stop after verb phrases and switch out parts of the exercise at the end.

10. The teacher and class then do the exercise together in whole class. The teacher projects the questions onto the overhead screen and records the correct answers on the transparency using colored markers (a different color for each type of phrase). Students can flesh out or correct their work from the model on the screen.

INTRODUCTION: DICTION

1. The teacher writes the word *dictionary* on the board and asks the class: What do you find in a dictionary? *(Words, of course.)* The teacher then explains that in literary terms, diction refers to an author's choice of words. In poetry, each word is significant and therefore carefully selected.

2. Each student receives a copy of the DICTION: THE ART OF CAREFULLY CHOOSING WORDS handout, and the teacher and class go over it together, pausing to discuss and clarify wherever necessary.

PRACTICE ANALYZING SYNTAX AND DICTION

1. The teacher explains that an awareness of syntax is essential to any critical analysis of literature and introduces students to the acronym PLOTS:

   P is for sentence PATTERNS
   L is for sentence LENGTHS
   O is for sentence ORGANIZATION
   T is for sentence TYPES
   S is for a SHIFT in any of the above (from short to long, from statement to question, and so on)

2. The teacher distributes copies of the SYNTACTICAL EFFECTS handout and goes over it with the students, defining and clarifying as necessary.

3. The teacher now writes a sample syntax question on the board and refers students to either an already-studied poem or a new one from the class anthology that lends itself to syntactical analysis.

   My favorite to use is "Warren Pryor" by Alden Nowlan. Here is the question for it: How does the poet's use of syntax underscore the feelings and attitudes of the people in the poem?

NOTE TO TEACHER: Before students can begin their analysis, they have to determine precisely whose feelings and attitudes are expressed in the poem, what those feelings and attitudes are, and toward what or whom they are directed. I generally provide some assistance with this and record possible answers on the board beneath the question before proceeding to Step 4.

4. Working in groups of three or four, students practice finding and analyzing examples of syntax in the poem, relating them to the question on the board. *(Allow about fifteen minutes for this activity.)*

5. In whole-class discussion, each group can then share its favorite (that is, strongest) example with the rest of the students, who can offer suggestions for extending and deepening the analysis.

6. The teacher now writes a sample diction question on the board and refers students to either an already-studied poem or a new one from the class anthology that lends itself to an analysis of diction.

   I like to use "The Dromedary" by Archibald Y. Campbell. Here is the question for it: How does the poet's use of diction convey the speaker's attitude toward the dromedary in the park?

   NOTE TO TEACHER: Again, it is important before beginning an analysis to define the terms of the question. In this case, the question tells us whose attitude it is and toward what, but students must still determine exactly what the speaker's attitude is.

7. Working in groups of three or four, students practice finding and analyzing examples of diction in the poem, relating them to the question on the board. *(Allow about fifteen minutes for this activity.)*

8. In whole-class discussion, each group can then share its favorite (that is, strongest) example with the rest of the students, who can offer suggestions for extending and deepening the analysis.

INTRODUCTION TO SYNTAX

WHAT IS A SENTENCE?

A sentence is a series of words that are organized in such a way that they express a complete thought or idea. A sentence always begins with a capital letter and ends with one of the following punctuation marks: a period (.), a question mark (?), or an exclamation mark (!). These indicate the sentence type.

A sentence always contains a verb. In fact, the shortest sentence possible in the English language is a one-word command, and that word is a verb: "Hurry!" "Look!"

Any group of words that does not contain a complete verb is not a sentence, but a sentence fragment:

> A small girl with a skipping rope.
> Going to the drugstore.
> The fluffy white clouds overhead.

Fragments may be used in written text to create interest or emphasis, but they need to be recognized as fragments when a text is being analyzed:

> The first one? Not the second?
> At last, a question!

THE PARTS OF A SENTENCE

In order to analyze an author's syntax, you must be able to identify the parts of a sentence by name.

The simplest way to divide a sentence is SUBJECT-PREDICATE. The subject is who or what the sentence is about. The predicate tells us what the subject does or is.

> *Karim* is very happy today.
> *We* have decided to visit Niagara Falls.
> *Regular exercise* will slow the aging process.

The most important part of the predicate is the VERB because it establishes the relationship between the subject and the rest of the sentence.

A TRANSITIVE VERB describes an action the subject performs directly on something or someone else (the DIRECT OBJECT of the verb). There may also be an INDIRECT OBJECT receiving the action.

(continued on back)

The first batter hit the ball right out of the park.
(Subject: the first batter)
(Transitive verb: hit)
(Direct object of verb: the ball)

I shall read you a story after lunch.
(Subject: I)
(Transitive verb: shall read)
(Direct object of verb: a story)
(Indirect object of verb: [to] you)

The sales clerk gave me too much change.
(Subject: the sales clerk)
(Transitive verb: gave)
(Direct object of verb: too much change)
(Indirect object of verb: [to] me)

The sales clerk directed me to the complaints desk.
(Subject: the sales clerk)
(Transitive verb: directed)
(Direct object of verb: me)

An INTRANSITIVE VERB describes an action without a direct object.

Tonya swims for an hour every day.
(Subject: Tonya)
(Intransitive verb: swims)

They reacted quickly when the fire broke out.
(Subject: they)
(Intransitive verb: reacted)

Some verbs can be either transitive or intransitive, depending on how they are used:

The children are playing in the park.
(Subject: the children)
(Intransitive verb: are playing)

He is playing the lead role in our school drama production.
(Subject: he)
(Transitive verb: is playing)
(Direct object of verb: the lead role)

(continued on next page)

A COPULA VERB describes a state of being or a transformation. It acts as an equal sign (=) between the subject and SUBJECTIVE COMPLETION of the sentence.

Adrian is becoming a very good skier.
(Subject: Adrian)
(Copula verb: is becoming)
(Subjective completion: a very good skier)

Laura is sad about the loss of her pet.
(Subject: Laura)
(Copula verb: is)
(Subjective completion: sad about the loss of her pet)

EXERCISE: Identify the subject, verb, and completion in each of the following sentences. Use the same pattern as shown on the previous pages.

1. Maria and her brother are building a tree house.

2. Yanno told the class an interesting story.

3. Knowing this information will help you in the future.

4. I am certain of this.

5. At midnight, the silver coach disappeared.

6. Giorgio has joined a health club.

7. Working part time is a valuable learning experience.

8. This new game is becoming very popular.

9. Lianne works best in a quiet place.

10. After dinner, I will show you my photos.

PHRASES ENHANCE SENTENCE MEANING

A phrase is a group of words that create meaning when they are put together but that do not have a subject or verb. There are different kinds of phrases, which should be identified by name when you are analyzing an author's use of syntax.

PREPOSITIONAL PHRASE

Prepositions are small words that indicate time, place, or relationships. A preposition plus its object(s) may be found anywhere in a sentence:

> Over that mountain lies a long-lost city.
> (Preposition: over)
> (Object of preposition: that mountain)
> (Function of phrase: adverbial—where)

> You may sign yourself out after third period.
> (Preposition: after)
> (Object of preposition: third period)
> (Function of phrase: adverbial—when)

> The electrical outlet beside the toaster is controlled by the light switch.
> (Preposition: beside)
> (Object of preposition: the toaster)
> (Function of phrase: adjectival—which outlet?)

NOUN PHRASE

Because English is a Germanic language, we have a tendency to pile up already-existing nouns to create new meaning:

touch-tone phone	service road	emergency response team
fleabag hotel	belly flop	pocket watch

Each of these is called a NOUN PHRASE.

VERB PHRASE

Verb tenses in English are formed using AUXILIARY VERBS, PARTICIPLES, and MODALS. Look at the following (italicized) examples of VERB PHRASES:

> I *will be expecting* you at three o'clock.
> Mister Jordan *has been waiting* an hour to speak to you.
> Kim *has to tell* you something important.

Have you *done* your homework yet?
I *did try* to contact you, but you *weren't accepting* any calls.

PARTICIPIAL OR GERUNDIAL PHRASE

A participle is formed from a verb and can take one of two forms: PRESENT PARTICIPLE or PAST PARTICIPLE. A participle acts as both a verb and an adjective. A participial phrase can answer any question except WHAT.

> *Believing himself alone*, he dropped all pretense of sadness or concern.
> (answers the question WHY)

> The tourists soon found themselves *stranded in a dangerous part of the city*.
> (answers the question WHERE)

A GERUND looks just like a participle but acts as both a verb and a noun. A gerundial phrase answers the question WHAT.

> We enjoyed *reading your latest letter*.
> *Making promises* and *keeping them* are two different things.

EXERCISE: Underline and label each of the phrases in the following sentences.

1. Rowing a heavy boat against the current is hard work.

2. She should have gone to the park with the children.

3. Here is the latest in kitchen utensils—a saucepan with built-in oven mitts.

4. Broken into pieces by the howling wind, our lawn ornament was soon adorning several properties down the street.

SYNTACTICAL EFFECTS IN POETRY

SENTENCE TYPES

- sentences may be declarative (statements), interrogative (questions), or exclamatory.
- shifting sentence types has the effect of (re)focusing the reader's attention.
- interrogative and exclamatory sentences used in poetry act to intensify the thoughts and emotions being conveyed (increasing evocativeness and provocativeness).

Rhetorical Question
- makes the reader think (an automatic response)
- stronger than a statement for making a point
- can, when several are used in a row, build drama or mystery
- depending on context, can be very effective at portraying a wide range of attitudes, intensifying the tone

Exclamation
- conveys a burst of strong emotion—"Alas, my heart!"
- especially effective when it breaks up a line of poetry or sits by itself in a short line—"wakes up" the reader
- may emphasize some aspect of the poem's main idea—"What a quagmire! What a mess!"

SENTENCE LENGTHS

- a shift in sentence lengths can signal a change in emotion or attitude
- very effective at communicating emotion (enhancing evocativeness) or focusing the reader on something important (increasing provocativeness).

Short sentence
- coming between longer sentences, may be used to present a key detail or idea
- used in series, will speed the pace of a passage but also chop it up, creating or heightening tension
- used in narrative dialogue or first-person writing, may indicate emotional tension (for instance, a series of short questions beginning "what if" to convey anxiety)
- coming after a series of long sentences, can signal the end of a lengthy and difficult experience

Long sentence
- slows the pace of a poem, may convey a lengthy process or a difficult struggle
- adds weight to the writing style, helps to establish a serious tone
- may be used in the form of a run-on sentence to convey excitement or imitate a speaking style

(continued on next page)

SENTENCE ORGANIZATION

The end of a sentence is the position of greatest emphasis; the beginning of a sentence is the position of second-greatest emphasis. Authors will purposely arrange the words and parts of their sentences in order to emphasize key thoughts or ideas.

Periodic sentences   –meaning is incomplete until the end of the sentence.
(e.g., Through the meadow and into the woods, to search for gold we go.)

Loose sentences   –meaning is provided at the beginning of the sentence.
(e.g., We're going treasure hunting in the forest beyond the fields.)

Natural order   –subject, verb, predicate (subject is important but the predicate is more important)
(e.g., The prize goes to the winner.)

Inverted order   –predicate, verb, subject (subject is most important)
(e.g., To the winner goes the prize.)

Similarly, in a list or series, authors will often arrange items in order:

Climactic order
- from least to most, lowest to highest
- builds drama, tension, suspense
- may be applied to individual words, phrases, clauses

Anticlimactic order
- from most to least, highest to lowest
- generally found in humorous or satirical writing
- may be applied to words, phrases, clauses

SENTENCE PATTERNS

- Sentences may be simple, compound, complex, or compound-complex.
- Varying sentence patterns makes a text more interesting to read.
- Sentence patterns become rhetorically important when they:
  - physically reflect the content of the text (for example, a series of compound sentences used to weigh the pros and cons of an issue);
  - occur with frequency in a passage (for example, an entire paragraph of simple sentences);
  - indicate the speaker's attitude or recreate his or her voice (For example, a five-year-old narrator will speak mainly in simple sentences; so will a speaker who is reluctantly or impatiently explaining something. A university professor, however, or someone who is trying to sound very intelligent will probably use entire strings of compound-complex sentences.).

DICTION: THE ART OF CAREFULLY CHOOSING WORDS

Authors (and especially poets) shop for words the same way you would shop for a piece of clothing: Is it the right size? A flattering style? This season's "in" color? How does it make you feel to wear it? How does it make other people feel to see you in it? When you are analyzing the word choices of an author or poet, look for the following:

POETICAL WORDS THAT MAKE MUSIC

Some words and phrases create a "sound effect" that enhances the meaning or message of a piece of writing. When describing a waterfall, for example, an author may choose words that sound like rushing water. To convey anger, an author may use a lot of short words with hard sounds in them.

WORDS AT DIFFERENT LEVELS

There are three levels of language: formal, neutral, and informal.

Formal diction creates an elevated tone in a piece of writing. This language is free of slang, idiomatic expressions, and contractions (such as "can't"). In dialogue, characters who use formal diction are usually highly educated (or want others to think they are) or are unfamiliar with the language.

Neutral diction uses standard language and vocabulary without elaborate words or slang, and it may include contractions. Newspapers and magazines use neutral diction.

Low diction is the language of everyday use. It is relaxed and conversational. It often includes common and simple words, idioms, slang, jargon, and contractions.

WORDS THAT ARE ABSTRACT OR CONCRETE

Concrete words name things that are tangible—that is, they can be experienced through the five senses. Abstract words name ideas, concepts, emotions, or conditions that are intangible. "Heart" is a concrete word; "love" is an abstract word. Concrete language draws a reader in, creating a strong sense of immediacy. Abstract language is less specific and more open to the reader's personal interpretation. It tends to keep the reader at a distance.

WORDS THAT HAVE MORE THAN ONE MEANING

In English, we have many words with multiple, sometimes wildly different meanings. Authors often take advantage of these meanings to add dimensions and levels of interpretation to their writing. Puns and double entendres are based on words having multiple meanings and are used to add humor to a piece of writing.

WORDS WITH CONNOTATIONS AS WELL AS DENOTATIONS

Denotation is the dictionary definition of a word. Connotation is the implicit meaning of a word and consists of the suggestions, associations, and emotional overtones attached to a word. For example, the word "house" has a different emotional effect on the reader than does the word "home," with its connotations of safety, warmth, and comfort.

SPECIALIZED LANGUAGE (JARGON)

Each profession, trade, or hobby has its own specialized vocabulary, or *jargon*. When an author uses jargon out of context, it's usually either to surprise the reader and make him or her think, or to create a subtext (a hidden message).

ASSIGNMENT 2: PRACTICE UNPACKING PROMPTS

1. The teacher hands out a copy of HOW TO READ A LITERARY QUESTION to each student and goes over it with the class, pointing out areas that students need to watch out for.

2. The teacher now reveals on the board or on the overhead screen a list of practice writing prompts based on short poems from the course anthology. Teacher and students together read the first prompt, identifying and highlighting the key word, object, and limiting factor.

3. The poem to which the prompt refers is read aloud by the teacher, who then models *defining the terms of the question* and emphasizes to students that while the terms of the question may be relatively vague, the terms of the written response must be focused, especially in a timed writing situation. In other words, before you can respond to a prompt about imagery used to create *atmosphere*, you need to decide what sort of atmosphere the poem contains: Is it an air of anticipation? A sense of great antiquity? A cloud of doom and foreboding? Defining the terms of the question is therefore an important first step in the process of planning a response.

   The teacher records the agreed-upon definitions on the board or overhead transparency, leaving room beneath the prompt for an analytical statement.

4. Referring to their anthologies and the list on the board or screen, students pair up to unpack and define the remaining prompts in the list. *(Allow about ten to fifteen minutes for this activity.)*

5. In whole class, the teacher and students discuss their definitions and decide on an *analytical statement* that could be made about each of the poems, based on the prompts. The teacher records an agreed-upon analytical statement underneath each prompt.

   Here are some prompts that I've used successfully with my students, along with a sampling of analytical statements.

   Read the following poem by Archibald Y. Campbell, titled "The Dromedary." Then write a well-organized short essay in which you analyze how the poet's use of diction conveys the speaker's attitude toward the dromedary in the park. (Analytical statement: Campbell uses language rich with connotation to share with the reader the proud desert ruler he sees when he looks at the dromedary.)

   Read the following poem by Alden Nowlan, titled "Warren Pryor." Then write a well-organized short essay in which you analyze how the poet's use of syntax underscores the feelings and attitudes of the people in the poem. (Analytical statement: In this poem Nowlan uses sentence length as an indicator of how trapped people feel in their lives.)

   Read the following poem by Louis Untermeyer, titled "Portrait of a Machine." Then write a well-organized short essay in which you analyze how the poet uses personification to issue a warning to humankind. (Analytical statement: Untermeyer personifies the machine as a resentful slave in order to warn us of the danger of becoming too dependent on technology.)

   Carefully read the following sonnet, titled "A January Morning," by Archibald Lampman. Then plan and write a well-organized short essay in which you analyze how the poet uses diction and imagery to create a strong contrast between the first eight lines and the final six lines of the poem. (Analytical statement: The words and imagery in this sonnet move the reader from pale stillness in the octave to noisy excitement in the sestet.)

   Read carefully the following poem by Anne Marriott, titled "Portrait." Then, in a well-planned and well-organized essay, analyze how the poet has used simile and metaphor to convey the speaker's attitude toward the individual being described in the poem. (Analytical statement: By comparing a librarian to the books and paper she works with, Marriott shares her perception of this woman as having no life.)

6. The teacher points out that the word *attitude* seems to come up often in timed writing prompts. Each student now receives a copy of the ANALYZING TONE IN LITERATURE handout and the teacher goes over it with the class. At the teacher's discretion, students may be given time to read over the list of "tone words" and look up the unfamiliar ones in the dictionary.

ANALYZING TONE IN LITERATURE

The TONE of a piece of writing is the ATTITUDE it expresses. An author or poet will have an attitude toward the subject matter but may also have an attitude toward the reader and/or toward himself or herself. The narrator of a story (or the speaker in a narrative or dramatic poem) will have an attitude toward the events, the characters, and/or the setting of the work.

Here are some useful TONE WORDS to help you analyze literary works:

angry	sad	sentimental	disapproving
harsh	whimsical	anxious	urgent
complimentary	playful	joking	condescending
indulgent	poignant	sympathetic	fearful
detached	contemptuous	happy	confused
apologetic	smug	childish	humorous
joyful	tranquil	contented	frustrated
mocking	sarcastic	sweet	objective
nostalgic	vexed	vibrant	zealous
weary	frivolous	irreverent	bitter
regretful	spiteful	dreamy	shocked
seductive	restrained	somber	candid
proud	giddy	pitiful	dramatic
provocative	impassioned	challenging	bleak
despairing	self-pitying	determined	arrogant

Use a dictionary to make sure you understand what each word means.

When analyzing TONE, it might be helpful to examine the following in addition to the range of technical, associative, and thematic literary devices:

DICTION   The words chosen by the author, as well as the characteristics of the language level(s) used: formal, neutral, and/or low.

IMAGES   The mental pictures painted by the author's choice and arrangement of words.

DETAILS   Pieces of factual information. Consider both what has been included and what has been purposely left out.

SYNTAX   This refers to the way words are put together to create meaning and includes such things as sentence length, organization, and the purposeful use of sentence fragments and run-on sentences for effect.

HOW TO READ A LITERARY QUESTION

A well-framed question will have three parts:
> a *key verb* and *object* that tell you what you are to do, and
> one or more *limiting factors* that narrow the question and make it more specific.

THE KEY VERB

The key verb is the most important part of a literary question. Here are some of the most commonly used verbs that you may encounter:

STATE: means to tell, as clearly and concisely as possible.
(Example: State two reasons for the protagonist's growing anger in this story.)

EXPLAIN: means to tell about something, providing enough detail to make it logical and understandable to another person.
(Example: Explain the point being made by the author in paragraph 3 of the essay.)

EVALUATE: means to rate something on a scale, giving reasons to support your judgement.
(Example: Evaluate the effectiveness of the metaphor in the first stanza of this poem.)

DESCRIBE: means to talk about something in some detail.
(Example: Describe how the setting of this story participates in the unfolding of the plot.)

DEFEND: means to support a position using quotations and/or specific references from one or more particular works.
(Example: Defend the publication of this essay on the front page of a daily newspaper.)

COMPARE: means to list or talk about specific examples of similarities and differences.
(Example: Compare the language used to express the speaker's attitude towards himself in the opening stanzas of these two poems.)

CONTRAST: means to list or talk about specific examples of the differences between items.
(Example: Contrast the ways in which these two story excerpts describe girls.)

EXAMINE: means to look closely and critically at the various parts of something.
(or **ANALYZE**) The focus you are expected to take will be given to you as part of the question: How, Why, To what extent, With what result.
(Example: Examine the relationship between the protagonist and antagonist in this novel. How does it affect the decisions they make?)

DISCUSS: means to formulate a thesis and support it using examples from the text.
(Example: Discuss the role played by travel in the lives of two characters in the novel.)

**Note: If the question has two key verbs – for example, "Identify and explain . . ." – remember to do both.)

THE OBJECT

The object of a question is its focusing factor. You don't just explain—you explain the author's methods. You don't just examine—you examine a character's attitude. To ensure that you are answering the question that is asked, you need to read the question carefully. To ensure that you're answering it fully, you need to make note of the focusing factor. Are you being asked to explain more than one method? Will you have to define or explain the character's attitude before you can analyze it? Together with the limiting factor, the object of the question will tell you exactly how much work you need to do.

LIMITING FACTORS

Limiting factors are included in literary questions to narrow a task and make it more specific and therefore more manageable. Remember that you have to answer the question that is asked. If the question specifies the first three paragraphs, then that is where you must focus your attention and find your supporting examples. If you're asked to support a discussion with examples of simile and metaphor, then those are the devices you should be looking for, ignoring everything else. Pay special attention to the limiting factor of a literary question, as it can save you a great deal of time and effort.

ASSIGNMENT 3: DEVELOP A SUPPORTING EXAMPLE

1. The teacher explains to the class that the "short essay" mentioned in each of the practice prompts will consist of an introductory paragraph ending with the analytical statement, followed by two well-chosen and well-developed supporting examples, each in its own paragraph.

   NOTE TO TEACHER: Since students writing the Advanced Placement English Literature exam are required to write three short essay responses in two hours, I decided to begin training my class of grade 11 pre-AP students to write a complete response in forty minutes, reasoning that if they entered the grade 12 AP course with this skill set already under their belts, they could focus more on the literature and ultimately do a better job on the AP exam. At the AP Summer Institute, I asked a workshop presenter what an acceptable length for a forty-minute essay response would be, and she told me that two or three well-developed examples would be considered sufficient for the body. So, the expectations outlined above are for an enriched grade 11 class. To prepare a nonenriched class for an end-of-semester English exam, I would recommend extending the time frame to an hour and asking for three body paragraphs.

2. The teacher moves to a clean panel of board or places a blank transparency on the overhead projector. The analytical statement for the first practice writing prompt is copied across the top of the board or transparency. The teacher and class then reread the poem to identify examples that support or illustrate the statement, and these are listed down the left-hand side of the board or transparency, modeling the format to be used by the students when quoting lines of poetry.

3. Together, the teacher and class discuss the listed examples, selecting the two strongest to include in a written response. On the right-hand side of the board or transparency, the teacher records notes based on the whole-class discussion about the effectiveness of these two examples, describing in detail the following:

   - what the example does
   - what it helps the reader to do
   - how it reinforces, supports, or illustrates the analytical statement

4. Students pair up with different working partners and each pair chooses or is assigned one of the remaining practice prompts on the board or screen. Referring to their anthologies and the modeled notes on the board or screen, student pairs select and develop two strong examples to support the analytical statement recorded beneath each pair's assigned prompt.

5. Pairs combine, forming groups of four or six, to discuss and compare their notes and offer one another suggestions for improvement.

ASSIGNMENT 4: ORGANIZE AN ESSAY-LENGTH RESPONSE (DFAR)

1. The teacher reminds the students that for the purposes of the English Literature exam, an essay-length response will consist of an introductory paragraph followed by two or three well-developed supporting examples, each in its own paragraph, and a concluding paragraph.

2. On the board or on a blank overhead transparency, the teacher prints the following:

   D
   F
   A
   R

3. The teacher then explains to the class while making notes on the board or transparency:

D stands for *defining* the question (as practiced earlier) and *deciding* on an analytical statement. This is what students will be doing in their introductory paragraph.

F means they'll be *finding* a strong example that supports or illustrates the analytical statement, then

A—*analyzing* the example, and finally

R—*relating* the example back to the analytical statement and the writing prompt. The second example should also be related back to the first example.

F - A - R represents a well-developed example and is what students will be doing in each of the body paragraphs.

R also stands for *repeating* the analytical statement, which is what the students will be doing to wrap up the response in their concluding paragraph.

4. The teacher points out that a well-organized, essay-length response will therefore have at least four paragraphs:

    1. Introduction—D
    2. Well-developed example 1—F, A, R
    3. Well-developed example 2—F, A, R
    4. Conclusion—R

Students should be given a few minutes to copy this information into their notebooks.

5. Students pair up with the same partners they had for Assignment 3 and take out their notes on their assigned poem and writing prompt. Working together, each pair is to first-draft a complete response using the work already done. *(Allow no more than fifteen minutes for this part of the activity.)*

6. Student pairs combine in groups of four to share their responses and offer one another suggestions for improvement. At the teacher's discretion, each group may wish to share its favorite body paragraph with the rest of the class.

ASSIGNMENT 5: WRITE A TIMED RESPONSE

Once students have practiced writing a complete essay-length response using the DFAR system, they are ready to begin a series of timed writing exercises. The teacher should ensure that each student understands the rules:

1. Each student will be working independently and will be in competition with no one but himself or herself.

2. The goal is to progressively improve one's skills, eventually becoming able to write a complete essay response in forty minutes or less.

3. Only forty minutes will be allowed for each writing exercise, start to finish. All work is to be done in class, and all work must be turned in to the teacher at the end of the allotted time.

4. The assessment done by the teacher following each exercise will be formative only, intended to help each student improve for the next time. No grade will be officially recorded.

NOTE TO TEACHER: To make the workload manageable, I recommend that each exercise be assessed on a single different aspect of the task. Provide two or three Level 4 (80–100%) grading criteria and highlight the ones that the student has not yet met. Create a bank of five or six suggestions for improvement and add one where applicable to each student's assessment slip. (Sample assessment sheets have been provided at the end of this module.) For my grade 11 students, I also selected four or five responses from each batch of submissions for a thorough read-through with detailed marginal comments and suggestions. By the end of the course, each student in the class had thus received at least one close assessment of his or her work.

5. Students will probably not have time to rewrite a good copy, so they would be wise to write the first draft on every second line, leaving space to make editorial changes if there is time. (*This also leaves space for the teacher to make comments and suggestions, should the student's work be selected for intensive assessment.*)

The timed writing exercise should be regularly scheduled at least six times during the course, using a different poem and prompt each time. This will provide students multiple opportunities to practice and refine their analytical-response skills before the end of the semester. (*My grade 11 students practiced every second week for a total of fourteen weeks.*)

Any students who actually manage to complete a response during the first or second exercise should be congratulated in whole class, as this represents a major accomplishment. By the end of the course, with regular practice, most if not all of your students should be able to finish within forty minutes.

TIMED WRITING #1   NAME: _____
ASSESSMENT: OPENING PARAGRAPH

Level 4 Criteria:
- The paragraph insightfully defines and discusses the terms of the question to be answered.
- The paragraph is logically and coherently organized.
- The paragraph concludes with a clear, focused, and firmly worded analytical statement.

*Highlighted criteria indicate areas that you need to work on for next time.

TIMED WRITING #1   NAME: _____
ASSESSMENT: OPENING PARAGRAPH

Level 4 Criteria:
- The paragraph insightfully defines and discusses the terms of the question to be answered.
- The paragraph is logically and coherently organized.
- The paragraph concludes with a clear, focused, and firmly worded analytical statement.

*Highlighted criteria indicate areas that you need to work on for next time.

TIMED WRITING #1   NAME: _____
ASSESSMENT: OPENING PARAGRAPH

Level 4 Criteria:
- The paragraph insightfully defines and discusses the terms of the question to be answered.
- The paragraph is logically and coherently organized.
- The paragraph concludes with a clear, focused, and firmly worded analytical statement.

*Highlighted criteria indicate areas that you need to work on for next time.

TIMED WRITING #1   NAME: _____
ASSESSMENT: OPENING PARAGRAPH

Level 4 Criteria:
- The paragraph insightfully defines and discusses the terms of the question to be answered.
- The paragraph is logically and coherently organized.
- The paragraph concludes with a clear, focused, and firmly worded analytical statement.

*Highlighted criteria indicate areas that you need to work on for next time.

TIMED WRITING #2   NAME: _____
ASSESSMENT: THESIS AND COHERENCE

Level 4 Criteria:
- The analytical statement is clear, focused, and firmly worded.
- It identifies the target aspect of the poem and answers the question contained in the writing prompt.
- Each paragraph in the body concludes by relating the example analyzed to the analytical statement and writing prompt.

*Highlighted criteria indicate areas that you need to work on for next time.

TIMED WRITING #2   NAME: _____
ASSESSMENT: THESIS AND COHERENCE

Level 4 Criteria:
- The analytical statement is clear, focused, and firmly worded.
- It identifies the target aspect of the poem and answers the question contained in the writing prompt.
- Each paragraph in the body concludes by relating the example analyzed to the analytical statement and writing prompt.

*Highlighted criteria indicate areas that you need to work on for next time.

TIMED WRITING #2   NAME: _____
ASSESSMENT: THESIS AND COHERENCE

Level 4 Criteria:
- The analytical statement is clear, focused, and firmly worded.
- It identifies the target aspect of the poem and answers the question contained in the writing prompt.
- Each paragraph in the body concludes by relating the example analyzed to the analytical statement and writing prompt.

*Highlighted criteria indicate areas that you need to work on for next time.

TIMED WRITING #2   NAME: _____
ASSESSMENT: THESIS AND COHERENCE

Level 4 Criteria:
- The analytical statement is clear, focused, and firmly worded.
- It identifies the target aspect of the poem and answers the question contained in the writing prompt.
- Each paragraph in the body concludes by relating the example analyzed to the analytical statement and writing prompt.

*Highlighted criteria indicate areas that you need to work on for next time.

TIMED WRITING #3   NAME: _____
ASSESSMENT: CHOICE AND DEVELOPMENT OF EXAMPLES

Level 4 Criteria: • The two examples are strongly related to the writing prompt.
                    • Each example is fully and thoughtfully analyzed.
                    • Each body paragraph concludes by firmly relating the chosen example
                      back to the analytical statement.

*Highlighted criteria indicate areas that you need to work on for next time.

TIMED WRITING #3   NAME: _____
ASSESSMENT: CHOICE AND DEVELOPMENT OF EXAMPLES

Level 4 Criteria: • The two examples are strongly related to the writing prompt.
                    • Each example is fully and thoughtfully analyzed.
                    • Each body paragraph concludes by firmly relating the chosen example
                      back to the analytical statement.

*Highlighted criteria indicate areas that you need to work on for next time.

TIMED WRITING #3   NAME: _____
ASSESSMENT: CHOICE AND DEVELOPMENT OF EXAMPLES

Level 4 Criteria: • The two examples are strongly related to the writing prompt.
                    • Each example is fully and thoughtfully analyzed.
                    • Each body paragraph concludes by firmly relating the chosen example
                      back to the analytical statement.

*Highlighted criteria indicate areas that you need to work on for next time.

TIMED WRITING #3   NAME: _____
ASSESSMENT: CHOICE AND DEVELOPMENT OF EXAMPLES

Level 4 Criteria: • The two examples are strongly related to the writing prompt.
                    • Each example is fully and thoughtfully analyzed.
                    • Each body paragraph concludes by firmly relating the chosen example
                      back to the analytical statement.

*Highlighted criteria indicate areas that you need to work on for next time.

TIMED WRITING #4   NAME: _____
ASSESSMENT: LITERARY ANALYSIS OF EXAMPLES

Level 4 Criteria: • Each analysis fully describes what the example does and what it helps the reader to do.
                   • Each analysis insightfully answers the question posed in the writing prompt.

*Highlighted criteria indicate areas that you need to work on for next time.

TIMED WRITING #4   NAME: _____
ASSESSMENT: LITERARY ANALYSIS OF EXAMPLES

Level 4 Criteria: • Each analysis fully describes what the example does and what it helps the reader to do.
                   • Each analysis insightfully answers the question posed in the writing prompt.

*Highlighted criteria indicate areas that you need to work on for next time.

TIMED WRITING #4   NAME: _____
ASSESSMENT: LITERARY ANALYSIS OF EXAMPLES

Level 4 Criteria: • Each analysis fully describes what the example does and what it helps the reader to do.
                   • Each analysis insightfully answers the question posed in the writing prompt.

*Highlighted criteria indicate areas that you need to work on for next time.

TIMED WRITING #4   NAME: _____
ASSESSMENT: LITERARY ANALYSIS OF EXAMPLES

Level 4 Criteria: • Each analysis fully describes what the example does and what it helps the reader to do.
                   • Each analysis insightfully answers the question posed in the writing prompt.

*Highlighted criteria indicate areas that you need to work on for next time.

TIPS FOR SUCCESS IN TIMED WRITING EXERCISES

1. CAREFULLY READ THE QUESTION, highlighting or underlining the key words. You are being asked to answer a question. There will be at least one limiting factor. Be certain you know what the question is and what the limiting factor is. Refer back to the question periodically as you write to ensure that you remain on topic and within the limiting factor. And don't change the question—if the word used in the prompt is "exciting," don't change it in your essay to "intriguing" or "puzzling."

2. PLAN BEFORE WRITING! Jot down notes. Better still, use a graphic organizer. The several minutes spent doing this represent an INVESTMENT of your time that will pay dividends when you begin to write.

3. WHEN YOU BEGIN TO WRITE, DON'T WASTE TIME OR PAPER DOING ANY OF THE FOLLOWING:

   - writing blurbs (for instance, "Using poetic devices, the author takes the reader on a truly thrilling journey through the story."). You're not promoting a movie. Keep "salesman talk" out of your essay.

   - teaching the reader about poetic devices (for example, "Alliteration makes lines of poetry memorable for the reader."). Assume that the reader already knows the basics and focus your attention on answering the question in the prompt.

   - making sweeping general statements. You need to be as specific as possible when analyzing.

4. WHEN QUOTING POETRY, DO NOT CHANGE THE FORMAT TO PROSE. The rules that apply to literary essays also apply to these timed writing exercises.

5. ANALYZE FULLY. Show, then tell. A well-developed example is one that has been accurately quoted, closely read, completely labeled, and then fully analyzed for the reader in terms of what it does and what it helps the reader to do. While analyzing the example, remember to relate it back to the writing prompt to keep yourself on topic.